Republican, First, Last, and Always

Republican, First, Last, and Always:
A Biography of B. Carroll Reece

By

F. Suzanne Bowers

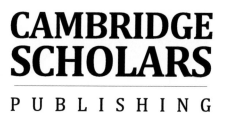

Dr. Norrell –
Thank you for always forcing me
to do better & do more. You taught
me what it truly means to be a
historian and made me a better
writer. I appreciate your constant
support & encouragement.
Suzanne ☺

CAMBRIDGE
SCHOLARS
PUBLISHING

Republican, First, Last, and Always:
A Biography of B. Carroll Reece,
by F. Suzanne Bowers

This book first published 2010

Cambridge Scholars Publishing

12 Back Chapman Street, Newcastle upon Tyne, NE6 2XX, UK

British Library Cataloguing in Publication Data
A catalogue record for this book is available from the British Library

ISBN (10): 1-4438-1916-6, ISBN (13): 978-1-4438-1916-9

TABLE OF CONTENTS

LIST OF IMAGES

ACKNOWLEDGEMENTS

There are many people I would like to thank for their gracious assistance in making this work possible. Professors Robert J. Norrell and Lorri Glover advised and mentored me during graduate school, where this work began as my dissertation. Both have made me a better writer and teacher. The Bernadotte Schmitt Research Award allowed me to spend extensive time at the Archives of Appalachia at East Tennessee State University, where Ned Irwin, Georgia Greer, and John Fleenor provided invaluable assistance during my research at the B. Carroll Reece Papers. Captain Brett Monette of the United States Army helped clarify army rankings and served as a resource for military questions. Jackie Laney edited and reviewed initial drafts, assisted me with research trips, and always provided moral support. My friends and colleagues Aaron Crawford and John Kvach read initial copies and offered excellent recommendations for improvement. Their support aided me in graduate school and continues today. I would also like to thank my sister, LaDonna Bowers, for her comments on initial copies and her tireless support of my scholarly pursuits, and my parents, for always believing in me. Numerous other friends have provided constant encouragement along my path. Everyone should have such champions for their cause.

INTRODUCTION

"I do not think we have a right to take our people's money and use it to try to raise the standard of living of the people in all the nations of the earth—we simply cannot carry the world on our back."[1] B. Carroll Reece wrote these words in a letter to a newspaper in late 1952, during the height of the Korean War. Although directly referring to the high cost in American lives during the fighting, Reece's words also defined his political viewpoint throughout his forty-plus years in politics. Born in a rural area of upper-East Tennessee, Reece rose to political dominance in the state's Republican Party and became a confidant of one of the nation's leading Republican figures. He believed that American democracy hinged on capitalism, and his extensive studies in finance and economics shaped his decisions throughout his career. Reece led one of the most virulent attacks against foundations during the 1950s because he believed these organizations used grant money to foster what he considered un-American ideals. Through Reece's career, it is possible to trace the fight against communism through an economic standpoint from the end of World War I to the downfall of America's most notorious anti-communist.

The struggle to maintain a balance between the Republicans in Reece's home district and their distrust of an expanding federal government characterized much of his political career. Reece lived in East Tennessee—politically defined as the First and Second Districts, stretching from Knox County eastward to the state line. Nestled in the Appalachian Mountains, most of the area remained skeptical of the strong federal government established after the Civil War. The economic and social problems that resulted from the war led a number of Americans to turn to local leaders to shield themselves from the many changes that followed. This attitude intensified during later crises, including the Great Depression and both World Wars, lending to the hostility that surfaced to the New Deal and to those considered outsiders. The region desired the money that came with federal programs but found the changes in social structure that came with the money intolerable. East Tennessee remained loyal to the Union during the Civil War, but it placed heavy emphasis on local autonomy. Once East Tennessee became associated with the Republican Party it rarely split its vote, which was characteristic of many Appalachian regions. This allowed local leaders to become almost immovable as long as they maintained community approval.[2]

Reece displayed an aversion to communism soon after his election to the United States House of Representatives. His experiences in World War I, combined with his father-in-law's hatred of communism and socialism, influenced him to become more dedicated to its eradication. The government proposal to operate the nitrate and power plants at Muscle Shoals, Alabama, in the 1920s seemed too similar to communism, prompting Reece to support private ownership of the facility. Although Reece worked to increase compensation and pensions for war veterans and to reduce high freight rates for farmers in his district, his stand on Muscle Shoals threatened his career in the House. His district desired the advantages of public operation, and his determination to submit a bill for private ownership appeared to his constituents to be a delay in resolving the issue. His actions continued to be a concern and a tool used against him in later elections, yet Reece stood by his decision and insisted that he based his actions on what he felt would prevent Communists from having the opportunity to damage private enterprise.

Reece's loyalty to his district and to the Republican Party secured his position in Congress, and he learned that East Tennesseans expected Congressmen to effectively balance national issues with local desires. He did this so successfully that he rarely returned home to campaign for reelection during his eighteen terms in the House. When the Old Guard Republicans tried to buttress their dwindling power within the party, Reece's banking background and organizational skills proved invaluable. Republicans selected Reece as chairman of the Republican National Committee in 1946, a shock to a number of leading Republicans in the nation. Many wondered how a congressman from a little-known area in East Tennessee with no major legislation bearing his name became the leading figure of the Republican Party. In addition to his relative anonymity in the national sphere, a number of newspaper articles reported Reece to have been a poor public speaker, and he most likely had a stutter.[3] The answer to Reece's selection lies in shrewd political maneuvering by Reece and the desire of the Republican Party to regain a majority in Congress. Reece made strategic political allies with men like Herbert Hoover and Robert Taft and placed himself in view of many of the nation's leading political figures. His ineffectual oratory forced him to compensate with other strengths, such as his firm grasp of economics and his keen ability to relate to people on a basic level. More importantly, the Republican Party saw Reece as a tool that could break the Southern stronghold and usher a return of black voters. Reece's private income became the decisive factor after he volunteered to serve as chairman without pay.

Robert A. Taft soon became the central influence in Reece's political career. Reece campaigned for Taft in hopes of helping him win the elusive Republican nomination for president. Many came to view Reece as little more than Taft's Southern mouthpiece. He earned a position on Taft's national campaign team in 1952, when Republicans determined to win the White House. Many blamed Reece for Taft's failure to secure the nomination, but in reality, the nation had moved away from many of the conservative ideas of Reece and Taft. Taft never blamed Reece publicly for his loss, and his letters to Reece evidence that their personal friendship remained strong through all their political turmoil.

The rise of the Soviet Union as a dominant world power after World War II became one of the central political issues late in Reece's career. Prior to 1917, communism seemed to be an unworkable ideal, but after the Russian Revolution it emerged as a real threat. In the United States, the Red Scare precipitated sixty years of suspicion and hostility towards communism. Americans feared that Communists planned to overthrow the American government through a variety of avenues. Thus, Congress and others in positions of power launched investigations through any facet that offered a weakness to communist infiltrators, including propaganda, Hollywood, educational facilities, and government employees. The Fish Committee, commissioned in 1930, analyzed communist activities within the United States and concluded following a brief investigation with minor recommendations. In 1934 Congress authorized a Special Committee to Investigate Un-American Activities, known as the McCormack-Dickstein Committee, to study Nazi propaganda, on the rise with Adolf Hitler's ascension to Chancellor in Germany. After the committee's one-year investigation, Congress did not sanction any other investigation until 1938, when Representative Martin Dies of Texas insisted that a special committee needed to resume the investigation into un-American activities and propaganda. The Dies Committee convened until 1944, when Dies decided not to seek reelection to the House. After American involvement in World War II and the threat presented by communist power in Russia, internal security became foremost among the minds of congressmen.

These investigations assumed a heightened importance in the decade after the war. Few remained outside the reach of those determined to prevent communism from destroying democracy. During the opening session of the 1945 House of Representatives, John Rankin of Mississippi proposed an amendment that created the House Committee on Un-American Activities (HUAC) as a standing committee of the House.

HUAC's investigations into labor, Hollywood, and government offices prompted the blacklisting and dismissal of a number of university professors and employees, making it increasingly difficult to express radical viewpoints or associate with communist groups. In 1950 the Senate created the Senate Internal Security Subcommittee (SISS) to investigate subversion, and Senator Joseph McCarthy declared to possess a list of communists working in the State Department.

Reece became consumed with rooting out Communist influence from every corner of American life. He enlisted the help of Republicans across the entire nation to support the fight against communism. In 1946 he led the Republican charge against Democrats in the congressional elections based on subversion and infiltration of the American government. Reece believed that large foundations represented one of the weaknesses through which communists could destroy American democracy. He implied that not only had subversives infiltrated foundations, but also that foundation trustees and directors made bad decisions with grant money through their choice of recipients. Reece attacked not the ideology of communism, but the economic decisions made by foundations that he believed fostered subversion and anti-American principles. In 1952 he served on the Cox Committee, which investigated tax-exempt foundations for subversive activity. The committee failed to find any evidence of illegal activity within foundations, and Cox's death in 1953 ended the investigation. Later that year, however, Reece introduced a bill to reopen the investigation on the premise that the Cox Committee had failed to complete its work. The House commissioned the Reece Committee in 1954 to investigate foundations and grants given to educational institutions. The Reece Committee's controversial public hearings lasted less than two months, during which time Reece accused well-known foundations—including the Ford Foundation, Carnegie Foundation, and Rockefeller Foundation—of fostering subversion.

The Reece Committee faced numerous troubles from its inception. Few believed Reece's assertion that foundations used grants to foster subversion in education. Most recognized the grudge Reece held toward liberal Republicans and his desire to avenge Taft's presidential nomination loss. The staff chosen to work on the committee increased its ineffectiveness by their obvious bias toward the foundations targeted. One Congressman on the committee, however, refused to allow the committee to assassinate the character of foundations without evidence. Reece supported the committee's critical final report, which went out of print shortly after its appearance and received little more than cursory notice from Congress. Throughout his final years, Reece maintained his belief that subversives infiltrated foundations, and subsequent investigations by Congress in the early 1960s must have seemed justification of Reece's vendetta.

Almost all of Reece's attempts to protect his district and American democracy turned disastrous. His effort to direct the operation of Muscle Shoals into the hands of private enterprise to promote the interests of his home state eventually cost him his seat in Congress. The creation of the power plants through the Tennessee Valley Authority (TVA), which brought less expensive electricity to his district and forced Reece to support government operation, flooded his hometown as part of its development. His desire to ensure the security of the nation and its educational systems prompted him to lead an investigation the same year that McCarthy and his supporters became discredited in the eyes of the nation. Reece became the leader of the Republican Party, yet few recognized his name and newspapers often misspelled it.

Reece's life and career reflect the complexities present in United States history throughout the twentieth century. A pocket of Republican power in East Tennessee had little influence on state elections, although Republicans increasingly carried the state in presidential elections. Republicans could, however, wield their power over their district representative to Congress. This led to an understanding between the party leaders in the state that often became the source of criticism from both parties. Reece exploited this agreement and his position to remain in office and also gain patronage for his district. His career revealed the complex dynamics that developed among mountain Republicans who disliked a strong central government but desired the advantages that such a government could provide. Newspapers that supported Reece portrayed him as a wholesome person who refrained from smoking or drinking. Articles lauded his military record, his family, and his faith in the Republican Party. Pictures of Reece during his tenure as chairman always showed him with a laugh or smile on his face. Those who opposed Reece depicted him as unintelligent and a bad speaker, with loyalty bordering on blind servitude. The truth of Reece's life and career exists somewhere in the middle. A look at his life reveals how both local and national politics merged to create a distinct political culture that had been building for decades. This unique culture foreshadowed the conversion of the South to conservative Republicanism. Specifically, Reece's political career traces a politician who molded his career around his belief that America's strongest defense against foreign threats was a strong economy.[4]

CHAPTER ONE

REECE, WHO ARE YOU?

Thirteen is not an unlucky number

In the rolling hills of East Tennessee, the Reece family sprang from humble origins to accomplish monumental things. In 1871, Rev. L.L. Maples founded Aenon Seminary in a remote area of Tennessee known as Butler. His daughter Sarah Emmaline Maples attended Aenon, where she met John Isaac Reece.[1] They married with only two assets: $150 in savings and a determination to raise a family. In 1876 seventeen-year-old Sarah bore John the first of their children, and in the following twenty-five years, Sarah gave birth to thirteen more children. Of the fourteen, only one failed to live past his first year at a time and place of high infant mortality. A local paper interviewed John about his large family and the challenges associated with it. "Thirteen is not an unlucky number," John replied. He and Sarah prided themselves on their ability to raise their children in what they considered to be comfort and informed the reporter that they had given "each a good education, at the same time saving sufficient money to buy a farm and build a house affording ample room for such a family." John owned 130 acres of land that he farmed to support his family. He made the children's shoes, and some had to go barefoot until well into the fall when he had time and money to complete them. All of the children worked on the farm and at other jobs to help support the family. Eight of the thirteen children attended college by the start of World War I, a remarkable feat for such a poor and uneducated area.[2]

Butler's origins trace back to the Revolutionary Era. Cherokee Indians named a river in northeastern Tennessee the Watauga, meaning "beautiful river." According to legend, Daniel Boone passed through this area in 1769 on his way to Kentucky. On his journey, Boone's favorite horse became lame, and he released her on the banks of a stream to fend for herself. The next year, this same horse, fully recovered and healthy, met Boone as he passed back through the area. Boone then named the creek "Old Roan," after his horse. Roan Creek flowed into the Watauga at the lower end of Butler. The area possessed many of the characteristics of an

Appalachian region—families centered on kinship ties and residents placed an emphasis on face-to-face interaction. Most worked to make ends meet rather than to make a profit. They often taught their children to hunt at a young age in order to help support the family.[3]

Butler remained a small town in the corner of upper East Tennessee. It consisted of mostly private homes, and many of the families had lived there for generations. The area contained few opportunities for industry until the arrival of the railroad in the early 1900s. The Whiting Lumber Company, J. Minish Furniture Company, John B. Wilson Casket Company, and Cozier Wood Package Company furnished Butler with factory jobs. The other businesses in the town included cafés, a general store, a drugstore, a post office, a filling station, barber and beauty shops, the Bluebird Tea Room, and Shupe's Hotel. Residents could attend Butler Christian Church, Butler Baptist Church, or Butler Methodist Church. The town had one school and two water fountains.[4]

The Reece family claimed a long history of military service both in Tennessee and in the nation. A great-great-great-grandfather, Captain Jacob Brown, reportedly founded the Nolachuckey settlement, the first in the East Tennessee section of the Great Smoky Mountains. Local historians credit Brown with the first store in this area, supplied with goods brought by packhorses from the Carolinas. Captain Brown fought with John Sevier, the first governor of Tennessee, in the Battle of King's Mountain during the Revolutionary War. Major General Brazilla Carroll McBride, the namesake and great-great uncle of Brazilla Carroll Reece, fought in the War of 1812 and married the sister of Revolutionary War hero Nathaniel Greene. John Reece's family continued this military tradition as five of the ten boys served in the military: Wilson Landrine and John Eggers during the Spanish-American War, Brazilla Carroll and Lemuel in the army during World War I, and Raleigh Valentine in the Army Air Corp during World War II.[5]

Born on December 22, 1889, Brazilla Carroll Reece entered the world at a time when America still nursed fresh wounds on its way to recovery from its most devastating and deadly war. The government in Washington officially ended Reconstruction in 1877, but few in the nation embraced the new citizens as equals. The South maintained a strong Christian heritage that stemmed from the Second Great Awakening and had been bolstered by southerners' growing respect and nostalgia for the past as embodied by the Lost Cause. Both of these are evident in the names given to the Reece children. The name Brazilla most likely comes from the Old Testament name Barzillai, meaning "iron" or "strong." The Bible records Barzillai as showing hospitality to the future king David when he fled from Absalom, but Barzillai declined the king's offer to spend his last days at court.[6] Although his Christian name inspired thoughts of integrity and strength, B. Carroll Reece chose to forego the use of his ancestor's first name in order to assert his own identity. His experiences during his first thirty years developed the perseverance and dedication that would later characterize his career in the United States House of Representatives.

J. I. REECE & HIS FAMILY

Figure 1.1 The Reece Family. Left to right: John Isaac Reece, Sarah Maples Reece, James Lafayette Reece, Wilson Landrine Reece, John Eggers Reece, Walter Jacob Reece, Joseph Isaac Reece, Amanda Catherine Reece, Asa Clayton Reece, Brazilla Carroll Reece, Lemuel L. Reece, Millard Brown Reece, Laura Ruth Reece, Anna Reece, and Raleigh Valentine Reece. Courtesy of the B. Carroll Reece Papers at the Archives of Appalachia, East Tennessee State University.

Education is what develops savage man into civilized man

Reece and his family placed great emphasis on learning, a rare trait in such a rural area. He began his formal education in the same school where his parents met. By the time Reece entered school his grandfather had sold Aenon, re-named Holly Springs College in 1886. After being purchased by the Watauga Baptist Association, it officially became Watauga Academy in 1906. Although Reece's parents had been able to send him to a public school five miles away, he had to work summers in the woods peeling tan bark for eighty-five cents per day in order to attend Watauga Academy. Twenty cents of that income supported the food and educational costs for eight of his siblings. Despite the difficulty of working while attending school, Reece became one of the first two graduates of Watauga Academy in 1908. His first teaching position paid him a salary of thirty-five dollars per month. After less than two years of teaching, he decided to continue his education at Carson and Newman College. He enrolled in a variety of courses, including psychology, debate, German, French, and pedagogy. Reece played basketball and served as captain of the football team. He earned high grades and graduated as valedictorian of his class in 1914 with a Bachelor of Arts degree. [7]

Figure 1-2. The basketball team at Carson-Newman College, circa 1913-1914. Reece is second from the left on the back row. Courtesy of the B. Carroll Reece Papers at the Archives of Appalachia, East Tennessee State University.

The assignments Reece completed during these early years revealed much about his developing character, idealism, and sense of morality. In a speech that debated the question of nature versus education in forming the character of man, he took the position of education and argued that once prisoners were educated they became law abiding citizens. "Education is what develops savage man into civilized man," Reece wrote, because "nature without education is blank." In one essay he recognized the need for many rural schools to incorporate advances in agriculture into their curriculum because of the monotonous nature of farm life where "the girls will become discouraged and the boys will become restless and leave for the city." Reece revealed his pride in being an American when he commended Theodore Roosevelt as "an example of the most modern Americanism" and lauded adversity as "the gateway to success and to greatness." Reece described education as a privilege, of which the recipients bore the responsibility to convey their knowledge to others.[8]

Reece wrote a number of essays that revealed his increasing belief of war as undesirable. Pointing to various wars in history, including the Peloponnesian War and the Boer War, he wrote that "taking human nature as a whole, its wars are its best protection against its weaker and more cowardly self, and that mankind cannot afford to adopt a peaceful economy." In a later essay he described war as "one of the greatest evils that has ever been intentionally maintained by man" because it separated the family, often took the lives of young men, and drained a country of its resources. Reece believed that God must have given man a spirit of war, though he questioned whether God "intended for man to rule by force of arms." Citing the Revolutionary War, he reasoned that some wars for independence were justified, but asserted war was no longer necessary because intelligent people responded to reason. "Now it is that all international disputes should be settled by arbitration and the people ought to no longer be burdened by war . . . they ought no longer in this new era of learning and civilization be forced to endure the attendant miseries of war."[9] This viewpoint became increasingly evident during the opening years of World War II, when Reece advocated isolationism rather than participation in what he often described as Europe's war.

Reece's essays also revealed his emerging viewpoint on government and America's position in the world. He called for support for America from all nationalities living within the United States and prophetically wrote that he could not "imagine any greater misfortune that can befall mankind than to have any two of the great nations of the world feel that their interests necessitate a trial of strength with each other." He predicted that this would involve all other nations of the world in a manner never seen. In an essay comparing the English system of government with the American republican system, he concluded that the cabinet form could not exist anywhere outside of England because of specific conditions that existed only within that nation. He concluded that the American form of government was better and was the model towards which other nations looked—a modern-day city on a hill. "Thus do we set the mark in legislation and government, and thus do we lead the world by reason of the able enterprise and sure judgment of the Fathers of our Government." This idealism about American government and capitalism influenced his ideas regarding communism and its spread throughout Europe and Asia during his Congressional career. Although written in his early years, Reece adhered to these principles throughout his life.[10]

Reece continued teaching after he received his degree from Carson and Newman College. Letters of recommendation written by faculty conveyed their high opinion of Reece and his abilities as both a teacher and a student. Former teachers described Reece as "an excellent instructor," "a young man of Christian ideals, of real worth and strength of character," "an unusually brilliant young man," and "a man of splendid ability and high ideals."[11] He made inquiries into a position as a high school principal in Cookeville, Tennessee, in 1914, and received a job offer from the Central Education Bureau in St. Louis, Missouri, in 1915 to teach mathematics and German at an annual salary of $1,200. He declined this position, as well as one in Mooresburg, Tennessee, to enroll in New York University (NYU) in 1915 to pursue a Master's Degree in economics and finance. At the same time, he received a Master of Arts degree from Carson and Newman in philosophy and English literature, although the school delayed reporting the official designation until 1920. When he graduated from NYU in 1916, Reece continued on at the school as Assistant Secretary and Instructor through 1917. As the United States entered World War I, Reece took a leave of absence from his post to enlist in the army.[12]

Our company commander, well, ain't he a fine fellow!

Europe maintained a precarious peace during the first decade of the twentieth century. Years of economic competition, a surge in nationalism, and a complicated system of alliances kept many European nations cautiously aware of their neighbors. On June 28, 1914, the assassination of Archduke Franz Ferdinand by a Serbian nationalist upset this delicate balance and became the catalyst for war. As the Austro-Hungarian Empire declared war on Serbia, alliances among Russia, Germany, Britain, and France drew most of Europe into the conflict.

The war that most assumed would end quickly turned into an impasse that lasted three years. New technology and weaponry made this war deadlier than any previous. Following the sinking of the *Lusitania* in 1915 and the *Sussex* in 1916, President Woodrow Wilson warned Germany against provoking American entry into the war. In February 1917, Wilson received a copy of a telegram that Britain intercepted from the German foreign minister, Arthur Zimmerman, which promised Mexico the territory in the Southwest that had been ceded to the United States if Mexico entered the war on the side of Germany. The telegram, combined with the March 1917 revolution in Russia, removed the last obstacle to American participation. Wilson appealed to Congress to declare war on Germany, and the United States officially entered World War I on April 6, 1917. America then faced the challenge of mobilizing an economy, the population, and a large army. Because of the immediate need for officers, the army rushed many through training in the Plattsburg style. This training was very basic, and bad weather or lack of supplies often prevented troops from completing their training.[13] Most of the soldiers arrived in Europe unprepared for the battles to come. Both soldiers and leaders had to learn "on the job," at the risk of high casualties.[14]

Reece followed in the footsteps of his older brothers as the United States entered the world conflict. On April 24, 1917, eighteen days after the United States officially declared war, he enrolled into the Plattsburg Reserve Officers Training Camp in New York. At twenty-seven, he weighed only 135 pounds and measured five-feet-nine-inches tall. At his graduation from training on August 10, 1917, Reece took an oath as Second Lieutenant, Infantry Section, Officers Reserve Corp.[15] In September, he received orders that assigned him to the Rainbow Division, 166th Infantry, Company A, under command of Major General Mann. The Rainbow Division deployed the following month to serve with the American Expeditionary Force in Europe.

Reece's keepsakes from the war reflect both his hurried training and his lack of experience. Among the tokens that survived were booklets issued by the army on visual signaling and the role of a Platoon Commander. The latter included important questions a commander should ask himself before taking over a trench, before an attack, and after gaining the objective of an attack. The necessity of this guide reflected the absence of combat time for officers and troops. One of the more interesting mementos was a personal notebook that Reece kept with military figures, lists of officers, times, and a personal note of caution: "Do not deficate [sic] around kitchen."[16] He remained with the 166th Infantry throughout 1917 and into 1918 when they entered the front on February 22nd. He then transferred to the 26th Division, 102nd Infantry on May 1st and continued as part of their offensive until the war's end.

Reece dedicated himself to both his military duty and his men. A June patrol order from the headquarters of the 3rd Battalion, 102nd Infantry, ordered Reece to command an exploring patrol into enemy territory in order to locate an enemy observation post and take prisoners, but his first true encounter in battle came at Aisne-Marne on July 18-26, 1918. His combat experience grew as General Pershing led American troops, including Reece, at St. Mihiel from September 12-16 in an attempt to drive the Germans away from Verdun. Before they could succeed, the Allied forces persuaded Pershing to reduce his objectives and turn his attention to the Meuse River-Argonne Forest region. The drive at St. Mihiel proved less successful than Pershing had hoped, but the troops learned much about war on the Western Front.[17] Reece earned the nickname "Pop" among Company M because of the way he tended to look after them. One report stated that after fighting at St. Mihiel, Reece attempted to rouse his troops for a return to the front with "Men, we are making history. Forward!" They demonstrated their fatigue with the war with responses of "The hell with history!" and "Go swipe us some chow, Pop."[18]

The Allied forces began a massive assault at the Meuse-Argonne front in late September that became the decisive battle of the war. The delay in transporting weapons and soldiers to the front caused fighting to stalemate, compounded by General Pershing's insistence that the American troops remain separate from those of the other Allied forces. The troops' dependence on the French for supplies and weapons, however, forced Pershing to finally agree to officially serve under Marshall Petain. After recapturing Verdun, the German forces withdrew to their second lines of defense. The job of attaining a key sector, Hill #360, fell to the 26th Division on October 24th. Woods covered the top of the hill, and remnants of trees destroyed by battle shadowed its slopes. German troops dug into pillboxes and trenches and continually rained heavy shells on the road leading to this hill, giving the area the nickname "Death Valley." American troops fighting from shell holes slowly gained the slopes of the hill, with heavy casualties. The battle raged during daylight, and troops attempted to recover their wounded under cover of dusk. The German flares and subsequent machine guns increased the difficulty of the rescues.[19]

On October 27th, 1918, the 102nd Infantry received a handwritten field order from headquarters to gain possession of Hill #360 in Bois d'Ormont after an artillery preparation against German forces. Reece and his men faced a hidden danger during this assault. Germany first used gas attacks on April 22, 1915, on an unprepared French and British military. Britain's retaliation caused Germany to develop a more toxic gas in the form of a liquid poison that turned yellow when exposed to the air. This mustard gas could penetrate clothing and remained active for weeks on the ground or on bushes, forcing Allied troops to be more cautious when they advanced. On October 12th, the Germans began a thirty-four hour bombing of Bois d'Ormont with mustard gas shells. Reece and his men likely suffered exposure to remaining traces of this gas. Reece led the offensive to the crest of the hill, but bursting shells threw him to the ground, twice knocking him unconscious. When he regained consciousness, he reorganized his command and held firm to his position. He braved machine gun fire several times to crawl in advance of the Allied front line in order to rescue wounded men hiding in shell holes. The strength of the German entrenchment and intense artillery fire finally forced the army to issue an order to draw back despite the advance. By November the Allied forces pushed German troops back to their own border and cut supply lines, prompting Germany to seek an armistice.[20]

Reece's actions during this assault earned him the Distinguished Service Cross, the Distinguished Service Medal, the French Croix de Guerre with Palm, and citations from Marshall Petain as well as the Division Brigade and Regimental Commanders. Marshall Petain described Reece as "an officer of great bravery . . . He gave proof of the finest devotion by going to look for the wounded of his Company left between the lines." The fighting temporarily placed Reece in command of the 3rd Battalion, which the commendation for the Distinguished Service Medal described as "a task of great difficulty" because the battalion became disorganized with high casualties. Despite these difficulties Reece "displayed marked ability and determination in reorganizing his command and moulding [sic] it into a good fighting unit, able under his leadership to achieve valuable results." He also received a commendation from the Major General of the 26th Division, who entered Reece's name and actions in the record of The Yankee Division. Reece retained command of the 3rd Battalion through the end of the war.[21]

The armistice designated November 11, 1918, as the end of fighting in Europe. Many in the military, however, lacked confidence in this agreement. Reece received orders on November 10th to take his men "over the top"—out of the trenches toward enemy lines—at 9:15 the next morning. Rumors of the armistice, to take place at 11:00 that morning, made him hesitate leading his men to possible death. He thus faced the dilemma of risking the lives of his men or openly defying a military order, an act that could have resulted in a court martial if rumors of the armistice proved false. Reece's solution entailed telling his men to go over the top but to find the nearest shell-hole and stay there for the next hour and forty-five minutes. Reece spent that time wondering if he would be court-martialed for failing to take his objective. At the designated time, both sides laid down their arms, and Reece and his men survived without loss of life or honor.[22]

Reece's stellar military reputation extended down to the common soldier. After fighting in the Argonne Forest, Sergeant Ramsay wrote to his brother Jack that "our company commander, well, ain't he a fine fellow! Gosh! Jack he is a prince. He takes such great pains in his men. When we went over the top the last time, he was right there with a bayonet and rifle, and I said to myself the first Dutchman that gets him does not go back to tell about it."[23] The loyalty that Reece inspired in his men lasted long after the war. When he decided to run for a congressional seat, the surviving men from his company submitted a letter to be used in publication. They described Reece as "like a father to us . . . a great fellow." They cited both his bravery and his loyalty as characteristics that set Reece apart from other candidates for office.[24] Reece reportedly never cursed at the men he led and told them that he would rather resign his commission than speak to them in the manner other officers spoke to him.[25]

Reece maintained a degree of modesty about his experiences during the war. Although his military record appeared in most of his election propaganda, Reece omitted exceptional emphasis on his actions. An interviewer in the early 1920s pointed out that Reece maintained the honor of being the only known soldier to have received the Distinguished Service Cross, the Distinguished Service Medal, and the Croix de Guerre with Palm. "A fellow don't deserve a medal for doing something anybody would do under the circumstances," Reece reasoned. In another interview, he maintained the same analysis of his actions, recalling "That wasn't anything so very unusual . . . You didn't see it happen every day, but you did see it once in a while. The concussion of a bursting shell would simply knock a man over . . . Then he'd get up and start again." The leadership experience Reece gained during World War I and his ability to place his actions in the greater context of the war proved invaluable in his congressional service and later appealed to top men in the Republican Party.[26]

Demobilization of troops at the end of the war signaled a new problem for the American government. For many soldiers, morale became a problem because of long delays before they returned home. After unsuccessful attempts with drills and sports contests, the army offered to provide instruction to those wanting to learn basic skills, such as reading and writing, as well as subjects ranging from elementary grades to college level. Approximately one and a half million troops took advantage of this by enrolling in courses at universities in both Britain and France while still on duty with their units.[27]

Reece capitalized on this opportunity and headed to the University of London School of Economics in March 1919. The journey itself proved somewhat precarious, evidenced by Reece's handwritten memo to the Board on Claims and Lost Personal Property at the end of April for lost items, including a uniform, shoes, boots, bed roll, blankets, etc. totaling $263. Reece secured a pass allowing him to travel at his own expense outside the university and visited much of Britain. These journeys permitted him to see the effects of the war on Britain's people and countryside. [28]

Following the armistice, the American military placed a temporary halt on all promotions. While in London, Reece asked his former commander Colonel Lewis about the status of his promotion based on his actions at Bois d'Ormont and Lewis' recommendation letter. In a prompt response, Lewis wrote a letter from Paris describing Reece as "a gentleman of the highest character . . . As regimental commander it was my intention at the first opportunity to recommend Lieut. Reece for promotion to Captain and later to Major." The war's end and Lewis' absence from the division prevented him from following through with his intention. Lewis added that "I consider Lt. Reece to have been deprived of well won promotion."[29] Despite his commendable military record, six years passed before Reece received the promotion he felt duly deserved.

After more than a year abroad with the army, Reece returned to the United States. On June 23, 1919, special orders relieved him from duty and ordered him to proceed to Brest, France, as the Port of Embarkation for return to the United States. Keeping in line with progressive ideals, the camp hospital certified Reece "free from vermin of any sort and all Venereal and Infectious Diseases" and allowed him to proceed to Camp Dix, New Jersey. On July 26th, he wrote to the Commanding General to request a formal discharge from the military in order to assume a position at NYU as director of one of its schools. He explained that remaining in active service would force him to "assume financial and professional risks" that he preferred to avoid. He offered to remain on the discharged list of officers or to go into the Reserve Corps. Two days later the 50th Infantry accepted his request and honorably discharged Reece from Camp Dix and the army on August 16, 1919.[30]

Reece returned to an America consumed by suspicion and fear. The United States recognized the provisional government established in Russia in March 1917, but in November another revolution replaced that government with the Soviet regime. The American government refused to recognize Soviet Russia and severed all diplomatic ties. Anarchists and other radical groups within the United States hoped other areas of the world would duplicate the Soviet revolution. In February 1919 a series of strikes spread across the United States, and the following April authorities discovered thirty bombs mailed through the postal system to people hostile to the anarchist movement. In June a series of bombs exploded across seven cities that targeted those involved in suppressing radicalism, including

Attorney General A. Mitchell Palmer. These bombings spread fear across America as all radicals—anarchists, communists, the International Workers of the World—became grouped together as a "red menace."[31]

The response to these attacks led many Americans to view radicals and immigrants as threats to security. The Attorney General authorized a series of raids in late 1919 through early 1920 in hopes of discovering those responsible for the bombings. A number of radicals faced arrest and deportation for possession of weapons or suspicion of radical affiliation. As the anarchist movement within the United States slowly declined, focus shifted to the growing communist movement. The initial terror associated with the Red Scare declined as post-war prosperity increased, but communism remained in the minds of many, including Reece, as a subtle but constant threat to American democracy. This idea may have explained in part why Reece maintained his affiliation with the military through the next ten years. On May 27, 1924, the Adjutant General appointed him Major, Staff Specialist of the Officers Reserve Corp of the Army of the United States for the duration of five years. The next March, he received appointment as Lieutenant Colonel, Specialist in the Army, to enter active duty when specially ordered.[32]

Ten Years in Congress is Long Enough for Any Man

One political party dictated the politics of most southern states after the Civil War. Once the Democratic Party overthrew Reconstruction governments, it presented a solid front to the nation on most issues, especially those regarding race. According to the historian V.O. Key in *Southern Politics in State and Nation*, the South may not have been an important region in national politics, but politics were important in the South. With one-party dominance, the primary election became the main contest in the southern states because the party nominee rarely faced opposition in the November election. In *Dixie Demagogues,* the authors describe the primary election as an entertainment and "an exchange of personalities in which the pot calls the kettle black." Within the Democratic Party, rival factions fought for the nomination on local levels and sought the support of the regional political boss.[33]

Tennessee followed this political model of the South with one important exception. The Democratic Party dominated the central and western parts of the state in the years after the Civil War, but the eastern part of the state remained loyal to the Republican Party both during and after the war. E.H. Crump of Memphis emerged during the first half of the twentieth century as the local Democratic political boss, and as a result of the limited number of Republicans in the state, he often garnered enough support from his district and those surrounding it to elect his favored candidate into state office. An informal agreement between the Republican and Democratic leaders of the state allowed East Tennessee elections to proceed unhindered by the Democratic Party in return for little or no opposition from Republicans in the senatorial and gubernatorial campaigns. This permitted East Tennesseans to elect Republicans from the First and Second Districts to the United States House of Representatives on a consistent basis. The political scientist William C. Havard characterized Tennessee politics as a double one-party state.[34]

After he left Fort Dix, Reece returned to serve as Director of the School of Business at NYU and maintained contact with men from the war and his home state. Reece wrote to Sergeant Alvin C. York to request a meeting when he returned to Butler in early April and provided York with a copy of his war record as incentive for the meeting. Reece also corresponded with his former commander, Captain Lewis, to discuss the actions of the 102nd Infantry on the day of the armistice. Although he lived in New York, Reece sustained a political connection with Tennessee. He announced approval that Sam R. Sells, the Republican congressman from the First District, insisted that delegates from the district support Major General Leonard Wood at the National Convention.[35]

Unhappy with their current Republican representative, a delegation from Tennessee visited Reece in 1920 and asked him to consider running for Congress on the basis that Sells had agreed to step aside if a war veteran wanted his seat. Shortly thereafter, he requested a leave of absence from NYU to return to Tennessee. This move seemed uncharacteristic for a person who had spent his life in academia, but in later interviews Reece disclosed that at the age of thirteen he told his brother Jim that he had decided to go into public office. He wanted to help people, but he had to wait for the opportune moment to enter the political sphere. Reece worked with the American Legion while at NYU, but this petition presented his first opportunity to hold a political office. After a local newspaper announced Reece's candidacy in the primary for the Republican nomination for the First Congressional District seat in the House of Representatives, tempers flared between Sells and Reece. When the two met to discuss their candidacy, Sells denied stating he would resign his seat. He then reportedly looked at Reece and asked, "Reece, who are you? You haven't any chance to win against me."[36]

The primary elections in East Tennessee involved heated campaigns for the few Republican positions left in the state. In 1920, when Reece decided to campaign for the representative seat from the First District,

Sam R. Sells had occupied the position for ten years. Playing off the report that Sells would step down if a real soldier desired his seat, Reece supporters touted his military record, recapped the actions that won him many medals, and used a snapshot of Reece in uniform as his campaign portrait. When Sells denied making the statement and refused to withdraw from the primary, Reece's supporters began to attack Sells' legislative record and his credibility. In a sworn statement published in local newspapers, Reece accused Sells of stating that he would pick his own successor to office and it would not be Reece. According to the statement, Sells declared that no man could break his organization and that his eventual retirement from office did not mean a political enemy would succeed him.[37]

The contest between Sells and Reece presented the first challenge to a primary nomination and the first real election campaign in East Tennessee in a number of years. Reece stated he hesitated to run initially, but after hearing that Sells would not run if a soldier entered the primary, he acquiesced. After local papers printed a number of attacks against Sells for his promise to step aside for a real soldier, he acknowledged the comment but stipulated that at the time he had a Major Caleb Hathaway in mind as his successor. Sells informed Reece that a candidate needed more than simply a military record to qualify for office.[38]

Sells' decision to remain in the race for the primary nomination prompted a new wave of attacks against his suitability for office. A large circular distributed to residents of Greeneville, Tennessee, listed a number of reasons why Sells should not be the choice of the people. The circular reminded residents that Sells' position as a manufacturer meant votes against the interests of the farmer, the laborer, and the poor. It asserted that Sells lacked a critical understanding of educational issues that Reece, a former teacher, possessed. One of the most damaging accusations was that Sells made more money during World War I than he had during his entire life, whereas Reece volunteered to fight. Representative of the intense religious nature of the area, a campaign pamphlet titled "Can Anything Good Come Out of Sodom" attacked Sells' military record, cited court records that showed Sells had been charged with public intoxication and disorderly conduct, and accused him of infidelity.[39]

Figure 1-3. B. Carroll Reece, circa 1919, with his military honors. He used this photograph as his campaign picture during the 1920 elections. Courtesy of the B. Carroll Reece Papers at the Archives of Appalachia, East Tennessee State University.

Reece supporters assailed Sells' legislative record. They charged him with selling the people of the First District to General Wood at the Republican National Convention in Chicago for $8,000 by switching his vote at the last minute. They also condemned Sells for using public money in the campaign by sending out campaign materials from his office in Washington with the aid of his clerks rather than volunteers. Campaign flyers described Sells' legislative record for the previous ten years as a failure and claimed Sells missed or was absent for approximately 500 votes. The flyers also highlighted that Sells continually voted against or missed measures in the interest of the farmer and laborer and hinted that he took money as a purchase for his nomination.[40]

Retaliatory charges from Sells forced Reece to defend his qualifications for office and his dedication to the district. Reece used his military record to refute accusations that he had never voted or paid a poll tax in the district. He claimed his absence was for the nation's safety and that such accusations insulted all soldiers. Advertisements reminded constituents that Reece had no commercial interests to handicap him or divert his attention and promised Reece would "stay on his job for 365 days in the year." Reece described being a congressman as a childhood ambition and vowed to "free the party from bossism and build up an efficient, just, and successful organization which will have in mind to preserve only the interests of the people." The campaign centered more on attacks against the candidates' suitability for office rather than issues, but in one speech Reece touched upon political concerns important to the district. He advocated improvement in public schools, better pay for teachers, federal aid for public roads, and rewards for "honest labor." "Ten years in Congress is long enough for any man," cried Reece supporters. Sells failed to bring enough benefits to the district, and the Reece campaign capitalized on this detail by attributing it to a length of time in office that had made Sells negligent to his district. The campaign tactics proved effective, and Reece won the Republican primary nomination in August, assuring him of the election win in November. Warren G. Harding, the Republican candidate for president, defeated the Democratic candidate with the promise of a return to "normalcy."[41]

During his first year in office, Reece attended a social function that became a pivotal point in his life. In 1921, the thirty-two-year-old Reece attended a dinner party at the home of Mr. and Mrs. Eugene Pomeroy in Washington, D.C. There he met Louise D. Despard Goff, a graduate of The Spence School in New York—an elite elementary and high school founded by Clara Spence in 1892 for women—who had spent six months abroad working on a committee for devastated France after World War I. Both would later admit that neither had wanted to attend the party, but it was the beginning of a relationship that would last more than forty years. On October 30, 1923, the two married in what newspapers called the social event of the fall. Reports of the event described Reece as the "baby member of the House" and Louise as a "successful debutant." The *Washington Post* considered the event "one of the most important of the autumn weddings."[42]

Reece's marriage connected him to a Republican family firmly established in national politics. Louise's grandfather, Nathan Goff, Jr., came from a wealthy West Virginia family. He served in the Union Army during the Civil War and was taken prisoner by Confederates. His war experiences helped him gain a strong local support base for his entrance into politics. Residents of his state referred to him as "General Goff," even though he only attained the rank of Major during the war. Goff maintained friendships with President Rutherford B. Hayes and President William H. Taft. President Andrew Johnson appointed Goff as United States District Attorney for West Virginia, a position he held—with one brief respite as Secretary of the Navy under President James A. Garfield—until President

Chester Arthur's administration forced him to resign in 1882 because of disagreements with President Arthur.[43]

Goff then returned to West Virginia and built up a strong Republican following. He ran for congressman in 1882 and served for three terms. He received a large family inheritance in 1885, which removed any worries regarding personal finance. In 1888, friends convinced Goff to run for governor of West Virginia. His ultimate dream was a Senate seat, but he decided to listen to his friends and won the gubernatorial election by 110 votes. Democrats contested the election and after a lengthy investigation seated their own candidate. This loss did not decrease his prominence, and he accepted a position as a judge of the United States Circuit Court for the Fourth Judicial District from President Benjamin Harrison in 1891. He served in this capacity until President Taft urged Goff to run for the United States Senate seat in 1912, a seat he held until his death in 1920.[44]

Nathan's son and Louise's father, Guy Goff, also built an impressive political resume. Guy Goff left West Virginia at the age of eighteen to attend Kenyon Military Academy in Ohio. He then attended Harvard Law School and opened his own practice at Boston to avoid practicing in his father's judicial circuit. He then moved to Milwaukee and received a 1911 appointment as United States Attorney in Wisconsin from President Taft. Close family ties between the Taft and Goff families played a role in the appointment, but Guy Goff also maintained a distance from factional disputes in Wisconsin politics that appealed to the president. At the end of his term in 1915 he returned to private law practice and then offered his services to the government at the onset of World War I. He served with General Pershing as acting Judge Advocate General for the American Expeditionary Force from 1919 to 1920. He returned to Washington, and in 1921 President William Harding asked him to serve as assistant to the Attorney General. While there, he worked to appoint former president William Taft as chief justice.[45]

The death of his father and brother forced Guy Goff to return to his home state, where he maintained the political dominance created by his father. West Virginia law required him to reside in the state in order to administer the estates of his father and brother. In the process of functioning as executor, he became known to a number of influential people. In 1924 he ran for and won the race for United States Senator from West Virginia. Residents viewed him as wealthy, experienced in Washington, D.C. politics, a good speaker, and removed from past West Virginia political frays. He established himself as a conservative voter and earned the support of his state, but failing health prevented him from running for a second term in 1930.[46]

Guy Goff became a national figure in the Republican Party and maintained a high degree of animosity towards communism. During his service in World War I, Goff wrote letters to his family about the destruction caused by Bolshevism and its proponents. He remarked that the "only way to meet Bolshevism is to crush it without the fear of what a noisy minority in England or America might say. Verily, this is not a tea party, it is neither Boston nor pink." The Goff family presented a bound copy of these letters to Reece, suggesting the importance of Goff's viewpoints to him.[47] Reece already had an aversion to communism from his own war experience and his extensive study of capitalism and economics. Goff witnessed first-hand much of the destruction caused by World War I, and his letters probably intensified Reece's conviction of communism as an impossible system of government. With Goff's guidance, Reece dedicated his career to defending capitalism from the threat of communist encroachment.

Reece's background in finance and economics and his later personal business interests enabled him to become sufficiently wealthy to spend time in a political career that provided only a small income, while rooting him firmly within his home district. This allowed him to garner enough prestige and support to win his district's seat for the United States House of Representatives, often with little or no campaigning. In order to understand how Reece translated this local influence into a force that seated him at the head of the Republican Party, it is important to understand the relationship between the local elections and Reece's specific actions during his first years of service in the House.

CHAPTER TWO

PASS PUBLIC OFFICE AROUND

What He Expects to Do That Counts

Reece's first term in office indicated an attempt to follow through on campaign promises to improve conditions in East Tennessee. Reece recognized that the people of the district would scrutinize his first term since he centered his campaign on his predecessor's inability to secure benefits and patronage. He had encouraged the district to "pass public office around" in 1920, and he hoped to prevent them from wanting to do so again in 1922. The House assigned him to the Civil Service Reform Committee, the Committee on Roads, and the Committee on Expenditures in the Treasury Department. In April 1921 he formally introduced a bill to appropriate money and to donate surplus war materials, including trucks and tankers, to states for use by their highway commissions. Republican Senator Arthur Capper of Kansas introduced a similar bill in the Senate, and the two bills merged into the Capper-Reece Road Building Bill—Reece's main accomplishment in his first term. Under its provisions, Tennessee received $729,000 in machinery for road improvements. President Harding disliked the idea of the money appropriated to states continuing beyond his administration, so Reece amended the bill to allow money given to states for highway construction to extend for only three years. The bill granted Tennessee around $15 million during that period. Reece called himself a "fanatic" about good roads because of the lack of well-maintained roads in his hometown of Butler.[1]

As the 1922 primary elections approached, Reece temporarily shifted focus to secure a second term in office. Opposed by W. B. Ellison, the mayor of Johnson City, Reece asked his constituents for another two years in office based on the custom of allowing a new representative a second term. He quoted Abraham Lincoln's adage of it never being a good idea to swap horses in the middle of the stream. Reece had achieved the position of a ranking member on all committees on roads, which he advertised as a great benefit to his district. Reece also broadened his campaign to include minorities. In one advertisement for a speech he made in Johnson City in

August 1922, the bottom portion noted that space had been provided for
colored men and women. At a time of segregation and Jim Crow laws, this
attitude of inclusion towards minorities stood out and later played a part in
his selection to chair the Republican National Committee. Reece defeated
his opponent in the primary election with more than a 12,000 vote
majority and returned to Washington for another two years.[2]

During his second term, Reece directed his efforts toward legislation to
benefit military veterans. Few of Reece's bills and proposals passed, but
he won the support and vote of veterans for his attempts. Perhaps recalling
the slight in not receiving a promotion at the end of World War I, he
introduced a bill to extend the time frame that Distinguished Service
Medals could be awarded to three years beyond the approval of the act.
Many World War I soldiers enlisted before reaching the minimum age of
eighteen, and law dictated that they be issued a dishonorable discharge.
Reece proposed a popular bill allowing for honorable discharges for these
men based on their service to the country. Reece campaigned for a
Veterans Administration at Mountain Branch Soldiers Hospital in Johnson
City, Tennessee, that came to fruition on June 6, 1930, when the House
passed a bill for $650,000 for expansions to the Soldiers Home. The
American Legion thanked Reece for his attempts to stand by service men
and women against "sordid and selfish opposition," and a campaign
pamphlet for veterans described Reece as "a friend to all veterans of all
wars."[3]

Throughout his career Reece maintained his commitment to help
veterans and soldiers. His work most likely stemmed from a true concern
for those who served as well as recognition of the political support
veterans provided. Reece supporters published a campaign pamphlet after
his 1932 return to Congress titled "Republicans Provide Veterans with
Benefits; Democrats Take Them Away!" In 1936 Reece received letters of
thanks for his actions in obtaining additional benefits for disabled
veterans. Reece announced to his district that "one of the most consoling
compensations of being in office is the opportunity which it has given me
to be of service to my disabled comrades and their dependents."[4]

During Reece's tenure, a proposed bill that paid a cash bonus to
veterans of World War I became a point of contention for many veterans
and legislators. At the end of his first term in January 1922, Reece
declared passage of a bonus bill as his first priority. The House acted on a
bill later that month, but members reduced the cash payments and
increased the offers of insurance and home and farm aid in an effort to
reduce the amount of initial revenue needed. The Harding Administration
waivered in support for the bill because it believed the cost involved

exceeded the nation's ability to pay. In late 1923 Reece worked to pass a bonus bill so veterans could receive their bonus before the Christmas holiday, but President Coolidge vetoed it. Representative Hamilton Fish presented a third bonus bill in 1924—a twenty-one year endowment life insurance policy to be paid in 1945—that finally met with approval. The onset of the Great Depression later that decade triggered the march of thousands of veterans and their families to Washington, D.C., in 1932 in a failed attempt to obtain immediate payment of the bonus.[5]

In addition to his proposed federal legislation, Reece worked with veterans on an individual basis throughout his career. In 1930 Reece supporters sent a mailing to notify veterans of Reece's success in getting a bill passed that allowed any veteran with a twenty-five percent disability to receive a disability allowance without providing proof of the injury's connection to service. The mailing included an application for the allowance along with a campaign letter. Supporters sent yet another mailing specifically to Spanish-American War veterans with an application for an increase in pension.[6] Reece began a twenty-year correspondence in 1924 with veteran S.C. Slagle of Jonesboro, Tennessee. The initial letters involved minor issues, such as Slagle's concern that he could not drive his tractor on the highway because of possible damage from its weight and its claws. Shortly thereafter, Slagle became concerned with laws regarding the amount of his veteran's compensation and its continuance. Reece assured Slagle that he would stand by him to secure his continued compensation and thanked Slagle and his friends for their actions on his behalf during Reece's 1930 campaign. In the later years of the Great Depression, Reece expressed sympathy at the closing of Slagle's mill as a result of competition, illness, and hard times. Reece's letters demonstrated a concern for various aspects of the veterans' lives, not just those concerning legislation.[7]

Major Paul E. Divine of Johnson City, Tennessee, sought Reece's help in 1935 with a land appraisal. That March, Reece appealed to the Deputy Land Bank Commissioner for a reappraisal of Divine's farm after the commissioner reported a reappraisal as unjustified. Reece asked for the second appraisal on the basis that the appraiser came from an outside area and did not comprehend all the factors that influenced appraisals in Washington County. Reece contended that these factors made the estimate too low. The fact that Reece expressed interest in obtaining Divine's "upper farm" most likely played a part in his request as well. Reece responded to letters from Divine's friends for personal requests, such as a bill that provided a memorial cemetery for Union supporters killed by Confederate soldiers and a recommendation to enter the military or naval academy. Reece often took advantage of opportunities to aid his constituents and garner political support.[8]

Reece felt comfortable with his growing command of First District politics and decided to continue his career in the House. Those opposed to Reece sought a challenger for the 1924 primary and settled on their former congressman, Sells. By the middle of March, ten of the twelve county conventions supported Reece as the Republican candidate. In 1923 President Harding became ill during a speaking tour and died on August 2nd. His vice president, Calvin Coolidge, completed his term in office and became the Republican candidate for president in 1924. Sells then withdrew from the race because he claimed an offer to be Coolidge's campaign manager in Tennessee would have created an embarrassing position if he remained in the contest.[9]

Shortly thereafter a Claiborne County resident, Will Jones, announced himself as a candidate for Reece's seat. Jones accused Reece of staying in Washington so long during the sessions that he became a stranger to his home. Reece vehemently denied the charge and became angered over attacks directed toward his wife and his reportedly lavish residence in Washington. "My home is on the Watauga at Butler . . . and I pray it may always be my home," Reece avowed. He reaffirmed this shortly thereafter when he purchased his childhood home in Butler and built a house in nearby Johnson City, Tennessee.[10] The hostility of Appalachian voters towards congressmen in Washington arose less from an aversion to long tenure than from the perception that extended residence in the capital caused a representative to neglect the needs of the district. Residents believed that their congressman needed to live among his constituents to truly understand their needs. The emphasis placed on personal interactions often proved an effective tool to generate hostility among voters and win an election.[11]

Reece attempted to combat these accusations of neglect by traveling across the district to speak at rallies, but a sudden accident altered his plans. On July 27th, Reece and his wife drove from Newport, Tennessee, to a speaking engagement at Tazewell in Claiborne County. As Reece pulled to the side of the road to let another car pass, his car skidded into a ravine and overturned. Reece and his wife, trapped in the car, had to be extricated with the help of onlookers. Louise broke her shoulder and Reece, knocked unconscious, suffered injuries to his face and back that kept him hospitalized until August 13th. With the help of his supporters, Reece won the primary election from the hospital and carried nine of the twelve counties in the district. The only other candidate in the November election, an independent, failed to break Reece's momentum in his endeavor to return to the House.[12]

Reece failed to distinguish himself during his next term in office but reappeared in the news as the 1926 elections approached. In August 1925, O.B. Lovette, the Greeneville Attorney General, and Joel N. Pierce, the Greene County School Superintendent, announced their candidacy for the Republican primary. Pierce obtained the support of former Congressman Sells and political leaders in both Knoxville and Memphis to exert pressure on voters by demonstrating his statewide appeal. He hoped this would produce enough support to defeat the Reece machinery. Reece bristled at the interference of outsiders and accused Pierce of contributing to a drastic increase in the price of textbooks while serving on the Tennessee Textbooks Commission in 1925. The campaign soon became two-sided, as Reece and Pierce attacked each other's credibility. During the 1926 contest, Pierce became the first person to make a campaign speech in Reece's hometown of Butler since 1920.[13]

Personal problems plagued Reece throughout the campaign but had little effect on his popularity. In August 1925, Reece's younger brother Raleigh accepted a position as science teacher and athletic coach at Rhea County High School in Dayton, Tennessee. He replaced former teacher John T. Scopes, who lost his job after being charged with violating the Butler Act by teaching evolution in school. In January 1926, Raleigh resigned his position in anticipation of dismissal from the school board after an incident at a party. The school omitted the specifics of the incident, described by a local paper as a prank, but the resignation news appeared in the *New York Times*. Reece's health became an issue, and he spent more than two weeks in the hospital during the campaign in July for an undisclosed illness that his campaign managers attributed to gas attacks he endured in World War I. Reece's doctors announced that Reece simply needed to rest in order to regain his strength. In early September, however, Reece collapsed shortly after he won the primary and remained in the hospital through the November election. Reports originally attributed his weakness to physical ramifications from the World War I gas attacks, but doctors later discovered symptoms of a goiter and operated on November 8th at Walter Reed Hospital in Washington.[14]

Reece and his supporters structured their campaign around legislation he had proposed to benefit his district. One campaign pamphlet advocated his reelection on the basis that most districts kept a person in office ten years or more. In stark contrast to his 1920 campaign, the pamphlet reasoned, "Why send a new man to Congress who would have to begin at the foot of the class?" Reece worked in early 1926 on proposed legislation establishing the Smoky Mountain National Park and providing funding for its development, which earned him significant support in the district even though the bill failed to pass. Supporters reminded constituents of efforts he made in his first three terms of office to allocate money for better roads and pensions for veterans. Reece won the primary by more than 6,500 votes, with a majority in all but two counties. Lovette finished third without carrying any county. Unhappy with the outcome, Pierce supporters tried to petition the vote, but the GOP primary board declined their request.[15]

Reece continued his efforts to enact legislation to benefit his district. In September 1927, he presented a bill to open up West Point to appointees from the Citizens Military Training Camps to recognize them as a source for regular service officers. Reece believed the measure would bring the army closer to the people, although it never came before a vote. Later that year, he proposed a bill that passed the House the following January to expand the 6th Circuit United States Court. This measure allowed a Tennessee judge to be appointed to the court since the state did not have a representative on the circuit. He hoped to improve local transportation with his 1928 Good Roads Bill, which provided federal aid in construction of secondary farm-to-market roads traversed by rural carriers. Both the Farm Bureau and National Association of Rural Letter Carriers endorsed the measure, which passed with similar measures from other congressmen.[16]

Reece became an avid proponent for the creation of a Merchant Marine. In a March 1928 speech, he appealed to Congress to maintain a Merchant Marine as an auxiliary to the Navy. Citing the cost of constructing transport ships during World War I, he lauded the Merchant Marine Act of 1928. Reece stated that although he resided in an interior state, he knew the economic importance of a Merchant Marine for the transport of surplus products to overseas markets. Aside from his support of these bills and proposals, Reece authored no substantial legislation. The effort to resolve operation of Muscle Shoals consumed much of his attention during his first decade in office. In an interview covering his war experiences, Reece explained his slight legislative record and perhaps his political philosophy when he stated, "it's not what a fellow might have done, but what he expects to do that counts."[17]

The Entire Proposition Originated in Red Russia

Before the First District elected Reece to Washington, Congress began the debate over what to do with the hydroelectric and nitrate plants at Muscle Shoals, Alabama. The area of Muscle Shoals extended thirty-seven miles along the Tennessee River in northern Alabama, and the history of efforts to develop the area stretched as far back as 1824 when the Secretary of War, John C. Calhoun, requested a survey of the area for military purposes. Over the next several years, the federal government surveyed and worked to improve navigation of the region. Congress authorized the Muscle Shoals Power Company to develop Muscle Shoals for power and navigation in 1899, but the company never took advantage of the privilege. In 1907, the Muscle Shoals Hydro-Electric Power Company, a subsidiary of the Alabama Power Company, submitted a proposal to build three dams at Muscle Shoals to develop power. In a 1909 report, a special board of U.S. Army Engineers expressed disapproval of the proposal because they believed it involved a government subsidy in an endeavor not commercially practical and beyond the government's responsibility to develop waterways.[18]

World War I intensified the need to resolve the issue of who would develop Muscle Shoals for transportation and power. The Army Chief of Engineers supported a new proposal from the Muscle Shoals Hydro-Electric Power Company in 1914, but the National Defense Act of 1916 suspended negotiations between the two. The Defense Act authorized construction of nitrate plants to lessen the country's dependence on Chilean nitrates and appropriated twenty million dollars for construction. It did so because one of the major types of explosives used during World War I contained nitrate, and command of the seas by another nation would have greatly hindered production of explosives in the United States. In July 1916 the Muscle Shoals Association formed at Nashville, Tennessee, to promote Muscle Shoals as a location for power, navigation, and fertilizer development. In 1917 a committee appointed by President Wilson determined water power to be the best method for developing nitrates, and in September the president authorized the construction of Nitrate Plants One and Two at Muscle Shoals. The government finished building both plants in 1918, the same year Europe and the United States signed the Armistice.[19]

World War I ended before the plants could benefit the government, raising the question of what to do with the nitrate plants that had cost more than $100 million to build. President Wilson intended to use the plants for government production of nitrates for explosives during war and production of nitrates for fertilizer during peacetime. The latter idea became very popular among farmers and agricultural groups as construction began on Dam Two, also called Wilson Dam in honor of the president. Unable to solicit private interests for operation of the nitrate plants, Nitrate Director A.G. Glasgow recommended the Wadsworth-Kahn bill for government operation of Muscle Shoals. The Senate passed the bill in May 1920, but the House adjourned before considering it. By April of the next year, a lack of funds forced a halt to construction of Wilson Dam.[20]

Henry Ford presented the first hope for private operation of the facilities and with it, the first in a long series of battles over Muscle Shoals. According to the historian Thomas McCraw, the Ford name in the 1920's was "magic." His 1921 offer to lease the plants from the government for 100 years stipulated that the government had to complete Wilson Dam. Other than a proposal to use Plant Two to produce nitrates for national defense and cheap fertilizer, his offer was vague and left out any binding provisions. The only promise Ford made involved building a city in the Muscle Shoals district that would become a great industrial center, prompting land speculation in the area. The same year, the Alabama Power Company submitted the only other proposal for private operation of the facilities. In 1922 both the Senate Committee on Agriculture and the House Military Affairs Committee visited the area. The Senate agreed on a bill presented by Senator George Norris of Nebraska that provided money for army engineers to complete work on Wilson Dam. The House accepted the bill but wanted to delay the availability of funds until later in the year. By June, the House Military Affairs Committee reported the Ford bid via the McKenzie Bill, but Congress adjourned before the Senate voted. The next month the Senate Committee on Agriculture recommended rejecting all bids to operate Muscle Shoals.[21]

Reece realized the implications of the Muscle Shoals debate for his district and positioned himself to be a central part of the process. At the beginning of his second term in office, he declined a position on the House Appropriations Committee to serve on the House Military Affairs Committee. Reece recognized that construction of dams in the Muscle Shoals area and river system would have a major impact on power supply for the Tennessee Valley. Without becoming an integral part of the discussion process, he would be prevented from guiding the project to the benefit of his district and would forfeit the resultant political support from his district. The debate over the Ford offer continued into 1923, and Reece, an advocate of the Ford bill, stated that it appeared Ford's offer would be accepted barring any better offer with a fertilizer guarantee. Reece never gave exact reasons as to why he supported Ford so vehemently, but it is likely that he felt that private operation would be more beneficial and feared that government operation lent itself too closely to communism. Government operation of power facilities directly challenged capitalist notions of free enterprise. Fearful of Ford's potential profit and citing the Water Power Act, the Tennessee Electric Power Company, Memphis Power and Light Company, and the Alabama Power Company presented an offer to lease the facilities early in 1924. Their offer made little headway because Reece used his weight in the Military Affairs Committee to influence the House to pass the McKenzie bill in March 1924.[22]

A series of setbacks stalled any progress on the Muscle shoals debate. When the House bill reached the Senate, the Senate Committee on Agriculture amended it by removing Ford's offer in favor of a federal power corporation operating Muscle Shoals. By October 1924, Ford tired of the delay and changes and withdrew his entire offer. Senator Norris, a member of the Committee on Agriculture, presented an amended bill to the Senate, but the measure failed to garner enough support to pass. While Norris worked to amend the McKenzie bill, Senator Underwood presented a substitute offer. Approved by President Coolidge, the new bill allowed the Secretary of War to lease Muscle Shoals for not longer than fifty years and stipulated that a government corporation would operate it with production requirements for fertilizer and nitrogen if no suitable lessee could be found before 1925. The Underwood bill passed the Senate but emerged from the House a much weaker bill, which allowed Norris to kill it with a filibuster. Following a 1925 recommendation of the House, Coolidge appointed a committee to determine the best solution to produce nitrates. The committee strongly recommended private operation.[23]

With the completion of Wilson Dam in 1926, the foremost question shifted from nitrate and fertilizer production to the development of power. Building the dam created a power source, even if it was not the main intent of the dam, and Norris viewed it as an "economic sin" and a waste of resources not to use the power. The option of selling the power wholesale to private companies for distribution allowed companies to profit from the development of public-owned resources. At the end of World War I, public disfavor of utility companies grew because utilities enacted rate increases at a time when other businesses improved service and lowered prices. In response, utilities created public relations companies to combat the negative image promoted by anti-utility groups. Utility magnate Samuel Insull created the Illinois Public Utility Information Committee, soon followed by others such as the National Electric Light Association (NELA).[24]

A 1926 joint congressional committee failed to reach a consensus on Muscle Shoals as various companies, including the American Cyanamid Company, proposed bids to lease the facilities. NELA lobbyists quietly tried to support a proposal by the Alabama Power Company to lease Muscle Shoals, but when the proposal became publicized, Norris tried to prove that the Alabama Power Company belonged to a huge power trust managed by General Electric—one of Insull's companies. Norris argued that the government should expand Muscle Shoals rather than lease it to fight this power trust. Reece opposed the American Cyanamid Company bid and authored his own bill to lease Muscle Shoals to Farmers' Federated Fertilizer Corporation for power distribution. The bill also allowed for the production of fertilizer to be sold to farmers at absolute cost through a board composed solely of farm representatives who would determine the cost structure. He believed the cost would have been ten to fifteen dollars per ton lower than the existing rate. The Military Affairs Committee disagreed and rejected both the Reece bill and the Cyanamid bid, the last major private offer.[25]

With the remaining private offer gone, Norris appeared to have the best solution for operation of Muscle Shoals. In late 1927, Norris presented a compromise plan in which the Secretary of Agriculture operated Muscle Shoals for power production and fertilizer research while surplus power produced in the process would be distributed to the public. The Senate passed the measure in March 1928, but in May the House Military Affairs Committee amended the Norris bill to change the operator of Muscle Shoals from the Secretary of Agriculture to the Muscle Shoals Corporation of the United States. The corporation consisted of three members appointed by the president. The amended bill also included two additional sections that allocated for the construction of Cove Creek Dam across the Clinch River, twenty miles northwest of Knoxville, Tennessee. The Military Affairs Committee intended the dam to produce 200,000 horsepower and to provide navigation channels.[26]

The Cove Creek Dam provisions became a major point of contention in Congress. In 1917, Tennesseans elected Democrat Kenneth McKellar of Memphis in the state's first popular Senate election. Previously, the state legislature selected senators, and McKellar thanked his voters by dedicating his career to handing out patronage. He understood that if he broke with the Crump machine he would need the support base he could generate from patronage appointments, especially those that Muscle Shoals would generate. McKellar expected to name the Tennessee employees, which would be advantageous since the current Republican administration allowed for few patronage opportunities for Democrats. He predicted low current rates, a manufacturing boom, and cheap fertilizer for the Tennessee Valley with government operation.[27]

McKellar attempted a filibuster to remove construction of Cove Creek Dam from the bill. He argued that neither senator from Tennessee asked for the measure because they realized it allowed the federal government to exercise eminent domain to condemn the land necessary for construction. McKeller stated the federal government did not have the right to take property, which would have amounted to the size of an entire county, from the state. When another senator pointed out the potential compensation, navigable waterway, and reservoir that would be constructed at government expense, McKellar responded that Tennessee did not consent to the seizure of their land. Norris added that only Reece wanted the dam constructed. In spite of the disagreements over Cove Creek, the measure passed both the House and Senate and waited only for President Coolidge's signature to enact the legislation. Coolidge allowed Congress to adjourn before he signed the bill, and his pocket veto forced the Muscle Shoals debate to continue into the next presidency.[28]

The 1928 presidential election brought out a host of candidates after Coolidge declined to seek the Republican nomination. Reece, with no opposition announced by March 1928 in his own primary, devoted his energy to the 1928 presidential race. Herbert Hoover emerged as the strongest Republican candidate, but opposition came from within the party in the form of "favorite son" candidates that hoped to gain control of enough delegates to stop the Hoover movement. Reece's father-in-law had contemplated seeking the Republican nomination since January, and in April Senator Goff formally announced his candidacy at the behest of many West Virginia delegates in Congress and what he described as other "prominent persons." Hoover assumed that West Virginia delegates would go uninstructed to the national convention and neglected to enter the West Virginia primary. Goff won by a wide margin and insisted that he was a "bona fide candidate" and not a tool of any other candidate. Reece, however, supported Hoover for the presidential nomination. He asserted he did not take the senator's race seriously and viewed Goff's candidacy as one of the favorite son movements designed to take away momentum from Hoover. In addition, Theodore Roosevelt, Jr., Robert A. Taft, and James R. Garfield—all sons of former presidents—spoke on behalf of Hoover. Although Taft's father and Goff's father shared a close relationship, he and Reece decided to support Hoover, most likely because they believed he stood a better chance of winning the election.[29]

Hoover's campaign committee took advantage of Reece's support and actively sought his help in the campaign. The Ohio Hoover Committee telegrammed Reece on April 18, 1928, to ask for a handwritten response in 100 words or less why he supported Hoover. Reece replied that Hoover possessed qualifications of training and experience to carry out the policies of Coolidge and that Hoover maintained integrity that would allow him to withstand attacks by Democrats. Hoover's campaign committee requested that Reece visit Ohio to make three speeches since many of Reece's fellow veterans from the 166th Infantry Rainbow Division lived in Ohio. Rumors spread that Hoover wanted Reece to succeed James W. Good as Secretary of War, but Reece avoided promotion of this idea. With the support of the Tennessee Republican Convention, Reece easily won the 1928 primary and general election as Hoover ascended to the presidency. Reece's involvement in Hoover's campaign marked his first experience with national political attention.[30]

The new year brought with it a new round of debates over the operation of Muscle Shoals and the start of America's worst financial crisis. The American Cyanamid Company again proposed leasing the facilities in a bill sponsored by Reece. Reece excluded the chairman and any members opposed to the bill in a "rump" meeting of the Military Affairs Committee and favorably reported the bill. This 1929 report contained amendments the committee designed to protect public interest, such as one that allowed the government to recapture the property if American Cyanamid failed to continuously produce fertilizer. It required a research lab on premises for fertilizer research and provided for the building of Cove Creek Dam and a public utility company for power distribution in East Tennessee. It also obliged American Cyanamid Company to certify itself as "an American-controlled corporation," emphasizing Reece's fear of communism. The committee ended the report with the assertion that the government could not "afford to junk our Muscle Shoals." Around the same time, the Federal Trade Commission began an investigation of utility companies that revealed graft and payoffs, which damaged any hopes for acceptance of the Cyanamid bill. Hoover still wanted to lease the power and fertilizer capabilities, but Norris reintroduced his resolution for government operation. The Senate approved Norris' bill in April 1930.[31] As Congress debated, the stock market began a sharp decline in October 1929, followed by a breakdown of the banking system. In a ripple effect, the collapse of the American financial system triggered economic failures worldwide—the Great Depression had begun.

The Republican-dominated House Military Affairs Committee appointed a subcommittee headed by Reece to draft an alternative to Norris' bill. In an effort to carry out Hoover's wishes, the subcommittee's recommendation allowed the president to appoint a three-person committee to negotiate a fifty-year lease for the property. This bill contained a number of stipulations regarding the lease: a requirement to manufacture commercial fertilizer; a limit of eight percent profit on fertilizer operations; prohibition against selling surplus power to private power companies until the demand of local municipalities and public agencies in the Muscle Shoals area had been met; the construction of Cove Creek Dam; and separate leases of the power and nitrate plants. Reece and the committee members adamantly declared that the bill itself did not constitute a lease but set the terms for one. Given the progress made in the last fifty years in transportation and technology the subcommittee believed fertilizer production would improve, thus it "would obviously be the height of folly to operate Muscle Shoals for an uneconomic purpose." One committee member dissented from majority opinion because he believed the facility should be leased only as a whole unit, rather than in parts. The subcommittee recognized that not all would approve of the recommendation but insisted that given the political atmosphere and conflicting interests the compromise represented the best possible option. Republicans influenced the House to accept the Reece Bill in late May 1930. The opposing Reece and Norris Bills forced a joint congressional meeting to work out the deadlock.[32]

The conflict over Muscle Shoals intensified hostility between Norris and Reece. Norris and his supporters in the Senate charged Reece with being a mouthpiece for Hoover. Reece attempted to discredit the Norris Bill by generating fear. He asserted that it contained un-American ideas spread by Norris "and his small group of radicals" and that "the entire proposition originated in Red Russia." He added that Bolsheviks spent millions to promote government competition with private industry, reminding his audience of Soviet ownership of power plants and farms. The NELA also characterized government ownership as "Bolshevistic, socialistic, inefficient, and generally odious." Reece contended that his bill focused on helping farmers—an idea he hoped appealed to those suffering from the Great Depression. When he returned to Tennessee to campaign for the 1930 primary, Reece discovered that the Muscle Shoals issue threatened his hopes of an easy re-election.[33]

A Man in Public Life Must Expect Defeat

The ten-year debate in Congress over Muscle Shoals proved to be a valuable weapon for Reece opponents. As late as May 1930, one local newspaper predicted no opposition for Reece as a result of his long record in Congress and his political strength. The next month, Republican Sam W. Price, a local attorney, announced his candidacy in the Republican primary on the platform of government ownership of waterpower projects like Muscle Shoals. Price advertised his campaign slogan as: "I am in favor of giving every man a fair chance, but surely ten years is time enough for experimenting." Reece's 1920 campaign to oust Sells by declaring ten years long enough for any man in Congress came back to haunt him. In 1928 Reece declared that development of Tennessee hinged on increased farm production through avenues such as cheaper fertilizer production via Muscle Shoals, construction of rural highways, and better school systems. Two of these elements became vital in the election results.[34]

During the summer campaign Reece fought a heated battle to defend his actions in Congress on the Muscle Shoals issue. The Norris bill promised $45,000,000 in federal money to the area for Cove Creek, and some constituents blamed Reece for delaying the project with his alternate bill. They remained bitter toward Reece even though Cove Creek Dam did not fall within Reece's First District, but in the Second District. By 1930, the Great Depression heightened interest in the power industry and desire for economic relief through public works. Although the poverty of East Tennessee made the depression barely noticeable in its early years, constituents saw the potential opportunity of large-scale construction and development of power to restore prosperity to their area. Price accused Reece of having nothing to do with the House bill and voting against Muscle Shoals in alliance with the power trust. One local article charged Reece with trying to destroy the Norris Bill for government operation based on several rumors regarding his father-in-law. The article reported speculations that Goff feared money leaving his home state, that he held stock in American Cyanamid Company, and that he expected a diplomatic post if Reece killed the proposal. Reece defended his actions with assertions that he first introduced the construction of Cove Creek Dam and only his bill guaranteed fertilizer production. He further added that government-owned power plants would be non-taxable, forcing farmers to make up the property tax loss, and asserted that the propaganda being spread against him had originated in Soviet Russia.[35]

The campaign in East Tennessee soon gained national attention. The *New York Times* summarized the contest in an article titled "East Tennessee Has Hot Election Ahead." Acknowledging that East Tennesseans tended to take state and local politics more seriously than national elections, the paper agreed that Reece's vote against the Norris compromise had created a bitter backlash. The article attributed much of the blame placed on Reece to bygone days of prosperity during the Coolidge administration. Reece reiterated his position that Hoover supported his bill and that only radicals and Democrats supported the bill conceived in Russia. Labeling Norris' bill as socialistic produced a sharp reprimand against Reece from one of his constituents in a local editorial. Even with the heated campaign, the *New York Times* still expected Reece to win the primary.[36]

A concerned Reece sought help from his Republican allies. On June 4th John Tilson, the Republican majority leader in Congress, sent Reece a letter for publication that lauded his actions on Muscle Shoals as the only practical measure and called an attack on Reece's bill an attack on the Republican Party. The letter did not convince all of his constituents of his dedication to the Muscle Shoals project, evidenced by an article that appeared in the *LaFollette Press* on June 19th calling Reece another "Benedict Arnold" and a "Judas to be dispised [sic]." In July President Hoover stepped in with a personal letter to Reece that applauded his efforts on Muscle Shoals and called the Reece bill "the only one that will secure an advancement of this development in the interest of the people of Tennessee." Hoover stated that the House would not pass the Senate plan, and if it did pass Hoover promised to veto it. Tilson included a personal note with Hoover's endorsement that advised Reece to wait until after the Senate adjourned session to publish the letter to prevent some of the senators and representatives from attacking both Hoover and Reece.[37]

Once the Hoover letter became public knowledge, the campaign and the Muscle Shoals issue took on heightened importance. In 1925 President Coolidge declared that the issue had grown out of proportion with its actual importance. By 1930 the Senate attempted to force Reece's hand when some members threatened to block Reece's bill on appropriations for improvements to the Soldier's Home in Johnson City unless he approved the Norris bill. Reece then charged Senator McKellar with trying to force socialism on the government as a means to dispose of Muscle Shoals. In response McKellar interpreted Hoover's endorsement of Reece as favoring the power interests over the people. Reece claimed to be startled by Hoover's letter because presidents rarely intervened in elections and often regretted it when they did. The national press debated the correctness of the president interfering in a local primary but continued to reprint the letter along with a "thank you" letter from Reece. The push from his Republican allies turned out to be enough for Reece to win the party nomination over Price in August with eight of twelve counties.[38]

Reece's primary election win gave him confidence he would retain his congressional seat, but he soon found himself in another fight to maintain control in his district. His Republican opponent, Sam W. Price, claimed the party nomination for himself amid accusations of fraud and corruption in voting. He charged Reece supporters with changing actual totals in favor of Reece between the poll closings and the official count and refused to concede defeat. One week later he announced his candidacy in the November elections as an independent candidate. Reece stated that Price failed to file official charges with the party because Price knew that his own transgressions would be brought to light. On October 17th, Price withdrew from the race in the interest of party harmony to help the chances of Republican victory in the state in the 1932 presidential election.[39]

The Republican unity lasted only a short while before voters dealt a devastating blow to Reece. Republicans and Democrats opposed to Reece urged O.B. Lovette, the Republican Attorney General in Greeneville, to oppose Reece in the November election as an independent based on a platform much the same as Price's. Since Lovette entered the race less than two weeks before the election, Reece did not take his campaign seriously. Reece believed his new opponent would not be strong opposition since Lovette's first attempt in 1926 garnered only about 2,000 of the 36,000 votes cast. Supporters made a last minute push to encourage votes for Reece, but when the polls closed, Lovette had defeated the ten-year incumbent. Reece made a futile attempt to explain his stunning loss. He argued that snow kept many voters in the mountains from traveling out because they assumed Reece would win. He asserted that more Democrats lived in urban areas and could vote in higher numbers despite bad weather. Reece found it hard to accept that his complacency toward his district's wishes on the Muscle Shoals power plants resulted in his loss. His concession speech to Lovette revealed humility and perhaps a comment on Price's primary campaign when he stated that "a man who cannot accept defeat graciously is not entitled to victory. A man in public life must expect defeat."[40]

The election outcome symbolized the importance of Muscle Shoals and the power issue in America. The *Washington Post* described the November election as a "stupid vote" by the district and claimed that the Reece bill could have had men already working in the area. The chairman of the Republican National Committee called the 1930 elections a "crazy quilt" because of anomalies like East Tennessee, where for the first time the regular nominee for Congress lost in an area that had been Republican since the nomination of Lincoln. An article in the *New York Times* considered two nation-wide principles to be of utmost concern: whether the federal government could operate the power plant and sell the product in direct competition with privately operated public utility interests; and the growing political battle between the private utilities—pejoratively called the Power Trust—and their enemies, which took on a new importance as it moved from local to state and national elections. The article predicted that the movement against private utilities would play as major a role in the 1932 presidential campaign as it had in the 1930 elections.[41]

Some Things Are More Honorable Than Being Elected

After his 1930 defeat, Reece continued to work on the Muscle Shoals project during the remaining months of his term. The structure of Congress meant that his session continued until March 4, 1931, so Reece began work on a new compromise bill in December 1930. Reece intended to amend Norris' bill to guarantee fertilizer production rather than promote government experimentation with production. It allowed the government to lease the power production with strict controls and stipulated that the government would construct Cove Creek Dam if no lessee could be found to build it. The compromise contained four major components: the government operated the dam and power generating facilities without the ability to create power transmission lines; the government leased the nitrate plants for fertilizer production with the encouragement of cheap fertilizer for agriculture; the government sold surplus power with preference to states, counties, and municipalities; and a definite provision for the creation of Cove Creek Dam. Even with Reece's work on a compromise, Congress still deadlocked at the end of 1930 over how to come to an acceptable solution.[42]

The following year brought temporary agreement in Congress regarding Muscle Shoals. In January 1931 the House conceded its main contention against the Senate plan and agreed to allow government construction of transmission lines out of the profit received from the sale of power. Reece still opposed government construction of transmission lines but believed there would be so little surplus power that the lines would not be needed. In consenting to this point, Reece and the House laid the burden on the Senate to agree to the compromise. By February both the Senate and the House came to terms with each other at a joint conference committee. Their proposal mandated the government to find a lessee within one year to operate Muscle Shoals for a fifty year lease or the government had to operate the nitrate plant itself. It gave the lessee preference on power produced for manufacture of nitrates and additional power up to fifteen percent of that used in manufacturing nitrates for other purposes. It also appropriated for the construction of Cove Creek Dam and created a board of three managers, appointed by the president, to build power lines and sell power to communities and other purchasers. The ten-year impasse in Congress over Muscle Shoals finally seemed to be at an end.[43]

Reece hoped to secure passage of a Muscle Shoals bill before his term expired. He and Representative Harry C. Ransley of Pennsylvania initially refused to sign the compromise. Aware of his district's strong feelings about the subject, Reece reported he would reluctantly endorse it as the best possible solution at that time. Hoover, however, disagreed and vetoed the bill, which many Reece supporters claimed as a vindication for Reece. In reality, the veto prolonged the controversy over Muscle Shoals and prevented Reece from claiming credit for resolution of the issue.[44]

Reece left office with the belief that he had worked for the best interests of his constituents. The day after Reece's term expired, Representative Ransley—the same man who had refused to sign the compromise along with Reece—prepared a speech for the House that praised Reece's career and gave him credit for the idea of building Cove Creek Dam. He believed the constituents of the First District had been misled by propaganda and a "socialistic phantom." Otherwise they would have realized the many advantages of the Reece bill for the South. Comparing Reece to Abraham Lincoln, Ransley described his 1930 loss as a fluke caused by snow-bound Republican voters in the mountains. As Reece expressed gratitude to his district and state, he asserted he held no bitterness, for "in this instance I felt honored in defeat. Some things are more honorable than being elected to office." He declined acceptance of any position that might have taken him out of his district and expressed his desire to live at his home "among my own people who have trusted and honored me and where I have found so much pleasure in serving." Reece avowed that the only means by which he would return to public office would be by the will of the people and not by party appointment.[45]

Although Reece failed to succeed on the legislative floor, he maintained an active and happy personal life. Presidents Harding, Hoover, and Roosevelt invited Reece and his wife to receptions at the White House. His first and only child, Louise Goff Reece, was born on May 18, 1928, and had the distinction of being the only child who had both a father and grandfather—Guy Goff—in Congress at the same time. She later attended Stephens College, a women's liberal arts school in Columbia, Missouri. Louise earned her pilot's license by the age of nineteen and flew her father to numerous campaign meetings and conventions. She named her plane—a graduation gift from her parents—"The Flying Elephant" and painted a white elephant and "Vote Republican" on the side. Her interest in aviation most likely mirrored Reece's fascination—he requested an

Figure 2-1. B. Carroll Reece and his daughter, Louise Goff Reece. Louise earned her pilot's license and often flew her father to political events. Courtesy of the B. Carroll Reece Papers at the Archives of Appalachia, East Tennessee State University.

autographed picture of Wilbur and Orville Wright's first ever flight with a human passenger in 1926. Louise continued her family's political legacy in college when she and a friend organized a pre-voting age political group to help the Republican candidate from Missouri get elected to Congress.[46]

Reece's first ten years in office produced little legislation but left him with a valuable political lesson. Reece worked hard to secure funding for public buildings and to build roads in his district, cooperated to build national forests and the Great Smoky Mountain National Park, and attempted to pass legislation for the benefits of veterans. This work ensured him local support, and his conservative voting record served him well until the issue became one of private-versus-public power. Reece then learned one of the contradictions inherent among Appalachian voters. They opposed government interference and control unless it brought money to their area, and only then if it did not bring policies that altered their existing social balance. Reece tested the tactic of labeling the Norris bill socialistic but learned that in 1930 his district cared more about potential prosperity for their area in a time of great depression than what they considered a foreign threat. Reece remembered these lessons in his later campaigns. In 1930, however, the people of the First District heeded Reece's 1920 advice and passed public office around.

CHAPTER THREE

UPON SAFE LEADERSHIP

I Was Duly Elected to Said Office

After his defeat, Reece turned to his father-in-law for political support. Reece asked Goff to contact Speaker Tilson to request that he go to President Hoover or the Secretary of War to secure a position for Reece. Both Goff and Reece believed that the election loss resulted primarily because he supported the president's views on the Norris Bill and therefore felt the president needed to assist Reece. Goff reported that Reece worked hard to secure pensions for his constituents and to ensure construction of the Soldier's Home in Tennessee and therefore deserved recognition. Goff called for "coordinated leadership in the Republican Party," which meant a helping hand for his son-in-law after his defeat.[1]

The Democratic surge that put Reece out of office allowed his older brother to enter politics. Joseph, one of the only two Reece children to identify themselves as a Democrat, received an appointment as Tennessee Commissioner of Insurance and Banking in July 1931. The appointment came from Gordon Browning, the Democratic governor elected to office in 1930. Joseph also graduated from Carson Newman College and spent almost thirteen years in educational administration before he returned to Johnson City to work in the insurance business. Joseph stated he never took an active role in public politics out of respect for his Republican family. The appointment angered many Democrats because they blamed Carroll Reece for the defeat of the Norris Bill.[2]

Carroll Reece's supporters pushed for his entrance into the 1932 Republican primary within a year of his return to Tennessee. Lovette knew that Reece maintained a large base of supporters and realized that since he had campaigned on the Norris Bill, he had to follow through on getting it approved. Lovette suffered a political setback in January 1932 when President Hoover appointed Reece's nominations for local postmaster positions. Shortly thereafter, nearly 1,200 Reece supporters met at a Morristown, Tennessee, rally and formally asked Reece to run for his former House seat. The Tennessee Republican Convention broke into chaos as Reece received their official recommendation. Lovette supporters responded with a walk-out in an attempt to conduct their own simultaneous meeting.[3]

The 1932 primary election resembled the heated campaign of 1930. After his 1930 victory Lovette declared that he did not know if he would vote with Democrats or Republicans once Congress convened in 1931. This proved to be a dangerous statement in a staunchly Republican area. Reece accused Lovette of siding with Democrats once he discovered Republicans to be unfriendly to him in Congress. Reece attacked Lovette's minimal legislative record and his vote against the amendment to the Federal Farm Loan Bill that advanced loans to farmers in their area. Lovette challenged Reece's Republican loyalty by reminding voters that a Democratic governor appointed his brother as Commissioner of Insurance. Reece argued that had he been reelected in 1930, there could have been hundreds or thousands of workers already on the Cove Creek Dam project. Reece also charged that Lovette lost most of the appropriations that Reece had secured for the Soldier's Home. In the final count, Reece won the primary election by less than 2,000 votes.[4]

Lovette followed the example of Price in the 1930 primary and charged Reece with voting fraud. Lovette contested Reece's win with the claim that "I was duly elected to said office." He accused Reece of submitting fraudulent poll-tax receipts and ballots marked with illegal voters and bribing voters with money and large quantities of whiskey. Reece denied all charges, adding that they were not specific enough to mount an official protest. Lovette once again talked of bolting the party to run as an independent, which some considered an unwise move in a presidential election year. The GOP asked Lovette to withdraw in September and again in October, but he refused on the basis that he won the primary. He believed massive fraud at the polls gave Reece the win. Lovette claimed he could not file an official protest because of the difficulty involved in gathering evidence and claimed his withdrawal hurt the party more.[5]

Reece believed that the lack of official charges meant Lovette had decided to support him in November. He soon realized that he faced another difficult fight to win the election. Reece criticized Lovette for promising to support the winner of the primary and then going back on his word. In the days before the November election, Reece and his supporters canvassed the First District in a motorcade to garner support. Their efforts proved successful, and Reece regained his old seat in the House against minimal Democratic opposition.[6]

A Period of Broken Promises

Democrats won vast majorities in the 1932 national elections as the economic depression worsened and spread to the international community. Hoover attempted to restore confidence in the American economy by increasing public spending to counter drastic cuts made by business leaders. His efforts failed, and the American people blamed the president for the crisis and his inability to provide relief. Cadres of homeless and poor gathered in make-shift towns known as Hoovervilles. The Democratic candidate for president, Franklin D. Roosevelt, promised a "new deal" for Americans. Roosevelt won the presidency in a landslide and surged into office in 1933 with a program to increase government assistance to the suffering and restore confidence in the federal government.

Reece faced personal tragedy in the months before he returned to office in 1933. His father-in-law, Guy Goff, announced in 1930 that his failing health prevented him from seeking reelection. He and his wife traveled to Europe and the Far East in an attempt to improve his health. Goff returned to the United States and worked to elect Republican candidates in the 1932 elections. His health took a sharp decline shortly after the elections, and he moved to Thomasville, Georgia, where he resided with his wife and daughter, Louise Reece, in an attempt to recuperate. On January 7, 1933, Goff died at his home with his daughter by his side. Condolences from President Hoover followed two days later. Reece lost not only a close family member, but also a strong political ally. Reece's wife and daughter inherited a large part of the Goff estate, which allowed Reece greater financial independence later in life.[7]

Reece's family experienced another devastating blow early in 1933. In late January, the Tennessee Insurance Department discovered a $100,000 shortage in bonds from the Blue Sky Division and charged Joseph Reece with its theft. Authorities in Washington, D.C., discovered $22,000 in cash in a safe deposit box in their brother Lem Reece's name and accused him of conspiracy to dispose of the bonds. The state believed that a third party—later identified as J.P. Bowers of Florida—sold the bonds in New York under the impression they belonged to a Memphis insurance company in need of cash. Joseph stated that the division had the bonds when he left office in January under the new administration and claimed his brother Lem had nothing to do with the bonds. The Department later found $10,000 of the bonds behind the office safe, but $73,000 had been sold. Guaranty Trust Company in New York possessed the remaining $17,000. Joseph waived extradition after his arrest in Washington, D.C., and pleaded not guilty to the charges. Tennessee's Assistant District

Attorney issued a warrant for his arrest, along with three others, on the assertion that they "conspired to defraud the State of Tennessee."[8]

Joseph's trial began in February 1934 in Nashville, Tennessee, and lasted almost two months. He originally declared the whole incident a set-up to frame him, but he later declared that he acted with the knowledge of the governor and claimed to be under the impression that the department did not own the bonds but kept them in trust. He asserted that the $22,000 found in New York belonged to campaign funds he collected for Hill McAlister's Democratic campaign for governor and for Carroll Reece's House campaign. Carroll refused to comment on the situation, which left people wondering if he would defend his brothers or remain silent. Joseph suffered a slight heart attack during cross examination on March 7th and spent the remainder of the day recovering at the home of a relative. Nashville papers claimed that Carroll Reece's failure to testify for his brother refuted Joseph's explanation of his actions. The court convicted Joseph and sentenced him to three to six years in prison. The judge later issued a warrant for the arrest of Lem, Joseph, Joseph's secretary, and J.P. Bowers for perjury on the stand. The judge placed Joseph in jail for pleading not guilty on the perjury charge, but Lem remained free on bond. Joseph offered a motion for a new trial in May 1934 with Lem as his attorney, but when Joseph failed to appear at court to hear the decision on his appeal, a Nashville judge affirmed his conviction and ordered his arrest. On July 6, 1935, Joseph entered the state penitentiary in Nashville.[9]

Roosevelt's first days in office marked the beginning of his New Deal Administration. He passed a series of acts and measures aimed at providing relief through public works projects and reorganization. This came into direct conflict with Republicans who had spent the previous decade fighting government involvement in the private sector and Muscle Shoals. The relief measures also presented a new dilemma for Reece. His stance against government operation of Muscle Shoals proved too conservative for those in his district who wanted the benefits that the completion of the dams would bring. Reece had to balance what his district wanted against his desire to adhere to the Republican platform on the New Deal.

In April 1933 the debate over operation of the Muscle Shoals facilities once again became a principal issue in Congress. *Newsweek* described it as a "post-armistice white elephant." Conservatives held that the federal government could not produce power as cheaply as the private industries that already existed. To succeed, the government would be forced to sell power at a low rate regardless of production costs, which would put private industry out of business. Roosevelt wanted a government-owned "yardstick" to determine the appropriate cost private companies should charge. Norris amended his bill to include Roosevelt's wishes to develop the Muscle Shoals Corporation and issue bonds to finish Wilson Dam. The amended bill contained four main provisions: that power would be transmitted through new transmission lines; that the government would produce nitrogen and fertilizer; that surplus power beyond manufacturing needs would be sold to states, counties, and municipalities; and that Tennessee and Alabama would be paid five percent of sales to make up for the loss in tax revenue. Private industry argued it could transmit power faster and at a lower rate than the government, which would keep private securities from plummeting. In the end, Roosevelt superseded all opposition when his New Deal administration passed the Tennessee Valley Authority (TVA) Act and developed the entire Tennessee River system in an attempt to create jobs.[10] The Act also ended any opportunity for Reece to claim credit for developing the area for the benefit of his district.

The TVA Act was a small part of Roosevelt's attempt to provide relief during his initial days in office. The administration tried to check the downward spiral in the economy by announcing a bank holiday, the Agricultural Adjustment Act, the National Industrial Recovery Act, and Farm Credit Act during the first 100 days of office. Although the economy showed slight improvement by 1934, a feeling of hopelessness pervaded the great number still without jobs. The Civil Works Administration and Works Progress Administration targeted many of these people, but unemployment remained high. The expansion of federal power created unrest among many of Roosevelt's opponents. Even though Roosevelt hoped for more radical measures to combat the depression, the Supreme Court kept executive power in check when it ruled some of the existing New Deal legislation unconstitutional.[11]

As the depression lingered, Reece and other Republicans attributed many of the nation's continuing social and economic problems to New Deal Administration policies. Reece blamed defense strikes on Roosevelt's inability to deal with the labor issue and a lack of courage. After the courts attacked his legislation, Roosevelt delivered a proposal to Congress that encouraged justices over the age of seventy to retire and gave him the ability to appoint new judges to the lower courts. This brought an onslaught of criticism from the public and Congress. Reece hinted that Roosevelt already had packed the federal courts by appointing almost two-thirds of the 300 sitting judges. The problem of big government, according to Reece, was that it regulated the actions of its citizens as well as its businesses. He described the New Deal psychology as "raise less and earn more; work less and prosper; do nothing and go forward; cheat and succeed; plant nothing and gather much; sleep all day and laugh at your neighbor who works in the sun; save nothing and retire on a pension; be lazy and thumb your nose at your energetic neighbor." In 1939, Reece asserted that eight years of New Deal policies had shown no record of prosperity, and he advocated a focus on the United States' prosperity over foreign entanglements. Reece declared that under the New Deal, the federal government became one entirely of checks, as opposed to checks and balances.[12]

Reece's experience in banking and economics fueled much of his criticism. In one Lincoln's Day address, he described the New Deal Era as "a period of broken promises, betrayal of trust, and of economic and political bondage." He calculated that while one-third of American income went towards the cost of government, the government spent only one dollar out of six for relief. Reece believed the government's increase in taxes for businesses resulted in high unemployment rates and that government competition in industry increased worries about business security. Reece asserted that taxation caused businesses to reduce the amount of private capital they invested, which halted expansion and let investment capital pile up in banks. The government, he argued, had embarked on a "business-witch hunt." In an address to NYU alumni at a 1940 anniversary dinner, Reece claimed that New Deal policies prolonged the depression. He reiterated his belief that government regulation harassed business and industry and that the government had become a competitor to private enterprise. He believed the administration's complacent attitude toward sit-down strikes encouraged bad labor relations.[13]

Reece always remembered to convey his opinions in a manner that his constituents understood. Few residents in the First District possessed both the money and opportunity to attend college. Most of these farmers appreciated the knowledge of those who did continue their education, but they resented those who characterized them as ignorant. Reece learned to strike a balance in his speech between complex political jargon and local vernacular. When he described the government's response to business leaders that proved untrustworthy, he described the situation as "a few of the cows in the business barn" that "gave sour milk." He asserted that the government had put businesses in a straight jacket and pointed out that a man could not work in a straight jacket—he needed overalls.[14]

No Tennessee Congressman Stays in Office
if He Does the Other Thing

Aside from his disparagement of the New Deal, Reece avoided major conflicts during his second tenure in the House. This ensured that local opponents had little ammunition to challenge him in First District politics, and as a result Reece faced no real primary opposition until 1946. Many accredited this to his good service to the district, but others considered it the result of a Reece machine no better than that of Mr. Crump in Memphis. Reece denied ever supporting Crump and his Democratic machine.[15]

East Tennessee remained a Republican area with little significant challenge from Democrats in local politics. After the 1942 elections, many in Reece's district considered it only proper that he retain his seat in the House. The *Johnson City Times* credited Reece's win to "the avalanche of public approval" given to him. The paper deemed the district lucky that it chose a man with Reece's good judgment and ability for Congress. The paper cautioned that the nation's destiny relied solely "upon safe leadership" such as that provided by Reece. By 1944 another local paper reported that under Reece's leadership Tennessee voters had proven that the Republican Party was no longer "chattel to be traded to Democratic bosses for the political advantage of a few party leaders." The article prided the state on its withdrawal from the political activity that characterized its "sister states" and credited Reece with advocating a true two-party system in Tennessee.[16]

The lack of local primary opposition permitted Reece to dedicate more time to national elections. In 1934 and 1938, Republican challengers withdrew from the local primary in the interest of party harmony after Reece supporters pointed out a new Republican would lose the veteran Congressman's senior committee assignments. Democratic candidates posed little challenge and in some instances actually aided Reece. In 1934 the Democratic National Chairman erroneously sent out letters endorsing Reece as the Democratic candidate in the First District. In national elections Democrats proved more successful, with Roosevelt winning reelection in 1936 and becoming the Democratic nominee again in 1940 for an unprecedented third term. In a 1936 article Reece attempted to damage Roosevelt's popularity by attributing his success to the support of the Soviet government. The growth of fascism and communism abroad in the mid-1930s troubled many Americans, even those who remained isolationist. Reece called for a withdrawal of American recognition of the

Soviet government and opposed a third term for Roosevelt as contradictory to the tradition set by Washington and Jefferson.[17]

Reece's loyalty to the Republican Party garnered increasing attention in national politics. In 1937 the National Republican Congressional Committee chose Reece as a member of its executive committee, made up of Republican Congressmen from each state to further the interest of the party in campaigns. In November 1939 the ranking Republican in Tennessee, Representative J. Will Taylor of the Second District, died and left Reece as the only Republican Congressman in the state. On December 2nd, the Tennessee Republican Committee unanimously nominated Reece to succeed Taylor on the Republican National Committee. Reece promised he had no personal ambitions but thought only of the good of the party. Reece's appointment made him head of Tennessee Republicans and gave him power to pick virtually all federal appointees in the state not tied up by civil service regulations. Many feared a concentration of too much power and hoped he would not create his own political machine or forge an alliance like that of Taylor and Crump. Taylor secured many favors and road improvements for East Tennessee but gave up primary votes for Crump candidates to accomplish this. In 1940 the Republican National Committee placed Reece on a committee to study publicity and considered him the high command in Tennessee Republican politics.[18]

Reece served on a number of committees during these years that allowed him to improve his legislative record without endangering his political standing. His involvement ranged from legislation that directly benefited his district to international councils. In 1937 he applauded the Great Smoky Mountain National Park in East Tennessee and expressed thankfulness that he served in a position to help enact the bill that created it. Later that year, Reece and six other congressmen traveled to the 33rd Conference of the Inter-parliamentary Union that opened in Paris on September 1st. British and French parliamentarians founded the union in 1888 to further the cause of democracy in the world. Delegates from twenty-three nations attended the conference, although the rise of dictatorships in the world made this number ten less than the last meeting held in 1927. The union claimed that a number of institutions resulted from their meetings, including The Permanent Court of International Justice and The League of Nations.[19]

Reece's background in economics led President Roosevelt to appoint him as the only Republican member of his Temporary National Economic Committee (TNEC) in 1938.[20] The president urged creation of the committee, passed by a joint resolution of Congress on June 16, 1938. The committee included members from both the Senate and the House, as well as representatives from several executive departments. Also known as the monopoly committee and anti-trust investigation, the TNEC studied all lines of business and industry and their relationship with the federal government. Reece added that they planned to study the needs of producers and distributors of commodities to see if stronger industries squeezed out weaker ones. The members insisted that the committee would avoid mud-slinging in their investigation. *Business Week* reported that the future relationship between private industry and the federal government lay in the fifteen-member committee and believed the committee, expected to take two years to complete the study, could present new legislation to clarify anti-trust laws. Reece considered it an honor to be named to the commission and attributed his appointment to his long-standing membership on the Committee on Interstate and Foreign Commerce and his experience at NYU. TNEC's hearings revealed an extensive monopoly problem in American business as well as unsound business practices and led to some prosecutions under the Sherman Act. Unfortunately, the committee released its final report in 1941, when the nation paid more attention to the growing war in Europe, leading many to write off TNEC as a failure.[21]

Reece refrained from allowing his political influence to determine Tennessee's vote in the 1940 presidential nomination. Tennessee leaned towards a Dewey nomination, but Reece informed the New York delegate, Russell Sprague—from Dewey's home state—of Tennessee's intent to send an uninstructed delegation to Philadelphia to cast votes. He asked Sprague not to interfere because other southern states believed Tennessee votes could be sold to the highest bidder and Sprague's presence, followed by a Dewey endorsement, would leave a wrong impression regarding control of the state. At the convention however, Wendell Willkie—a dark horse candidate and former Democrat who had never held public office—emerged as the Republican candidate for his tough criticism of Roosevelt and support for the British war effort. Reece reported that since the Republican National Committee selected Willkie by an overwhelming majority, he supported the candidate with as much energy as Willkie put forth in securing the nomination. Newspapers praised Reece for not using his influence to sway Tennessee votes at the convention. Although some southerners resented Willkie's recent conversion to the Republican Party, others commended the effort of Willkie because they believed his campaign worked to break down political intolerance. One North Carolina attorney lamented that the South had "been cursed long enough with this one party system and anything offering hope for some relief is to be encouraged."[22] Roosevelt defeated Willkie in the election, though Willkie fared better than the 1936 Republican candidate.

Reece maintained his focus on domestic legislation as the world became entangled in war. In 1940 Reece and Senator Robert Reynolds sought legislation to scientifically determine the degree of intoxication for drunk drivers, but criticism of its inadequacy prevented its acceptance. The House Committee on Interstate and Foreign Commerce began consideration in October 1943 of the Lea Bill that proposed Federal control of aviation and airports and excluded ground transportation companies from aviation. Reece countered with a minority bill that allowed corporations to participate through railroads owned by the companies. The minority bill asserted that the Lea Bill gave a monopoly of aviation control to the federal government whereas the Reece Bill protected and preserved states' rights. The next year Reece joined a bipartisan group that sponsored a bituminous coal bill that fixed minimum and maximum price levels in an attempt to end war profiteering. The group designed the bill to aid in coal production for the war and to assure production at fair prices when the demand ceased without a pattern of government regulation of the industry. None of these bills passed, but they revealed Reece's determination to focus on problems within the United States. His isolationism matched that of most Americans during the early years of World War II.[23]

Reece deviated from the Republican Party agenda in matters involving the Tennessee Valley Authority. He realized the importance of the project to his district and often solicited votes for TVA projects. Having learned a valuable lesson from his earlier defeat, Reece explained his actions of going against the Republican Party with his "theory being simply that no Tennessee congressman stays in office if he does the other thing." In 1940 the TVA proposed construction of a dam to control flooding after one of the many floods that plagued the Watauga Valley washed away numerous homes in the nearby city of Elizabethton and the railroad tracks that led to Butler. TVA approved the Watauga Dam and Reservoir Project in 1941, but a focus on World War II temporarily halted work on the project.[24]

From late 1943 to early 1944 Reece repeated requests for resumption of work on both the Holston and Watauga Dam projects for flood control. The area contained key war industries—Holston Ordinance Works in Kingsport and American Rayon Corporation in Elizabethton—and Reece asserted dams could provide additional power possibilities and storage. The delay on constructing the dams continued through June 1946 when the House removed a nine million dollar appropriation for them. Both Reece and Senator McKellar promised to do what they could to restore the appropriation in the Senate. Work resumed on the projects in 1947, and

TVA completed the dams the following year. Reece had obtained the dam for his district, but in the process lost his home town. The construction of Watauga Dam created Watauga Lake directly over the town of Butler. On December 1, 1948, the flood gates closed and what became known as Old Butler sat beneath Watauga Lake.[25]

Nobody Ever Wins a War

Reece maintained a position of non-intervention as the world became embroiled in a devastating conflict. He demonstrated this belief as early as 1937 when he signed a bill that prevented Congress from declaring war without a national referendum except in cases of an invasion. As Hitler moved into Poland in 1939 and began his drive to conquer Europe, Reece expressed opposition to United States involvement in World War II. He advocated a neutral course in which politics remained separate from matters involving national defense or foreign affairs. In a commencement address at Sevier County High School in his home district in May 1940, Reece vowed to oppose American involvement in foreign wars for as long as he served in the House. He warned that freedom disappeared in areas ruled by Communists, Nazis, and Fascists. Only if the United States became threatened by an invasion within the area of the Monroe Doctrine zone would Reece agree to fight. In his closing remarks, he encouraged graduates to "meet life unafraid."[26]

Reece remained hopeful that the Allied forces could end the war without American involvement. In July 1940, he assured his constituents that Great Britain possessed the equipment and materials to successfully resist a German invasion. He believed Allied resistance successfully weakened Germany, a nation he believed desired peace in order to avoid the harsh penalties of war. Reece felt that the Democratic administration was leading the United States into the European conflict and that its policies toward private business threatened labor rights and social gains. He warned that entering the war meant fighting Germany, Japan, and Russia as well and that "it is a lot easier to get into a war than get out of it." He proposed aid to Britain without direct involvement as a safer alternative.[27]

Reece's voting record during the early years of the war reflected his isolationist stance. His votes mirrored the views of the Republican Party, which insisted that the United States could avoid war in Europe. Many Republicans realized that the importance of keeping Japan's imperialism under control meant the United States had to build a big Navy and avoid appeasement of Japan. Reece favored a strong military for the United

States—he supported a twenty-one percent expansion of the Navy in 1938 and voted against a motion to cancel an appropriation to improve the harbor at Guam—but he remained opposed to direct intervention. Reece voted to retain an embargo against the sale and shipment of arms to any belligerent and warned that Roosevelt's policy of lend-lease would result in a "New Deal dictatorship" and increase the national debt for future generations. When Reece participated in a round-table discussion with other representatives debating the Conscription of Industry Amendment to the Conscription Bill in 1940, he took the position that the nation's economy was disrupted each time a worker was taken from his job and conscripted into the army. He warned that this small encroachment on liberty could become dictatorial. According to Reece, the conscription bill and the ability to commandeer plants comprised two of the steps that led toward the enactment of a Mobilization Plan, which would make the president an "absolute military dictator." He opposed conscription, an eighteen-month extension of the draft, and the Price Control Act. Reece attributed his anti-interventionist stance to his experiences in World War I and claimed many other veterans felt the same.[28]

As support for the war increased during 1941, Reece held firm to his belief that the United States should avoid involvement. In a Mother's Day speech, Reece related the stress his mother experienced during World War I with two sons fighting. He pledged to do everything within his power to prevent other mothers from having to imagine what their sons experienced in war. Reece, along with many others, thought that World War I had been the end of all wars and expressed sadness that "once again Europe is wantonly squandering the blood of her men in one of her periodic wars." He noted his disagreement with leaders who urged participation in the war rather than patient watchfulness to determine the reach of the conflict. He compared wars to forest fires, spread by hate and a lack of reason. Reece avoided commenting on the right or wrong of the war because he believed all wars ended at a peace conference. "I know that nobody ever wins a war; that millions of humble people must weep and mourn while a few others get rich."[29]

The day that Roosevelt declared would live in infamy became the day Reece finally relinquished his isolationist views. Two years of indirect assistance to the Allied forces through the cash-and-carry and lend-lease programs changed overnight when Japan made the fateful decision to bomb a sleeping Pearl Harbor. The success of the oil embargo imposed by the United States on the island nation suspended plans for a Japanese attack on Russia but led Japan to see a strike against the United States as its only alternative. Reece, as a member of the Republican National

Executive Committee, stated that he had hoped the day would not come when Congress declared war against Germany. After Pearl Harbor, he believed that the United States must join the war with men and resources. Reece and other congressmen spoke with confidence that "divine guidance" ensured maintenance of the nation's traditions. He encouraged unity after the attack and urged citizens to accept responsibility and purchase war bonds to avert the danger of losing the war. The Reece family became supporters of America's efforts when Raleigh entered the army in 1942—the fifth Reece son to serve in the military.[30]

Reece took a cautionary and realistic approach to the United States' entrance into war. He maintained his belief that the Communist Party desired to overthrow the government of the United States and therefore gave an added reason to fight. In April 1942 Reece called for the government to cut non-defense expenditures and dismantle programs instituted to alleviate the depression. He opposed the build-up of civilian employees because he did not think it would win the war. Reece's first-hand knowledge of war and the men and material required for the war effort led him to warn against the expectation of miracles from General McArthur in the Pacific, even with McArthur's military prowess. He cautioned that the American military forces faced a "tremendous land campaign" before victory would be declared. Roosevelt emphasized victory in European operations over a Pacific thrust. Debate over American interests and strategy limited military cohesion during the initial months of participation. Reece attributed the lack of progress at the end of 1942 to costly delays in decision making and a lack of total preparation.[31]

In 1942 Reece began an earnest effort to help one of his constituents secure a discharge from the army. Dayton E. Phillips of Elizabethton, Tennessee, received his draft notice in 1942 at the age of thirty-two. World War II threatened to cut short his eight-year term as district Attorney General, so Phillips wrote to Reece for assistance. Shortly thereafter Reece explored the possibility of securing Phillips an assignment to a Counter Intelligence unit. Reece encouraged Phillips to continue with basic training while he kept in contact with the Counter Intelligence office and the Judge Advocate General's office. Reece requested that Phillips continue writing to him even if nothing significant occurred and promised to update Phillips as the army processed Reece's requests. He advised Phillips that another man, badly in need of money, had been appointed to serve in Phillips' position. Reece continued his endeavors through 1943 for a Judge Advocate General appointment for Phillips to no avail.[32]

Phillips deployed to Europe before Reece could secure a better position for him. Reece wrote in October 1944 that he had hoped the war would have ended or ebbed to the point that some of the older men could return to the United States. Reece attempted to influence the war department to pass a regulation that returned district attorneys and other elected officials to their civil positions. Reece regretted that the war continued into the winter of 1944 and recognized that its end would come only with a major development. Phillips remained in Europe until the war ended and then asked Reece to make whatever attempts possible to secure his discharge. Reece worked to gather support from the district judge for a discharge on account of Phillips' age, poor physical condition, and potential service to his home state. Reece expressed a sense of obligation to those in the service and felt he should do his part to return Phillips to his elected office, but Phillips remained in the army until October 1945. Reece wrote to Phillips with gladness that he had returned to Tennessee and empathized with Phillips' military experiences.[33]

Reece's correspondence with Phillips expressed a true concern for the welfare of his constituent. Reece wrote to Phillips after long periods without contact, which suggested the two maintained a good relationship. One year after Phillips returned to the United States, he succeeded Reece as the House Representative from the First District. Most of the press dubbed Phillips as Reece's hand-picked candidate, but Reece soon learned that Phillips followed his own path. Reece and his supporters backed another candidate who lost to Phillips in the election. The friendly correspondence of WWII changed drastically when Reece decided to return to the House. Reece used his work on behalf of Phillips during World War II as political ammunition to attack Phillips' character.

The close of 1943 brought anticipation of an end to the war as Congress focused on the post-war world. The House formed a Post-War Economic Policy and Planning Committee to serve as a vehicle to return the nation to prosperity at war's end. Sam Rayburn, the Speaker of the House, appointed Reece as one of its eighteen members. The committee possessed the power to summon and interrogate witnesses, release surplus commodities, and gather information on reemployment, foreign trade, and materials. In 1944 the committee asked governors, county executives, and mayors of cities of over 10,000 people to provide information on public-works construction planned for after the war. The main focus of the group was to make reports to Congress rather than formulate legislation. Reece also served on the Republican Post-War Advisory Council, formed to address reconstruction at home after the war. Reece praised the committee and listed post-war industry and employment, social welfare, federal administration, finance and currency, agriculture, and international economic problems as its chief concerns.[34]

The Allied forces opened a Second Front in Europe with the landings at Normandy on June 6, 1944. One of the greatest feats of the war, the Operation Overlord landing involved massive amounts of troops and supplies. Although the poor weather hindered troops and movement, Americans finally broke through the German lines, putting the German army on the run. The public considered the landings a success and believed that the war's end was imminent. The Allied forces experienced some setbacks, but by the time the November elections arrived the outlook remained hopeful.

Roosevelt's continuing popularity prompted Reece to take a leading role in the 1944 presidential campaign. His local appeal became apparent when the *Chattanooga Times* conducted a state poll in 1943 and reported that Reece received two votes for the 1944 presidential nomination. John W. Bricker, the Ohio governor, emerged as a leading candidate, and speculation began that Reece would serve as his campaign manager. Tennessee endorsed Thomas Dewey, governor of New York, for president as Reece predicted a Republican win. In July 1944, Dewey named Reece as one of fifteen executive committee members directing his presidential campaign. According to *The Knoxville Journal*, Reece's appointment constituted recognition of Reece as a national figure after twenty-five years of service in Congress. Two years later, this support promoted Reece to an even more prominent position in the Republican Party.[35] Democrats felt certain that Roosevelt would again win the presidency, but his apparent declining health led many to oppose Wallace as his running mate. At the Democratic convention, delegates chose Harry S. Truman to run as the vice presidential candidate. Roosevelt easily won his fourth term as president, but a fatal stroke in April 1945 left Truman to end the war.

The tide turned toward the Allies in Europe in early 1945 as American and British troops moved east and Soviet troops marched west. Germany exploited all of its resources in a futile attempt to win the war, despite widespread destruction from British bombings. A lack of oil and military personnel signaled the imminent fall of the Third Reich. Hitler committed suicide in his underground bunker days before Germany's surrender in May 1945. Japan fought fiercely in the Pacific, which made a land invasion appear necessary to force surrender. In August Truman made one of America's most controversial decisions and authorized the use of the world's first atomic bomb at Hiroshima, followed three days later by one at Nagasaki. On August 15th the Japanese Emperor surrendered—the war had ended.

In 1945, when victory seemed almost certain, the leaders of Britain, Russia, and the United States held a series of talks to determine the shape of the post-war world. In February Churchill, Stalin, and Roosevelt met at Yalta to develop a plan for military occupation of Germany after the hostilities ended. The three agreed to a partition of Germany into four separate occupation zones, prosecution of war criminals, and the destruction of Germany's military-industrial capacity. Critics charged that the concessions made to Stalin left east-central Europe open to communist domination and established the basis for the Cold War. Anticipation of victory made all of the attendees relatively cooperative. In July Stalin, Truman, and Churchill—replaced midway through the conference by Clement Attlee, who defeated Churchill in Britain's post-war election—met at Potsdam in a less hospitable atmosphere. Stalin feared that his capitalist allies would turn against him. With little unity apparent, the three focused on how to implement earlier agreements on the division of Germany and post-war territory. While some nations wanted to destroy any possibility of future German aggression, others realized the growing power of communism meant Europe needed a strong Germany to keep the balance of power. The result of negotiations placed East Germany and East Berlin firmly in control of Russia and the communist government it established there. Conflicting visions over economic policy, Poland, and the future of Germany led to a Cold War that lasted for more than forty years.[36]

The end of World War II signaled a shift in the Reece family's focus to domestic political issues. Louise Reece spent most of the war volunteering with Red Cross as chairman of surgical dressings. She taught numerous classes, recruited volunteers, and chaired the Red Cross headquarters in Johnson City. Her work increased local support of Reece as a representative dedicated to his community. Speculation arose in early 1946 that Reece would face opposition in the primary for the first time as a result of "cross-party friendship" between Reece supporters and the state Democratic machine led by Thad Cox, Crump's successor. Reece and his wife turned their attention toward local politics without two of his ardent supporters. Reece's mother, Sarah Maples Reece, died on March 16, 1943, after a long illness. Raleigh returned home from World War II but died on July 19, 1946, at the Veterans Administration Home in Johnson City, Tennessee, built through Reece's appropriation efforts.[37]

Reece's return to office in 1932 should have been cause for celebration, but his brother's conviction, the Great Depression, and a Democratic congressional majority tempered his enthusiasm. Reece proceeded with a degree of caution in his legislative duties and avoided conflict with his party and his constituents. He continued his work with veterans and supported the TVA and its potential to aid his district's economy. Although Reece garnered little attention with his legislation, his loyalty secured the notice of prominent Republican Party leaders. Reece voted along Republican Party lines in opposition to Roosevelt's New Deal Administration and advocated non-intervention during the early years of World War II. Once the United States became involved, Reece worked to ensure Allied victory. The Soviet Union emerged as one of the two dominant world powers after the war, and disagreements over the post-war settlements contributed to a reemergence of hostility toward communism in America.

CHAPTER FOUR

VICTORY FOR REAL REPUBLICANS

Republican without Ifs, Ands, or Buts

Republican Party members recognized the importance of the 1946 congressional elections in shaping post-war policy and began working on their campaign strategy early that year. Tired of fourteen-year Democratic electoral dominance, Republicans looked to their National Committee to lead the party in the right direction for a win. Republicans needed twenty-seven seats in the House and eight in the Senate to achieve a majority. In December 1945 Republicans laid the foundation of their campaign platform and party policy in a declaration of principles drafted by the Republican members of Congress. Herbert Brownell, the Republican National Committee Chairman, endorsed policies of opposition to a "socialist planned economy," good relations between labor and industry, and "equal chances for all citizens, no matter where they came from or what their color or religion."[1]

By March the Republican Party chances seemed threatened as opposing forces within the party fought for control. Brownell resigned his post as chairman in early March to devote more time to his law firm, amid speculation that Governor Dewey would appoint Brownell to head his reelection campaign in New York. Party leaders believed they needed a Congressman to win in the upcoming elections. Reece and Clarence J. Brown appeared at the top of the short list of potential candidates. Brown, in his fourth term as representative from Ohio, previously served as lieutenant governor and secretary of state of Ohio. Papers described Reece as "a lawyer-banker-teacher-legislator" in his thirteenth term in office. [2]

By the end of the month the party divided over the leading candidates. Brown dropped out of the running because he expressed an unwillingness to resign his seat in the House and because John Bricker, the former governor of Ohio, emerged as a potential candidate for the 1948 presidential nomination. The party felt that having a chairman and presidential candidate from the same state would appear biased to voters and party members. John Danaher, the former senator from Connecticut

and Republican National Committee liaison with Congress, replaced
Brown as one of the top two nominees for the job. A congressman from
Indiana announced interest in the position as well but posed little real
threat to Reece or Danaher.[3]

Two powerful political figures battled over control of the Republican
National Committee and the nomination. Governor Dewey, with the
support of the liberal wing of the party, backed Danaher for the
chairmanship. Dewey had lost the 1940 Republican nomination for
president to Wendell Willkie and the 1944 presidential election to
Roosevelt, but he remained one of the foremost leaders in the Republican
Party. Robert A. Taft, Ohio senator and son of former president William
H. Taft, favored the more conservative Reece. Taft attracted attention in
Congress immediately after he arrived in Washington, and his
conservatism had earned him the nickname "Mr. Republican" among
fellow party members. Taft led the Old Guard forces of the Republican
Party behind Reece. Both Dewey and Taft held ambitions for the 1948
presidential nomination and saw control of the Republican National
Committee as vital to securing the party's support.[4]

Reece held great respect for Taft and developed a strong loyalty to the
senator. The relationship between William Howard Taft and Nathan Goff
led to a close friendship between Reece and Robert Taft when Reece first
went to Washington as a representative in 1921. In a letter dated 1958,
Reece provided insight into his long-standing devotion to Taft. Reece
wrote that Taft's victory in the 1938 senatorial race over his opponent,
who was supported by the party organization, "caught the imagination of
the people." He believed that Taft became a leader "in sound constructive
thinking," reinforced by the people's confidence "in his honesty and
integrity as well as his ability." Reece thought that the nation needed a
president who had "developed a philosophy of government, had a clear
governmental objective in mind, and who knew government on the
operating level well enough to drive towards that objective without being
dependent upon others." Reece saw him as "the one outstanding leader of
the party over all the lean New Deal years" and "the great hope of the
children in the wilderness of the New Deal."[5]

Republicans believed the selection of a new chairman would determine
the direction of Republican Party policy for the next presidential election.
A young progressive faction wanted a strong program of affirmative action
and policy making. The conservative Old Guard faction hoped to
capitalize on Democratic mistakes to win elections. Bricker joined forces
with Taft as Reece became a front-runner in the race. At the April 1st
meeting, Clarence Brown nominated Reece for chairman. The Ohio

primary election had ended and election laws prevented the Republican Party from nominating another candidate to run in Brown's district if he campaigned for chairman. A small amount of time remained until the Tennessee primary, and if Reece became chairman, the party could find another Republican to run for his congressional seat. Reece received forty-six votes to Danaher's thirty-one, falling short of the fifty-three vote majority needed to win the election. A second ballot mirrored the first. Reece supporters embarked on a heavy campaign to persuade Republicans to vote Reece into office. On the third ballot, nine of Danaher's supporters and three other voters switched to Reece to give him fifty-eight votes and the chairmanship of the Republican National Committee.[6]

The following day the press scrambled to answer how an obscure congressman known only to insiders and his own constituents became the national leader of the Republican Party. A large part of the answer came from Taft's support and the immense influence he possessed within the Republican Party. This victory of Old Guard Republicans gave Taft a perceived edge in directing the party to a Taft presidential nomination in two years. The Committee decided that the chairmanship should be a full-time position, and Reece's independent wealth allowed him to volunteer to serve without pay, as had his predecessor. Reece also expressed a willingness to resign his seat in the House to devote his energies to the Republican National Committee, which appealed to the business-sense of Republicans.[7]

Many papers heralded Reece as the first southerner to hold the position of chairman in an attempt to heighten the importance of the election. Others correctly identified Reece as the second southerner, recalling President Hoover's appointment of Claudius H. Huston of Chattanooga to the chairmanship in 1929 following the resignation of Dr. Hubert Work. *Time* magazine called Reece "something of a rarity in politics: a popular and successful Republican below the Mason and Dixon line."[8]

Reece's selection stemmed from a strategic move on the part of the committee to expand the Republican voter base. The other candidates came from areas that garnered more total votes, but Republicans hoped that the election of Reece would end the one-party system of the South. The party recognized that unless it acquired the support and votes of former Democrats there was little chance it would win the national election in 1948. Critics, however, reminded the committee that President Roosevelt could have been elected without a single electoral vote from the South. Reece maintained a "guarded optimism" that he could break the Democratic hold on the South by winning at least two states, but he acknowledged that others before him had tried and failed to win the South.[9]

Republicans also hoped to win back much of the black vote captured by Democrats during the New Deal administration. Reece fought for repeal of poll tax requirements and for a federal anti-lynching bill as well as for the Fair Employment Practices bill. The party hoped his legislative support on issues important to black organizations would draw out a larger vote. A Tennessee paper reminded voters that "colored citizens of Tennessee have found Mr. Reece on the right side of most issues with which they were vitally concerned." A Mississippi delegate predicted a "general homecoming of black Republicans in the fall of this year." One political leader from Missouri believed Reece took the party "out of race and color and put it back on the grounds of its birth and success." Reece's voting history for civil rights served the Republican Party well during the elections. Their attempts to reclaim black voters, however, later proved to be little more than campaign promises. When Truman desegregated the military in 1948 a number of Democrats bolted from the regular party during the presidential election, but it marked a step forward in civil rights. The Democratic Party took the lead on true civil rights reform in the 1960s, erasing any gains Republicans made among black voters during 1946.[10]

Reece's chairmanship placed a wedge between the liberal and progressive factions of the Republican Party. Political analysts recognized this as definitive proof that the Old Guard Republicans held firm control of the party organization. They concluded that this left Governor Dewey "with no more than one small, well-polished shoe in the door." Harold Stassen, the former Minnesota governor and 1948 presidential hopeful, emphasized that the selection of Reece did not set the party's policy or platform. He asserted that the primary elections and upcoming conventions would decide the direction of the party. An open member of the liberal wing of the Republican Party, Stassen stated he disagreed with Reece's stand on many issues in the past but would cooperate with him as chairman. Reece denied any party rift between himself and Stassen. "I don't know anyone who has been in Congress for 25 years whose record I wholly approve," Reece asserted, "even my own." Reece managed to successfully control some of the damage, and Stassen received criticism for his public statement of disharmony with Reece.[11]

Other liberal party members mirrored Stassen's disappointment with the new chairman. The lack of legislation bearing Reece's authorship and his limited experience in debate drew sharp criticism from those concerned with the party's future policy making. Newspapers described Reece as "one of the most reactionary men in Congress," the least capable of the two choices, and "a man with as sorry a record as one could find in the halls of Congress." Party liberals, including Wayne Morse, the Oregon senator, considered the conservative victory a "grand flop" that indicated the Republican National Committee intended to elect a Democratic president in 1948.[12]

Taft and Bricker's sponsorship became a point of contention among party members. Critics declared Reece a "thoroughly disciplined student of the Taft-Bricker-Landon school of thought in his party." Even Reece had to recognize that Taft's authority influenced his selection and possibly the 1948 presidential election to his own favor. Reece refused to be labeled a "Taft man" and insisted that he belonged to no one. He adamantly refused to "sharpen anybody's ax for 1948. I am going to devote myself to the congressional elections of 1946 and the Republican campaign for 1948." His dry wit, which became more noticeable in his later years, appeared in his acceptance of the chairmanship. Aware of the dissent that followed his election, Reece thanked "all those who voted for me on the first ballot—and also those who switched to me at the appropriate time."[13]

Supporters agreed that the leader of the Republican Party should clearly be a Republican, although not necessarily one that blindly followed the party line. For many, Reece unmistakably fit this description. One national committeeman compared it to a Baptist church in need of a new minister. He remarked that the church would not consider hiring a Methodist because it would be considered disloyal. A Kansas City paper called Reece "a man of seasoned judgment" that did not espouse radicalism, and the Bristol, Virginia, *Herald Courier* described him as "a fine type of American citizen" that rose to prominence and success "by dint of his own intelligence and energy." Conservatives considered Reece's election a "victory for real Republicans and a distinct setback for the Me-Too Republicans" that wanted the party to follow New Deal policies. Hamilton Fish—former representative and head of the 1930 Fish Committee Investigation—praised Reece's congressional record as being in line with his own and called Reece a "splendid choice." Estes Kefauver, a Democrat from Tennessee, described Reece's ability and integrity as unquestionable.[14]

Newspapers concluded that although the Republican National Committee could have chosen a better chairman, it also could have chosen someone much worse than Reece. Both critics and supporters acknowledged him as a party man with a conservative voting record but ceded that the Republican National Chairman should be just that. Danaher immediately offered his resignation as Congressional Aide to allow Reece to pick his own staff, but Reece persuaded Danaher to remain in his position to unite the party efforts in the upcoming elections. Although many liberals would rather have seen a more liberal person elected to the chairmanship, they could not, declared one newspaper, "lament the election of Mr. Reece." They acknowledged that Reece may not have been the best choice for chairman, but in the words of one newspaper, Reece "is Republican without ifs, ands, or buts," which was more than could be said for his predecessors who leaned towards support of the New Deal. Robert Taft predicted that Reece would be a "very able Chairman" because he was "quiet and determined, and a good organizer." Referring to Reece's inability to speak well in public, he ceded that Republicans needed "all those qualities rather than the qualities of a speech maker."[15]

Reece's resignation from Congress remained a question throughout 1946. He first took the position that he would maintain his seat because he could be of more service to his district in the House. In March Reece reported that he was willing to resign his seat but did not immediately offer a formal resignation. The governor of Tennessee announced that the state would call a special election within thirty days of Reece's resignation to fill the vacancy. When Reece failed to give a specific date, speculation circulated that he would keep his seat until his term expired in January 1947 since Congress expected a long summer recess beginning in June. Reece placed his resignation at some time before the end of 1946 but later announced he would keep his seat but not run for reelection. He cited the difficulty of calling a special election in time to name a successor for the current session in Congress. Because of concern for the expense to the state, Reece decided to remain in office so that the August primary could name his successor.[16]

The Choice Between Communism and Republicanism

Former chairman Brownell created an effective communication network to disseminate the party's news and platform to other party members. The *Republican Rural News Service* sent press releases and campaign material to over 4,000 small newspapers in the country to increase the party's exposure. Brownell wrote an editorial in the Republican monthly newsletter—*The Republican News*—sent to almost 200,000 Democrats and Republicans across the country. The Republican National Committee also sponsored *The Chairman's Letter,* sent to approximately 20,000 Republican members and contributors to provide background materials on the Republican Party for discussion and forums.

Figure 4.1. B. Carroll Reece with his collection of elephants. This publicity shot appeared on the front cover of *Newsweek* magazine during his chairmanship of the Republican National Committee. Courtesy of the B. Carroll Reece Papers at the Archives of Appalachia, East Tennessee State University.

Reece used Brownell's entire network immediately after taking office and greatly increased its circulation.[17]

The Republican National Committee insisted that the party needed to focus on the upcoming congressional elections before giving any thought to the next presidential campaign. Reece's first *Chairman's Letter* noted his plans to remake the American political landscape. He wrote that only the Republican Party worked to defend individual liberties against the encroachment of the federal government, an idea that appealed to his home district. Reece asserted that the New Deal pitted race against race and class against class. He and his supporters blamed the New Deal for its inability to handle the post-war economic situation. Fred McWane, a close friend of Robert Taft and Chairman of the Finance Committee for the Republican Party in Virginia, believed that the Republican Party could overcome the "spirit of defeatism and hopelessness" that pervaded American society with a strong show of leadership. Reece accused Truman and the Democratic Party of campaigning on fear and dire predictions of what would happen if Republicans won a majority. The Republican National Committee, however, used the same tactics in its drive to take control of Congress.[18]

Communism proved to be a valuable tool of the Republican Party because of the intense hatred building in America against anything associated with the Communist Party. Before World War II the splendor of the 1920s and the Great Depression overshadowed the issue of communism, but in the first election after the end of the war everyone recognized that the Soviet Union had become the other major superpower in the world. World War II forced the United States to cede aid to the Soviets in order to prevent fascists from winning control of Europe, but Americans remained suspicious of the Communist Party's goals after the end of hostilities. Many recognized the desire of the Soviet Union to create a buffer zone of friendly states in East-Central Europe to protect it against possible attack in the future.

The panic created by the Red Scare in 1919 never completely faded from the political arena. The Fish Committee and the McCormack-Dickstein Committee investigated communist and Nazi activities in the United States in the early 1930s, but the House did not seriously consider the recommendations of either committee. Animosity towards the New Deal and President Roosevelt spurred Representative Martin Dies to create the House Un-American Activities Committee (HUAC) in 1938 to investigate Communists he felt had infiltrated the government and society—"the pink fringe around the Red core of communism that really headed America for disaster." The Dies Committee soon began attempts to undermine the New Deal policies and faced accusations of attacking only Communist subversives while ignoring Hitler and Nazism. The committee investigated the CIO, Hollywood, and numerous government agencies. The Dies Committee investigation ended with Dies' resignation in 1944, but a last-minute proposal by Representative John Rankin in the opening days of Congress made HUAC a permanent committee in 1945. The publicity HUAC garnered in the press allowed Republicans to take advantage of the public's growing fear of communism.[19]

Reece strengthened his support of the Dies Committee as his fear of communism intensified. In 1942 he voted to lengthen the investigation of the committee. He commented on the Dies Committee in his weekly newspaper column and noted that its extension in the House resulted from public favor in support of the investigations. He pointed out that the Justice Department found radicals in government service two years prior to Dies and warned against allowing these radicals to involve the government in foreign entanglements. He asserted that the New Deal administration had formed an alliance with the Communist Party, made possible by the large number of Communists in the national government. Reece's actions and remarks on the committee indicated his belief that a degree of popular support justified the narrow focus of the committee. He thought that the threat of communism necessitated such investigations to combat subversion.[20] Reece believed that the Communist Party attempted to overthrow capitalism by financially supporting American Communists and that every effort needed to be made to prevent this.

Reece's first task as chairman was to prepare Republicans for victory in their efforts to regain control of Congress. Reece and the Republican Party had to articulate their distinctions from the Democratic administration and New Deal policies to win. Reece immediately identified anti-communism as a major component of the Republican platform in his first public speaking engagement at a NYU alumni banquet. He asserted that American citizens needed to oust Democrats from power to ensure survival of the American system of government because, according to Reece, the Republican Party was the true liberal party. Democrats, he asserted, had allowed Communists to infiltrate their party, and only the government plus a complete Republican victory could save the nation.[21]

Reece carefully distinguished members of the Democratic Party from the Democratic administration in his attacks. He acknowledged that not all Democrats became Communists or communist sympathizers, but he insisted that the Democratic administration let itself get in a position "where the communist tail is wagging the Democrat donkey." Reece believed that a radical fringe of the Democratic Party followed Communist Party doctrine and had managed "to insinuate its members in key positions in the policy making level in the Federal Government." Reece avoided labeling all Democrats as subversive because he hoped to persuade a number to vote Republican in the upcoming election. He advertised the

Republican Party as the "one uncompromising and constant enemy of communism."[22]

Republicans targeted Truman as the root cause for the administration's failure to prevent the spread of communism. In a speech discussing the peace conferences at Teheran, Yalta, and Potsdam and the Cairo Declaration, Reece argued that "the principles of the Atlantic Charter were sold down the river behind the backs of the American people." Even though the Teheran Conference and Cairo Declaration occurred before Truman ascended to office, Reece held him responsible for what he considered diplomatic blunders. He believed that Truman's desire for political support led to his association with radicals that would destroy America's representative government. Reece argued that the resulting struggle among the communist reactionaries in the Democratic Party prevented the administration from providing good government in line with American ideals of freedom.[23]

Certain members of the Democratic Party fueled the Republican charge of subversion within the government. Henry A. Wallace served as vice president under Roosevelt from 1940-1944, but a public disagreement between Wallace and high officials led Roosevelt to name Truman as his running mate in 1944 and relegate Wallace to serve as secretary of commerce. Wallace continued his discord with the Democratic administration under Truman when he openly disputed Truman's policy towards Russia. Wallace believed that the United States should avoid a hard-line approach towards Russia to preserve relations. Republicans immediately pronounced this as certain evidence that Wallace sympathized with Moscow and communist ideals and blamed Democrats for allowing Wallace to stay in a position of power. In an attempt to salvage the party's chances in the 1946 elections, Truman asked Wallace to resign his post on September 20th. Wallace complied, but Reece still publicized the situation as another example of the effect of the alliance between Democrats and communist radicals. Reece reminded voters that although Wallace had left the government, Truman and other radical forces still held power. Reece believed that Wallace had done more for the Soviet government than any secret agent but conceded that only Wallace could answer if his actions intentionally caused harm to the American government.[24]

Reece developed his own style of language when speaking of communism during the 1946 campaign. He consistently spoke of the Democrat Party, rather than the Democratic Party, because he felt that the policies and actions of the Democrats no longer held true to American principles of liberty and representative government. He believed that

Democrats had been so thoroughly infiltrated by Communists that they no longer constituted a democratic party in which all members held an equal vote—Communists and communist sympathizers had taken control of the party. Reece also spoke of republicanism as the opposite of communism, a system in which the government controlled not only the policies of the nation but also the lives and well-being of its citizens. He defined republicanism as a government in which "every citizen is free to order his own life as he sees fit . . . the worker may enjoy the fruits of his toil . . . he may provide security for his family . . . there are no class distinctions and no distinctions of race or color . . . the citizen is a free man, and not the ward of the state."[25]

The Republican attacks against the current administration and inferences of communist infiltration generated criticism of the Republican campaign strategy. Carl Hatch, a Democratic senator from New Mexico, called the communist platform a "phony Red Issue" and criticized the GOP for relying on it. Papers criticized Reece for evading real issues to rely on a Red Fascist claim without any real proof. The York, Pennsylvania, *Gazette and Daily* stated that Reece "deliberately and maliciously set about a Red-baiting campaign as a substitute for a program."[26] Reece recognized that Republicans could not win the campaign based solely on the nation's growing fear of communism and turned to other issues, often still linking them with communism, to increase voter support.

Reece attempted to break the Democratic stronghold on southern voters by arguing that the South had been ignored in politics during the Democratic administration. He reminded voters that no southerner wanted Wallace in office, but Wallace served as vice president for four years and would have been president had Roosevelt not replaced him with Truman. In the June 1946 issue of *The Republican News*, Reece condemned the one-party system that existed in many southern states. He claimed that the Democratic Party consisted of three elements: "the Solid South, held in bondage by the chains of racial discrimination; the big machines—Kelly, Hague, Flynn, Pendergast; and the radical group devoted to Sovietizing the United States." Reece asserted that only a two-party system could rescue the South from this bondage and called for the South to "cast its own votes in national politics instead of having it cast for them by men who do not represent the real sentiment and the real feeling of the South." He stated that as a southerner, he understood the plight of southern states—the dominance of the radical group in the Democratic Party left the voters with "the choice between Communism and Republicanism."[27]

Reece concentrated on other areas that had traditionally voted Democratic in order to increase Republican appeal. In early August he spent three weeks in the West campaigning for Republican candidates. The reception he received led him to believe that Republicans would indeed gain control of the House and possibly the Senate. He believed that a "Republican swing almost everywhere" indicated success in November, including the election of four new Republican senators from the West. As he traveled back through the South, he keynoted the state convention in Birmingham, Alabama. The local radio station broadcast the convention for thirty minutes free, which relieved Reece from some of the stress involved in getting the needed funds to conduct an effective campaign.[28]

Reece also appealed to blacks to vote Republican. On August 27th he addressed an Elks club in Buffalo, New York. He stated that the Democratic Party failed to look out for the interests of blacks. The Republicans were their true friends, he argued. He stated that racism and discrimination were still practiced in the country, but not in areas where the Republican Party controlled the government machinery. Reece reiterated that the ex-slaveholding South, big city machine, and red-fascist factions controlled the Democratic Party. He advised the Elks not to make their decision on race alone but on what was best for the country. Reece stressed that the Republican Party worked for the good of all citizens because the nation could not exist one-half free and one-half Bilbo—a reference to Theodore J. Bilbo, the Democratic Mississippi senator and an avowed racist and defender of segregation.[29]

While Republicans hailed Reece's address as a valid attempt to include blacks in the campaign, others criticized it as a façade to win votes. The *Chicago Times* called Reece's speech partisan campaigning that began candidly but became "extremely tiresome." The paper compared Reece's legislative record to Bilbo and found that Reece had only one chance to vote on racism in the 79th Congress—the issue of prohibiting federal funding to schools that discriminated against race or creed in handing out free lunches. Reece voted against the measure. Black voters also recognized that Reece made this speech in New York, not in the South, where Republicans hoped to sway loyalties. Blacks could have interpreted this as reluctance to upset the balance of support that Reece obtained from Democrats in his home state of Tennessee. A letter to the editor of the *Chicago Sun* in September 1946 called Reece's attention to the fact that the New Deal administration had enacted more permanent legislation to help blacks than any other administration.[30]

The party's attention shifted from voter demographics to price controls and the high cost of meat as the elections drew near. Fear of inflation during World War II forced Congress to pass the Anti-Inflation Act in 1942, creating the Office of Price Administration (OPA) to establish controls over prices and wages. Americans resented the OPA and created a black market for goods, but the OPA enabled the nation's economy to meet war needs. When the war ended, demand for consumer goods contributed to high inflation. In July 1946, Congress submitted a bill to extend the authority of the OPA to combat increasing prices. At the last minute, Truman vetoed the bill and blamed Taft and his amendment to the bill, which allowed manufacturers to enact price increases based on 1941 profits, for the failure of the bill. Truman explained that this amendment would allow for billions in price increases and provided "a sure formula for inflation."[31] The House sustained Truman's veto and the OPA bill went back to Congress.

Republicans quickly attacked Truman for allowing price controls to lapse. Taft called Truman's veto unfair and a partisan attack. He stated that Truman possessed the ability to prevent speculation and an increase in prices and rents but "chose to take all the chances of chaos, followed by speculative rises in prices." Reece, reacting in part as chairman and in part as Taft's confidant, responded that "the President has now, apparently, lost control of himself." Reece claimed that Truman's action showed that radical advisors dominated the White House because Truman failed to follow the advice of his party's leaders. Reece warned that Truman's actions exposed veterans and other citizens to danger of eviction and a continuation of strikes and the black market. For Republicans, no price controls posed a greater threat than the moderate ones proposed by Taft.[32]

Inflation immediately followed the removal of price controls, and Republicans blamed the Democratic administration for high prices. Commenting on the inflation, Reece asserted that "what this country needs is a good five-cent nickel," which he believed would not happen under a Democratic administration. High prices forced Truman to sign a new OPA bill in August that deviated little from the first OPA bill. By the end of September, the nation's supply of meat dwindled, and many citizens asked that OPA controls over scarce foods be lifted. The army placed an order for twenty-five percent of all meat available to feed troops, and Americans cried that a meat famine would result. John McCormack, the Democratic House Majority Leader, called for a temporary lift of price controls on meat, which Reece pronounced a campaign tactic since the lift would end right after the November elections.[33]

President Truman debated how to respond to the problem without damaging his party's chances in November. He wanted to keep controls because he viewed the meat shortage as a result of the large slaughter of meat in July and August and the rush to the market right before the administration restored price controls. Truman argued that had this not occurred, the cattle would have been fattened and come to the market in September and October at heavier weights. He accused producers of holding back livestock in hopes of higher prices at a later date. In a fifteen-minute radio broadcast on October 14th, Truman reprimanded the public for their attitude towards controls and agreed to lift the controls on meat and other products in an orderly manner.[34]

Reece demanded equal response time to Truman's price control speech because Republicans viewed it as a clear political tactic to garner more votes in the upcoming election. In an official Republican reply he stated that at any other time, Truman's stabilization efforts would have been accomplished at his desk rather than on a radio broadcast. Reece argued that Truman's restoration of price controls in September after he let them lapse by vetoing the first OPA bill caused the shortage in meat supplies. According to Reece, Truman's radical advisors wanted to retain unjustified controls over America's productive system. He lamented that the meat shortage became a political issue and declared that had Truman listened to the Republican members of Congress, the crisis would have been averted. Truman, he asserted, took a step in the right direction but responded too late to the problem—"Truman is locking the barn door after the horse has been taken to the butcher shop."[35]

Reece remained steadfast that Republicans would win the elections and a majority in Congress. He based the Republican campaign on what he called the Four C's that prevailed in Washington: Controls, Confusion, Corruption, and Communism. Reece stressed that voters recognized the Republican Party as the "champion of the American form of government." He believed that Americans saw confusion and a lack of leadership in Washington that led to increasing corruption. Reece claimed that voters had become tired of controls that came directly from Moscow and had realized that elements antagonistic to the American form of government dictated policy-making. For these reasons, Reece avowed that voters would make a change in Congress.[36]

In return for voter loyalty, Reece made numerous promises on what Republicans would accomplish in the next legislative term. As he traveled the nation to stump for local candidates, Reece summarized Republican promises into eight main policies that those in Congress would follow. Four of the policies had immediate and viewable effects on the population. Reece promised a reduction in the number of governmental departments, an early end to controls on production and distribution, an immediate reduction of individual income taxes, and an end to deficit spending. The final four policies dealt more with the administration of government than concrete issues. Reece avowed a removal of legal red tape that hampered efforts "to exterminate the subversionist [sic] rats gnawing at the timbers of the ship of state," opportunities for World War II veterans to gain employment, protection of states' rights, and an "end to secret dealings with foreign governments which have done much to destroy respect for the American government internationally." Reece declared that a Republican Congress would work in areas of production, taxes, inflation, labor, and security to "build houses instead of asking veterans and their families to live in blueprints and on promises."[37]

Reece attempted to convince the public that the Republican Party worked for the best interests of the people. He described a liberal as "one who fought to curb the exercise of absolute power by kings or aristocracies . . . one who is willing to fight to protect the liberties of the citizens against actual or threatened infringements by government." Reece claimed his definition applied to the Republican Party, while the Democratic Party followed the Communist Party ideology. Robert Taft supported this idea when he agreed that a liberal was "one who opposes measures which restrict personal freedom, grants others the right to disagree and is open-minded in his acceptance of new ideas." This tailored definition of "liberal" won Reece the respect of those in his own party and earned harsh criticism from those outside GOP circles. Democrats challenged Reece's voting record and questioned how Republicans could consider southern Democrats outside the liberal definition when they often voted with Republicans in Congress.[38]

In the final weeks before the election, both Reece and Robert Hannegan, the Democratic National Committee Chairman, emphasized the distinctions between the two parties. Hannegan questioned whether America would follow the progressive program of the Democratic administration or submit to the will of a few who wanted personal profits. Reece summarized the issues as a series of choices between "houses or blueprints, sound currency or inflation, government by majorities or pampered minorities, abundance or shortages, balanced budgets or deficit spending, Americanism or communism, full production or restricted production, free economy or planned economy." Hannegan played a recorded voice of President Roosevelt during election speeches, which Reece denounced as a cheap trick. One report circulated that Reece and Hannegan ran into each other at the Press Club, where Reece inquired of Hannegan who the 1948 Democratic presidential candidate would be. Hannegan evaded a direct answer on a specific candidate, stating that they "may have to dig him up." "Well, I hope you don't do that," Reece countered, "He might win again."[39]

Papers criticized Reece for evading real issues, but he accomplished the party's goal of increased publicity. Reece appeared on the cover of *Newsweek* and *United States News,* which characterized him as a hard worker and "master organizer." They detailed his strategy of concentrating on areas where Democrats won by less than five percent in 1944. Reece's tactics worked, and in the 1946 congressional elections Republicans picked up fifty-five seats in the House and twelve in the Senate—giving them a majority in both houses for the first time since 1930. In Tennessee, though, Reece's precinct voted for the Democratic candidates for governor and senator for the first time in eighty years. Reece's political influence in the area ebbed when he resigned to work with the Republican National Committee, and the new Republicans in charge proved unable to direct the vote as had Reece and his machinery.[40]

The 1946 congressional elections focused on the shortcomings of the Democratic Congress and administration. Republicans appealed to voters on issues of fiscal responsibility and the need to limit the power of organized labor. Both political parties also had the 1948 presidential election in mind. The increased role of the government in society during the New Deal increased federal debt when paired with years of budget deficits. Because Congress delegated more authority to new government agencies, some believed Congress less able to exert supervision over them. The Republican victory forced Democrats to move temporarily to the right of the New Deal program in order to reorganize alliances and increase Truman's popularity. Republicans responded in kind with a determination to enact campaign promises in order to present their accomplishments to voters in 1948. A significant consequence of the 1946 elections was Joseph McCarthy's defeat of Senator Robert LaFollette of Wisconsin, the only Progressive Party member in Congress. Reece campaigned for McCarthy, whom he described as a good man. Voters elected some of the most conservative representatives to Congress, determined to change Truman's fiscal policies.[41]

With the help of conservative forces, Reece secured the highest position in the Republican Party. He focused intently on the 1946 congressional elections so that Republicans could end fifteen years of Democratic rule in Congress. Reece played on the nation's fear of communism and discontent over the slow recovery after the war. He used these feelings to convince voters to choose Republican candidates. Republicans tried to influence southern and black voters with promises of greater inclusion that they later failed to keep. The outcome of the elections appeared to be a real victory for the Republican Party and placed Reece in an excellent position to use his influence to further Taft's political ambitions.

CHAPTER FIVE

TO ELECT AND NOT TO SELECT

Now Let's All Roll Up our Sleeves and Get to Work

Reece rejoiced over the Republican win but cautioned legislators against a careless attitude. He reminded Republicans that Democrats still controlled the executive branch and that Democratic presidents had appointed the majority of the judiciary. Reece called for cooperation between the Democratic executive branch and the Republican legislative branch, which he believed would happen if each avoided encroachment on the other's duties. The November and December *Chairman's Letter* pointed out that initiating legislation laid outside the president's duties and that Congress reigned supreme in matters of legislation. He asserted the president's main duty involved execution of laws regardless of his approval of them. Reece claimed that the legislature rather than the Republican National Committee would set out the party program but at the same time rallied Republicans with a cry of "Now let's all roll up our sleeves and get to work to put the Nation back in order."[1]

Republicans desired complete control of all branches of the government, but Reece warned party members to put the legislative program ahead of the 1948 presidential election. Democratic Chairman Hannegan warned of the great responsibility that came with the GOP victory. Reece considered the November elections a fork in the road where voters turned to the right. He initially acknowledged that the Republican National Committee could focus on the 1948 election but later insisted that Republicans concentrate on fulfilling their legislative program. When questioned about a possible candidate, Reece insisted that the function of the committee and its chairman was "to elect, not select" the candidate.[2]

Reece viewed 1947 as a foundational year to prepare for the following year's presidential election. The first opportunity for Republicans arrived with the mayoral election in Chicago. Reece traveled to Cook County, Illinois, on January 18th to speak to Republican precinct workers about the importance of the election and to campaign for the GOP candidate, Russell W. Root. Newspapers considered the election part of the Republican plan to gain support, and Reece called it an "important preliminary engagement" in the battle for the White House. Reece reminded voters that the Chicago "Kelley machine"—operating under former Mayor Kelley—had a new candidate, and although he appeared respectable, he would have to follow the directions of the machine to gain support. He referred to Chicago as the "warming up for the big game next year." Reece's insistence on the importance of Chicago turned disastrous when the Democratic candidate for mayor won by almost 265,000 votes. Reece recanted his claim that 1948 hinged on the Chicago election with a recollection that Chicago had elected a Democratic mayor for the previous twenty-five years. He learned, however, that Republicans made a mistake by campaigning on national issues rather than local issues and by making sweeping predictions.[3]

Reece's criticism of the Truman Administration provided a means to enhance the Republican chances in the next presidential election. In January 1947 Reece disparaged Truman's State of the Union address as vague with no specific recommendations for laws to alleviate the nation's problems. He accused Truman of trying to appeal to the radical North and the racially intolerant group of the Solid South in the Democratic Party to get support for 1948. These were two of the divisions that Reece asserted destroyed the Democratic Party and allowed Communists to infiltrate the government. These were also two of the groups that Reece courted to win votes for the Republican Party. Reece touted the Republican Party as the party formed to abolish slavery, which he equated with communism. He argued that thousands of fellow travelers still held positions in government office and allowed radicals to dictate policy in order to remain in power. According to Reece, only Republicans could restore good government.[4]

Reece implored the Republican legislature to restore confidence in the Republican Party through legislation. In January, Reece sent a letter to 7,500 Republican office holders in Congress to encourage them to act on campaign promises. He reiterated the importance of this in his *Chairman's Letter* and called for the Republican Congress to uphold campaign promises of reducing federal expenditures, cutting individual income taxes, and reducing the national debt. Reece asserted that these measures would prevent an economic tailspin from the increased spending during the New Deal similar to what had happened ten years after World War I. Truman opposed an immediate tax reduction in the fiscal budget to allow any surplus to be applied to the public debt. Reece insisted the government needed to be returned to one based on law rather than on the whim of bureaucrats. He believed that the new legislators needed to "clean up the mess inherited from fourteen years of Democrat confusion and misrule and to set the nation on the high road to prosperity."[5]

Even though Reece attempted to focus the attention of the Republican Party on legislation, the press speculated early in 1947 that the party favored Taft for the next presidential nomination. In a January interview with *Meet the Press* Taft evaded a direct answer on his candidacy because he believed it would depend on how well Congress did in the upcoming year. When questioned about Southern delegates, Taft insisted he had no hold over them but had many friends among the national committeemen that held a degree of influence over them. He acknowledged that the South alone made a tenuous foundation for a delegate and often voted in its own best interest. Having his close friend Reece as RNC chairman, however, gave him a perceived advantage in swaying the vote.[6]

Reece appealed to Republicans to work together to dispel any rumors of division within the party. Reece's March editorial in *The Republican News* likened the job of the GOP to a football team and emphasized the necessity of working out differences "before the plays are called." He feared that Democrats would use dissent within the party to divide the Republican vote and perhaps gain some of these votes to elect a Democratic president in 1948. A rift within the legislature also jeopardized its ability to enact positive measures. His comments received wide coverage in the press as evidence of a party split. Readers assumed that Taft bore the responsibility of quarterbacking the team and criticized Reece for emphasizing the party by asking Congress members to follow the party line.[7]

The most damaging criticism of Reece emerged from within the Republican Party. Wayne Morse, the senator from Oregon, refused to stand by party decisions with which he disagreed. Morse considered Reece's attitude that of a "chore boy" to the Republican Party and stressed that this attitude failed to represent that of the majority of Republicans. He called for Republicans to move forward with Republican liberals rather than backwards with Republican reactionaries. Reece tried to dispel rumors of tension within the party by stating that although Morse did not always agree with party leaders, there was "room in the party for people with different views. In fact, it is a healthy thing for a party." Reece feared any indication of weakness in the party or its leader transferred to the capability of Republicans to effectively run the government.[8]

Reece's first opportunity to enhance the image of the Republican Party came from the hands of the new Democratic National Committee Chairman. In March 1947 Chairman Gael Sullivan sent Reece a draft letter that called for bi-partisan support of the Truman Doctrine to extend aid to Greece and Turkey in order to prevent the spread of communism. Sullivan claimed that Arthur Vandenberg, Republican senator from Michigan and a staunch supporter of the Truman Doctrine, approved this measure as an incentive for Reece to sign the letter. Although this would have seemed to be of great interest to Reece because of his ardent hatred of communism, he used Sullivan's letter to create an embarrassment to the Democratic Party.[9]

Reece chided Sullivan and his letter as a political tool to gain power. Reece noted that Sullivan issued a statement to the press at the same time he sent the letter to Reece, who was out of the office. He claimed that Sullivan knew that if the GOP complied and signed the letter, it would appear to be a "me too" party. If it refused, it would suffer criticism as being isolationist. Senator Vandenberg asserted that Sullivan used his name without his knowledge or permission, and Truman announced that Sullivan had failed to discuss the letter with him. Reece responded that policy must be approved by the appropriate branch of government, which excluded the national committees. He maintained that committees served the parties as tools rather than as governors. "Since I do not own the Republican Party," Reece declared, "I do not propose to be put in the position of selling it or giving it away." Newspapers publicized the incident for days and called it a "brash scheme" and the "No. 1 Blunder of 1947." Reece successfully avoided forcing Republicans to make an international commitment to fight communism abroad and at the same time debased the Democratic Party.[10]

Charges of communist infiltration during the previous campaign had prompted Truman to create the President's Temporary Commission on Employee Loyalty to set loyalty standards and establish procedures for removing disloyal persons from federal jobs. The commission's findings caused Truman to issue Executive Order 9835 on March 21, 1947. This order established a loyalty program as a requirement for holding a federal job and commenced the first widespread investigation into possible subversives in government. Some Republicans viewed this program as proof that subversives had penetrated the highest ranks in government. The order received bipartisan support in Congress, but Reece uttered a backhanded compliment of the effort. He commented that if the order meant what he hoped it meant, which was a true effort "to drive out those subversive termites who have been using positions of power and influence under the present Administration to undermine our form of government—then I am glad the President, however belatedly, has adopted this important part of the program supported by the Republican Party and its candidates in the 1946 campaign."[11]

In interviews the following month, Reece expressed doubt that Truman's loyalty order would be a success. He still assured Republican cooperation with the administration to purge the government of subversives, a problem that he insisted Republicans had been complaining about for years. The responsibility for administering the plan fell on the heads of various departments of government, and Reece claimed that these very departments permitted radicals to infiltrate the government in the first place. Reece also questioned Truman's commitment to the purge since Truman wrote a letter the previous month to George Earle, the governor of Pennsylvania, and referred to the problem as a "Communist 'bugaboo.'" Reece asserted that this indicated Truman's lack of concern about communism being a serious issue.[12]

Once Truman addressed the issue of subversion, Republicans alleged that the president hindered their goal of restoring prosperity to the United States. Reece led the fight in highlighting Truman's attempts to "sabotage" Congress in enacting legislation it viewed as beneficial to the nation. The new Congress suffered criticism for taking a long time to enact positive legislation, but Reece attributed this delay to caution and desire to avoid hastily enacting new legislation as the New Deal administration had done. In the April issue of *The Republican News*, Reece credited rumors that Truman would veto Republican legislation to the same people who claimed the Republican Congress had done nothing. He noted that it appeared to be an inconsistency, "since if Congress did nothing, there would be nothing for the President to veto." Reece pointedly dared Truman to veto any of the legislation based on campaign promises involving tax cuts, labor curbs, and a ban on portal-to-portal pay suits. Reece acknowledged that Truman would be acting within his rights as president but would fail to discharge his duties in a proper manner since voters approved of the measures.[13]

Truman vetoed a number of bills passed by Congress that eliminated some of the New Deal reforms. Reece accused Truman of fighting "with every weapon at his command" to prevent legislators from reducing high prices, expenditures, and taxes. When Congress failed to override Truman's veto of the tax reduction bill, Reece attacked Truman for trying to prevent the fulfillment of a 1946 campaign promise. Reece claimed that Truman's veto kept the nation under a wartime economic structure even though the war had ended. He reasoned that the Treasury would not have lost money because low taxes would have resulted in more business activity. Truman stated that he vetoed the tax reduction bill because he feared it would bring on a recession. Reece claimed that Truman's veto continued the "tax and tax, spend and spend, elect and elect philosophy of the now discredited New Deal" and asserted that Truman would propose another similar reduction right before the next election.[14]

Concern over economic issues extended to the international community as well. As the Soviets began creating the Eastern Bloc, the need for economic recovery in Europe and a strong German economy to combat the spread of communism became apparent. In a commencement address at Harvard University in June George C. Marshall, Truman's Secretary of State, emphasized the need to foster European recovery by funneling monetary aid to nations in an attempt to restore stability. The Soviets viewed this act as an attempt to create an anti-Soviet bloc in Europe and rejected the proposal. Other European nations agreed on a plan for recovery and presented a proposal to Truman for funding.[15]

When Truman presented a bill to Congress it met with much opposition from the Republican Party. Republicans chastised Truman for excessive spending on New Deal programs and resisted the idea of sending more money abroad. Taft spearheaded much of the opposition to the bill. Taft believed that communism and the Soviet Union were not synonymous. When queried he described friendship as the best response to Russia. To defeat communism he believed America needed to develop its present government and business system to the point that people understood they were clearly better off than they would be under communism. He insisted peace could come if communists confined their ideology to their own country. Although Reece too believed that communism could be defeated by a strong economic system, it is likely his concern about communist infiltration within the United States and his isolationist stance would have led him to oppose passage and vote against the bill had he been in Congress. The bill continued to meet with resistance until the communist party overthrew the government of Czechoslovakia in February 1948. The Soviet Union's blockade of West Berlin the following June in response to the Marshall Plan and the introduction of a new currency in West Germany solidified the belief in the need for economic aid to oppose the spread of communism.[16]

The most prominent attack against New Deal legislation came with the Labor Management Relations Act of 1947, commonly referred to as the Taft-Hartley Act. A criticism of the Wagner Act of 1935, the Taft-Hartley Act made a closed shop illegal, allowed states to pass right-to-work laws, and gave the president the power to call for a cooling-off period before a strike that would endanger national safety or health. Truman immediately vetoed the bill because he said the bill was "unfair, wouldn't work, would promote strikes and labor discord, and would plunge the hand of government further into the affairs of working people and their employers." His veto also served as an appeal to organized labor to support the Democratic Party.[17]

Truman's veto provoked outrage from the Republican Party. Defending his good friend and co-author of the bill, Reece called Truman's veto a bid for a fifth New Deal term and an attempt to maintain an alliance with the subversive elements of the CIO-PAC. He equated an individual's right to work with the importance of the right to strike. The House majority leader insisted that radicals and Communists who wanted to see the economy falter influenced Truman's decision. Republicans threatened to propose an anti-lynching bill in retaliation against southern Democrats unless they voted to override the veto. They had used this tactic when they introduced an anti-poll tax bill after Democrats "helped kill the income tax reduction bill." Both houses of Congress overrode Truman's veto the same day, and the GOP claimed victory.[18]

The Taft-Hartley bill became one of the crowning achievements of the Republican Congress. Taft considered the bill "an attempt to restore some equality between employer and employee" that allowed for free collective bargaining without government interference. Taft recognized the power of labor leaders but wanted to prevent their power from becoming arbitrary. Hartley believed that "America wanted a new labor law. America needed a new labor law." Both Taft and Hartley asserted their bill eliminated the elements that caused industrial conflict. Reece later applauded the inability of future Democratic Congresses to amend the Taft-Hartley bill.[19]

The organizational responsibilities of his chairmanship forced Reece to turn his attention to the selection of a city to hold the 1948 Republican National Convention. Chicago and Atlantic City emerged as early choices, and then one congressman telegraphed Reece that Philadelphia would be timely as the birthplace of American independence, especially since the party was trying to make the 1948 campaign about returning the government to the people. By the time the April 21st meeting arrived, the choice had narrowed to Chicago and Philadelphia. Taft supporters wanted Chicago as the convention site since it was nearer to his home state of Ohio, while Dewey supporters chose Philadelphia for the same reason. Philadelphia offered the convention $200,000 as an incentive to hold the convention, and Chicago offered $100,000 plus a rent-free convention hall with decorations. Reece claimed that he favored Chicago because it was a more logical choice from the standpoint of geography and facilities, but in truth he wanted to give Taft an advantage in the presidential nomination. At the vote, Philadelphia's large donation became the deciding factor in choosing that city over Chicago to hold the 1948 convention. Reece's only consolation at losing the Chicago convention site came when the executive committee gave him the authorization to appoint the committees on arrangement, rules, and contests for the convention, which in essence allowed him to stack the committees in favor of Taft.[20]

One aspect of Reece's role as chairman involved tempering any extremes in the public's perception of the Republican Party. George Van Horn Moseley served as a General in the United States Army and won both respect and numerous commendations for his wartime service. He also blamed Jews for the Russian Revolution and other economic problems in the world. He corresponded with Reece to advise him on guiding the Republican Party platform against communism and the New Deal and requested that Reece publish his views. Reece respectfully acknowledged his letters but advised Moseley to make his own statement rather than utilize the Republican Party or Reece's name to propagate his position. Reece refused to associate the party with anti-Semitism. Reece also faced hostility from some within the RNC who either resigned or lost their administrative positions. One woman asserted that Reece forced her resignation from her post and then lied about it to other members. Reece denied her allegations and refrained from further comment. He feared that any controversy placed "the Party in an awkward position." Reece focused on maintaining unity for the good of the upcoming convention.[21]

The stress Reece encountered in his position failed to diminish his hopes for a Republican victory. In August 1947 he took his wife and daughter on a promised trip to South America as a graduation gift to his daughter. Reece noted to a friend during his trip that his job as chairman was "a heavy and burdensome one." Upon his return he renewed his belief that the American people wanted a change from the New Deal. Reece projected optimism, even denying that the influx of candidates seeking the nomination would cause dissension in Republican ranks. The months leading up to the convention indicated his optimism was premature.[22]

Price controls continued to be a source of contention for most Americans. Reece again tried to connect high prices to communism, calling price controls a "favorite weapon of the red fascists because it gives them power to control the lives of all people." He blamed high prices on the administration, reasoning that they resulted from too much money in circulation and the increasing cost of production brought on by wage increases. He believed New Deal programs resulted in Americans not working as hard as they used to work because of the numerous government handouts. Reece reasoned that price controls not only limited the price on the final good, but also controlled the price of everything that went into making it and prevented free exchange among people. After the president removed and then reinitiated the price control on meat, he opposed the president's power to fix prices and wages as a "cop in every kitchen" philosophy.[23]

Reece recognized a limit existed on his ability to associate the Democratic administration with communism before he would anger the entire voting population. He acknowledged that not all members of the Democratic Party were Communists or subversives and admitted that he knew many Democrats in Congress who were very patriotic. Reece also shied away from directly charging the president with having communist sympathies. "I am not accusing President Truman, or his immediate advisors, of any conscious purpose to subvert our form of government or to destroy our economic system," Reece proclaimed. "Mr. Truman, I am sure, is no more of a communist than I am." Reece realized that "communists in government" allegations made issues more vital to the population, but accusing the nation's leader of being a Communist made the Republican Party look scandalous.[24]

While dismantling the New Deal and thwarting communism took center stage in national politics, Reece's home district focused more on the actions of the TVA. During 1947, Reece corresponded with many of his former constituents about the TVA proposal to build a power line through much of Johnson City. They expressed dismay that the proposed power line would take a right-of-way through much personal property and the heart of town. They pleaded with Reece to work with the TVA to reroute the line so that it would lessen the division of personal property. Reece, however, failed to persuade the TVA to alter its plans. His inability to enact legislation that controlled the development of the Tennessee Valley continued to plague him.[25]

Many Tennesseans feared and disliked TVA programs to improve literacy and education because they felt it extended the reach of the federal government too far. Guy L. Smith, the editor of the *Knoxville Journal,* wrote to Reece that the TVA proposed "another one of those . . . schemes to further socialize the American scene." Reece refused to comment on the appointment of David Lilienthal, director of the TVA, as chairman of the Atomic Energy Commission because he asserted it went beyond partisan issues. It is quite likely, however, that he strongly opposed the appointment because of a personal grudge against Lilienthal. By mid-1947, a story began circulating that Reece tried to prevent TVA from building power lines in East Tennessee in 1943. The existing power provider, East Tennessee Light and Power Company, reorganized, and communities petitioned TVA for cheaper power. Reece urged Tennessee legislators to create a new utilities district in upper East Tennessee controlled by a board of three men, with Reece as chairman. This would

Figure 5.1. B. Carroll Reece at a campaign rally on the steps of the Cocke County Courthouse. Notice the gentleman to the right of Reece who was unwilling to have his photograph taken. Large crowds usually gathered to hear Reece in his home district. Courtesy of the B. Carroll Reece Papers at the Archives of Appalachia, East Tennessee State University.

have allowed him to keep TVA out of his district. Lilienthal opposed Reece's plan and helped defeat it in the state legislature. Many credited Reece's opposition to Lilienthal, and later that of Robert Taft, to political retribution.[26]

Reece's job of campaigning for Republican candidates became more difficult as divisions deepened within the party. In March, Reece received a letter from newly elected Senator Raymond Baldwin of Connecticut and fifteen other new senators complaining that Eugene Milliken, the chairman of the Senate Finance Committee, failed to consult with the new Republicans in policy-making. Reece replied to Baldwin with a courteous letter that offered research and publicity facilities of the national committee. Reece cautioned that Congress needed time to adequately consider legislation before approval and acknowledged that Republican constituents were becoming impatient. He offered to consider Baldwin's ideas in founding the party program. Baldwin replied that he was pleased Reece agreed to closer communication between the national committee and Congress.[27]

Reece pacified the new congressmen with promises of things to come, but he failed to achieve the same result with veterans of Congress. In November, George Aiken, the Republican senator from Vermont, advised Reece to resign his post as chairman of the Republican National Committee. This followed an article in the *New York Times* that labeled Reece a "Republican albatross" that was responsible for putting the party's "worst face forward." Senator Aiken declared that Reece failed to win the confidence of the public and considered it a mistake to leave him at the head of the party. Senator Charles Tobey, from New Hampshire, requested that Reece issue a manifesto assuring the nation that Republicans were Americans first and not blind followers of the party platform. Tobey wanted the American public to understand that Republicans would cooperate with Democrats on matters of foreign policy. He accused Reece of discounting the general public and using sarcasm and innuendo rather than common sense in Republican policy statements. Aiken received little support among Republicans because many considered him a party irregular and one of the more radical members of the party. Reece's victory in 1946 also gave him good standing within the party. Reece refused to resign, and although many assumed he would be encouraged to limit his statements to safer subjects, he prepared for the upcoming fight for the presidential nomination.[28]

We Are All Republicans Together

By early 1948 four men had announced their candidacy for the presidency. In late 1947 Robert Taft gathered a group together to assess the possibility of his nomination and embarked on a trip across the nation under the obvious guise of promoting the work of Congress. He relied on his friends in Ohio to run his campaign, and they worked to humanize Taft to the voters. Thomas Dewey, the governor of New York, also decided to run for the nomination, leaving Republicans with the choice between Taft and Dewey. In July 1947 Republicans acknowledged that the Democratic candidate would be President Truman and criticized him for working on his campaign rather than running the government. Henry Wallace, Roosevelt's second vice president, emerged as the fourth candidate when he formed a new Progressive Party. Reece announced that Wallace's candidacy marked the separation of the "Moscow wing" of the Democratic Party from the "Pendergast wing." His remark intimated that communists and the political machine built by Tom Pendergast dominated the Democratic Party. He hoped that this division would allow the Republican Party to win a majority of the votes and the presidency. When Truman tried to coerce Wallace back into the Democratic Party in early January 1948, Reece pronounced it an attempt to restore the Moscow wing of the party.[29]

Reece again tried to portray the Republican Party as a liberal party. He declared in February that all Americans, regardless of party affiliation, lived on the same boat. "If we go on the rocks," Reece declared, "we all sink together." He believed it therefore necessary to elect a Republican president they could trust since the Republican Party "has always defended the peoples' rights against abuse or attempted abuse by their government. That is why it is the Liberal Party." Reece tried to convince the voters that during the last two Democratic administrations the nation had become engaged in war but lost the peace. Reece's conservative Republican assertion that his party epitomized liberalism convinced few voters, forcing him to utilize other tactics.[30]

A number of events in 1948 increased concern about communism in the American government. HUAC asserted that it sought to "ascertain facts relating to subversive activities and propaganda" rather than charge any individual with a crime. HUAC's 1948 hearings, however, became more widely publicized and sensationalized than any in its past. Espionage hearings began when ex-communist Elizabeth Bentley testified that she received confidential information from a government official and communist agent, William Remington. The FBI forced Remington's ex-wife to testify and followed his attorney to gather enough evidence to convict Remington, who was beaten to death in prison the following year. Another ex-communist, Whittaker Chambers, identified government employee Alger Hiss as an informant from whom he received numerous confidential documents. Chambers' testimony elicited little more than skepticism until he produced the "Pumpkin Papers," seemingly concrete proof that Hiss had supplied him with government documents.[31]

Reece and the Republicans played on fears generated by these incidents to attack the Democratic Party. His February 1st *Chairman's Letter* proclaimed "general agreement that the greatest menace confronting our nation today is world communism." He attempted to inflame the situation the following month when he predicted that if World War III occurred, it would be between the United States and Russia. This, Reece asserted, increased the need to remove all Communist Party members and fellow-travelers from government in order to prevent espionage. He asserted that the administration possessed evidence of subversives in government employment but had become too tolerant to do anything to combat the problem, a charge that resounded among anti-communists for the next six years.[32]

Reece advertised a Republican president as the only means to rid the government of subversives. He stressed that Communists damaged a nation by destroying four crucial elements: a worker's job loyalty, the belief in private property, the value of money, and the belief in God. Reece tried to reverse his isolationist label by stating that neutrality in world events had become impossible and that communism could be the common enemy that would unite nations aside from past tensions. He defined American support of communism as "nothing more than organized treason" and blamed the New Deal policies and administration for the threat of advancing communism in the world. Reece asserted that only a Republican president could meet the challenge of ensuring safety at home and preventing the spread of communism abroad.[33]

Tension between the administration and Congress over subversion reached a breaking point during HUAC's investigation of Dr. Edward Condon. The atomic scientist faced accusations of turning over secrets regarding the atomic bomb to the Communist Party. J. Edgar Hoover, the director of the FBI, submitted a letter regarding Condon's loyalty to Truman, which he subsequently refused to disclose to the congressional committee. Reece proclaimed this withholding to be a direct challenge to the right of representatives in Congress to full information regarding public offices. He stated that Congress created the FBI and considered it "completely ridiculous to argue that the Congress which created these agencies of government is not entitled to know how they are being administered." Reece insisted that the issue involved the structure and powers of the government rather than political parties, but he accused Truman of adhering to New Deal philosophy that the "President is the government." Although he did not advocate impeachment, Reece listed it as among the recourses that Congress could take to force Truman to release the information. Truman refused to budge, and HUAC failed to convict Condon of wrongdoing.[34]

Reece recognized that some voters desired a more concrete reason to vote for the Republican Party than a rehash of the 1946 campaign. Members of his own party cautioned him against pressing too hard on the communist issue. One party member stated that although no one wanted to see communism spread in the United States, campaign promises of doing what the Democrats did in a better way would fail as well. Reece's solution to this was to associate the Truman administration with the Pendergast machine in Kansas City. Tom Pendergast had long dominated politics in Kansas City and supported Truman's nomination as senator. Many considered Truman his hand-picked protégée. When Pendergast died in 1945 Truman attended the funeral. Reece accused Truman of maintaining a close association with the corrupt machine and hinted at vote fraud in the 1946 election. Reece claimed that the defeat of the Pendergast-backed congressional candidate in 1946 showed that Kansas City voters disapproved of Truman. The March 1948 *Chairman's Letter* stated that the time had come to remove the radical Pendergast influence from the administration, as the presidential race had become one of "Republicanism vs. Pendergastism." Ignoring the fact that he had his own "machine" in his home district, Reece altered his "changing horses mid-stream" adage by claiming that the horse should have had enough sense to get out of the stream by that point. He attempted to play on the American animosity towards politically-dominant machines to garner votes and portrayed the Republican Party as machine-free.[35]

In June, Truman announced a non-political tour through the West. Reece immediately attacked this as a misuse of public funds and commented that the tour was as non-political as the Pendergast Machine, a quote widely reprinted in newspapers. Truman stated that a congressional fund established for presidential duties funded his tour, even though Reece felt that everyone clearly saw it as a stumping tour for Democrats. Reece speculated that Truman would try to explain his non-cooperation with Congress and his vetoes. He sarcastically remarked that Truman omitted Kansas City on his tour schedule, even though "it might have been assumed that the President would want to pause in Kansas City long enough to lay a few wreaths on the tombstones of the ghosts who voted for him in such large numbers during his campaigns for the Senate in 1934 and 1940."[36]

The upcoming Republican National Convention again forced Reece to turn his attention momentarily to organizational obligations. The committees handled much of the work, but Reece had to devote some time to coordinating committee members and activities. Reece attended to matters regarding convention committees, songs to be sung, the inclusion of women and blacks, the appointment of pages, and the use of motion picture cameras at the convention. The GOP Victory Club, under his direction, sent desk elephants to national committeemen as visual reminders of their goal. Reece sent a form letter to each state's finance committee for distribution to request a "replenishment" of operating funds. He indicated that the cost of making "firm stands on behalf of *economy, tax reduction,* and *equitable labor-management relationships*" in Congress exceeded projected expenses and pleaded with recipients to contribute to the RNC in order to enable the party to run an effective 1948 campaign.[37]

The first real challenge to the convention came when competing Republican factions fought for delegate seating. As early as February 1948 the selection of delegates provoked conflict among Republicans in Alaska. Taft wrote to Reece inquiring about the status, and although Reece omitted the nature of the conflict, he responded that the action being taken fell in line with convention rules. In May, two Georgia Republican factions clashed over which would be seated at the convention. One faction favored Dewey for the presidential nomination, while the other favored Taft. Although Georgia's Republican National Committeemen favored the Dewey faction, the Taft faction possessed a telegram from Reece recognizing it as the official delegation from Georgia. The following month, newspapers reported that a secret vote taken at the convention seated the pro-Dewey faction of delegates. In retaliation, Reece accused one of the Georgia delegates of "having tried to browbeat him in his office."[38]

Reece opened the convention on June 21st with the declaration that the Republican Party and the Communist Party formed the two most powerful political forces in the world. He called fellow travelers the "typhoid Mary's of communism" that had assimilated into the New Deal administration and insisted that a Republican president constituted the first step to eradicate the problem of communism. He claimed that the current administration had been in power too long to combat the spread of communism. Reece acknowledged dissent among Republicans for the first time and stated that although many disagreed on method, "they never disagree as to the final objectives." He declared that the Republican Party had "no radical wing, no Moscow wing, no Pendergast wing. No right wing, no left wing." The convention responded to Reece's address with a five-minute standing ovation.[39]

Tennessee showed its support for Reece by nominating him as a "favorite son" candidate for the presidential nomination. Tennessee Republicans began the drive as early as February 1947 without any outward show of support from Reece. They credited Reece for the party's success in the November 1946 elections and began activity on his behalf. Few truly believed that Reece could win the nomination and considered the movement complimentary to show that Reece maintained control of the state. In late April 1948 Reece had to work to repair a three-way split among Tennessee Republicans regarding who would be named as delegates to the state convention. The group divided over the federal civil rights program and the federal poll tax repeal bill. The RNC Arrangements

Committee planned to have "some of the leading negroes from the Southern States at each opening day," prompting controversy among some party members. The delegates decided to back Reece on the first ballot for president but voted against the federal program because of a fear that the federal government would extend its influence into other areas of life.[40]

Although Reece favored the civil rights program, he wanted his name on the presidential ballot because of the influence it would have on his political standing if a Republican won election to the White House. He declared that he would remain neutral and outside of the discussion, but in the end he allowed the delegates to announce their support for him on the ballot. The *New York Times* declared the move to allow the favorite son vote a "situation without parallel in the modern history of the Republican party." It acknowledged that Washington recognized the absence of Reece's presidential ambitions but knew that Reece wanted to hold the delegation together so its vote could be used for another candidate on subsequent ballots.[41]

Throughout his chairmanship, Reece adamantly declared that he remained free of bias regarding the presidential nomination. Everyone who knew him, however, recognized his devotion to Taft. Actions such as his support of Chicago as the convention site and the favoring of the pro-Taft delegation from Georgia clearly illustrated his preference to Taft and made his proclamations of neutrality less authentic. On the fourth day of the convention, the first ballot showed fifteen of the twenty-two delegates from Tennessee for Reece. Dewey garnered 434 votes to Taft's 224. On the second ballot, thirteen of Tennessee's delegates obediently switched to Taft, but his 274 total votes failed to win him the nomination. With 515 votes, Dewey accepted the Republican nomination for president as Taft conceded defeat.[42]

True to his Party, Reece supported Dewey's nomination and remained positive that Republicans would carry the South and the presidency. In his last issue of *The Republican News,* Reece acknowledged that the convention would be hard fought and that the voters would determine the fate of the nation in November. He pleaded with Republicans that "when it is all over, *let us remember that we are all Republicans together.*" Reece hid his disappointment at Taft's loss to don the veneer of loyalty to the party. His position as Republican National Chairman proved to be of little use to Taft because his support for Taft opened Reece to more criticism than Taft supporters could overcome.[43]

Dewey's nomination for president meant that Reece's time as chairman had come to an end. Dewey praised Reece for his effectiveness in winning the 1946 elections and organizing the party for the upcoming presidential election. Dewey took advantage of the option to select a chairman who would provide more momentum for his campaign. Reece resigned from the chairmanship and planned to return to his Tennessee district. Dewey immediately asked for his assistance in the presidential campaign and speculation arose over the possibility of Reece running for senator. Reece's national prominence ebbed, but his local dominance remained strong.

You've Got to Measure the Cloth Before you Cut It

After his resignation, Reece initially claimed that his political career had ended. Before the elections, he wrote to a fellow Republican that after he gave up his congressional career for the chairmanship, his political ambition ebbed. "I am not running for office, am not running anyone for office," Reece asserted, "and do not expect to ever hold office. After we win in 1948 I plan to go back to the Great Smokies and enjoy myself for a few years." [44] Reece made this statement at a time when he expected to help Taft win the presidency and thus a cabinet post for himself. Taft's failure to capture the Republican nomination for president forced Reece to reevaluate his decision to retire completely from public life.

Reece's friends in Tennessee also felt that Reece needed to remain in public politics. In January 1948 GOP leaders in East Tennessee consulted with those in West and Middle Tennessee to discuss the possibility of Reece running in the senatorial race that year. The idea originated with Guy Smith, editor of the *Knoxville Journal* and friend of Reece. The group talked about the possibility of Reece's candidacy without formally consulting him regarding his intentions. Tennessee law allowed a person to qualify for a primary without candidate consent, so the group decided to enter Reece in the senatorial primary. After his resignation, rumors began to circulate that Reece would indeed run for the Senate seat. When questioned about his candidacy, Reece responded that "You've got to measure the cloth before you cut it . . . I've got to do a little measuring." [45]

Reece soon realized that the Senate seat would be his only chance to return to Washington in 1948. The campaign for his House seat had been well under way for a number of months, and Reece may have felt that returning to that position would reduce his political standing more than his failure to secure the presidential nomination for Taft. Reece had the support of the GOP for the Senate seat, but he would have to campaign against his Republican successor in the primary and against the Democratic nominee in November to return to the House. On July 19th Reece announced that his name would be on the ballot for Tennessee's

Senate seat. Reece supporters immediately referred to his service as chairman of the Republican National Committee as reason to elect him. They noted that he left his successor $800,000 in the treasury and had become a force in the party. These skills, they argued, would greatly benefit him in the Senate.[46]

Republicans felt relatively certain of their ability to elect Reece as a result of a split among Tennessee Democrats. Estes Kefauver, a Chattanooga attorney, first ran for political office in 1938, when he announced his candidacy for the Tennessee State Senate. He lost to the incumbent but remained involved in state government as Finance and Taxation Commissioner. Samuel McReynolds, the Democratic U.S. Representative, died in 1939, and Kefauver decided to run for his vacant seat. With the support of Memphis' Crump machine, Kefauver went to Washington, where he made a name for himself among Democrats by supporting TVA and the New Deal and voting independently. In 1946 Kefauver supported an anti-Crump candidate for Tennessee's Senate seat, Edward W. Carmack of Murfreesboro, and earned the animosity of Crump Democrats.[47]

When he decided to run for the Senate in 1948 without Crump's approval, Kefauver braced for a fight. Crump attacked Kefauver as a "pet coon" and soft on communism, prompting Kefauver to don a coonskin hat that he wore around the campaign trail, giving him state-wide recognition. The Democratic primary involved Kefauver and two other candidates— one who had lost Crump's support because of political blunders and another supported by Crump. Kefauver won forty-two percent of the state vote and shattered Crump's stronghold in Tennessee. He criticized the long-standing agreement between East Tennessee Republicans and the Crump machine that prevented true two-party politics. Republicans saw Kefauver's win as a great advantage to Reece. They assumed that Crump forces would either support the Republican candidate or stay away from the polls. In early October rumors circulated that Crump agreed to back Reece, but Crump denied making a deal with anyone and stated that he held no interest in politics. In the end, Crump agreed to a truce with Kefauver—Crump denied his support but withdrew any opposition to him.[48]

As the campaign started in earnest, Reece again turned to fear of communism to gain voter support. He proclaimed the foremost question to be one of whether voters could stop the "collectivist movement in our government" rather than one of differences between political parties. He considered liberals, radicals, left-wingers, reds, and pinks to be all of the same camp wanting to rule the people through Washington. He declared his opponent—Reece never called Kefauver by name during the campaign—

was held captive by left-wing forces. He accused Kefauver of being part of the problem in Washington that led to an increased number of Communists in government offices. According to Reece, the struggle came down to a fight "between the American way of living, the Southern way of living, and an alien force that was born behind the Iron Curtain of Europe."[49]

Reece embarked on a cross-state tour of Tennessee with Roy Acuff, the GOP gubernatorial candidate and a country music star. Acuff brought his band, the Smoky Mountain Boys, with them on their tour and entertained the crowds with music and antics such as balancing his violin bow on his nose. Acuff rarely ever spoke on current issues or his stance on these issues. While it would seem that voters would be put off by such unconventional campaigning, these shows actually garnered more attendance than most Democratic functions. Unfortunately for Reece, many in the crowd came more to hear Acuff's performance than Reece's speeches, and some cried for Reece to finish so they could hear the show. Acuff often played with his band in lieu of a formal speech, and some papers actually began to consider Reece a liability to the Acuff campaign. The only negative response the campaigners received came at a rally in Kingsport, Tennessee, on September 7th. A few in the crowd met Reece and Acuff with a barrage of eggs, tomatoes, and grapefruit, but local officials quickly subdued the disgruntled voters.[50]

Reece encountered a number of problems when voters questioned his legislative record. The most intense criticism of Reece came from those who accused him of changing his viewpoints once he became a senatorial candidate. Opponents of Reece charged him with becoming a states' rights proponent after voting for the federal anti-lynching law and for the repeal of the poll tax in federal elections. The TVA again appeared in the election campaign when campaign material noted that Reece voted against the Norris Bill. His actions to unite the Republican Party hurt his local credibility. Democrats reminded voters that although Reece claimed to be a southerner, he declared at the Elks Club in New York that the southern block of the Democratic Party plunged the nation into war. One local paper claimed that Reece's attachment to the Acuff band presented the best way for people to listen to him since he preceded the performance. Had it occurred in the opposite order, the paper speculated, very few would stay to hear Reece "turn his back on his Republican record in congress in favor of his apparently recent 'conversion' to TVA, democracy, and other Democratic principles."[51]

Reece recognized that the influence he carried in his home district might not extend to the entire state, and he needed to ensure that he took the right steps to present his record and his strategy in the best light. For the first time, Reece hired a professional publicist to help in the campaign. His independent wealth again became a factor when critics complained about the amount of money he spent on the statewide campaign. Opponents publicized Reece's votes against New Deal legislation that affected farming, banks, and public utilities. Reece responded to his attackers by speaking against the Fair Employment Practices Commission being imposed on states. He called it another avenue to destroy states' rights and a deceptive New Deal scheme. He spoke in support of the Taft-Hartley Act and promised to work for the advancement and expansion of the TVA. In a desperate attempt to tarnish Kefauver's reputation, he advertised that his opponent voted against HUAC, the only organization trying to bring subversives to light, and also took money from the CIO.[52]

Reece requested the support of national Republicans to bolster his campaign and his chances for election. In September Reece flew to New York to seek the help of presidential candidate Dewey. Dewey agreed to support Reece's candidacy, but in his senatorial aid campaign Dewey pointedly avoided a stop in Tennessee, which many interpreted as recognition that Kefauver would win the state. To combat rumors that Dewey responded with a lukewarm reception of Reece because of his support of Taft, Herbert Brownell, Dewey's campaign manager and former GOP chairman, urged Tennesseans to vote for Reece to ensure unity between the White House and Congress. Local papers pointed out with a hint of irony that the last time Reece requested support from a president, he lost the campaign.[53]

In October Taft flew to Tennessee to remove suspicion that he blamed Reece for his failure to capture the presidential nomination. Rumors circulated that some Taft supporters charged Reece with not using his influence in the right way, particularly after the deciding vote for seating the pro-Dewey Georgia delegation came from the Tennessee member of the credentials committee. Taft spoke at rallies in Nashville, Crossville, and Knoxville and urged voters to elect Reece, whom Taft claimed to have the interest of Tennessee at heart. He accused Kefauver of being a staunch supporter of the New Deal and working against the Taft-Hartley Act. Even though Taft's presence garnered large crowds at the rallies, some citizens took offense at Taft's appearance in a state campaign and questioned his authority to involve himself in their election.[54]

As the election neared voters questioned why the candidates had failed to organize a joint debate. In September Kefauver challenged Reece to a public debate, but the GOP stalled giving their consent. On September 14th Reece accepted Kefauver's challenge but suggested a state-wide hookup to a Nashville radio station with each candidate paying for half of the costs. Kefauver favored a platform debate with the opportunity for voters to pose questions to the candidates, but he agreed to a radio debate if it could be opened to the public. Newspapers published a number of articles crediting both candidates with a call for the other candidate to "put up or shut up," increasing the confusion over who agreed to a debate and what format would be used. On September 22nd, Kefauver announced he would call off the entire debate if Reece would not work on any terms but his own. Reece, perhaps wary of having to answer voter questions without a prepared script because of his speech impediment, avoided the public debate while attributing the cause to a difference in the set-up of the debate platform rather than his unwillingness.[55]

Across the nation Republicans felt confident that they would emerge victorious from the elections. The Reece-Acuff campaign ended in Nashville at a rally with close to 10,000 attendees, and both candidates felt positive that they would win their respective offices. Polls showed Dewey with a substantial lead in the presidential race. The Democrats contended with both Wallace's campaign and a States' Rights Party that emerged when a number of angry Democrats walked out of the Democratic National Convention over the adoption of a civil rights plank in the platform. The Dixiecrats, as they came to be known, nominated Senator Strom Thurmond as a Third-Party candidate. The *Chicago Daily Tribune* printed its next day's issue on election night announcing Dewey's win. The final vote crushed local Republican hopes when Acuff lost to the Democratic candidate and Kefauver defeated Reece by over 120,000 votes. Truman surprised almost everyone by capturing 303 electoral votes to Dewey's 189 in the presidential campaign. The Republican victory of 1946 proved to be short lived as Democrats regained a majority in Congress. Democrats maintained control of Congress through 1994, with the exception of Eisenhower's first term from 1953-1955. Kefauver telegrammed Reece and thanked him for the "hard clean campaign" that he ran and his "good sportsmanship." He requested Reece's cooperation as the nation united behind their new president.[56]

In two short years, Reece rose and fell from the highest position in the Republican Party. His organizational skills and determination helped Republicans win a majority in Congress in 1946, but he failed to win the presidential nomination for his close friend and political ally, Robert Taft. Dewey's win became both Taft's and Reece's loss, as Reece resigned the chairmanship in place of someone more favorable to Dewey. He returned to Tennessee with hopes of a return to politics through Tennessee's senatorial race. The machine that Reece built in the First District had saved his career a number of times in the campaign for U.S. Representative but fell short in a state-wide election to convince voters he was anything other than a reactionary conservative from the Old Guard. Even the heavy machinery of Taft and Dewey failed to aid Reece any better than Hoover's support had in 1930. For only the second time since 1920, Reece returned to Tennessee without any political office. Reece could neither select nor elect the winner of the Republican nomination for president or Tennessee's senator.

CHAPTER SIX

MORALITY MUST BE RESTORED

An Almost Unprecedented Demand That I Run

Dewey's loss in the 1948 presidential election brought turmoil to the Republican National Committee. Anti-Dewey forces within the Republican Party blamed Reece's replacement as chairman, Hugh D. Scott, Jr., for the defeat. Rumors circulated in late December 1948 that Reece might consider an attempt to regain the chairmanship. Scott refused to resign his position on the basis that he received a four-year appointment. By January 1949 an increasing rift in the party became apparent as Taft and other Republicans censured Scott for the amount of money he spent in what they considered a "me too" campaign. They also condemned Scott for staffing the executive committee with Dewey supporters, a violation of his former pledge of neutrality. The *New York Times* quoted an editorial in the *Chicago Tribune* that "Scott is through" and that "the man to replace him is Carroll Reece, the only National Chairman in twenty years to lead the party to victory in a national election." Despite this commendation, Senator Taft recognized the improbability of reinstating Reece as chairman.[1]

A formal movement to replace Scott as chairman made his position increasingly tenuous. Reece and Harrison E. Spangler, a former national chairman from Iowa, both announced their belief that Scott should resign. They criticized him for maintaining his seat in the House of Representatives while he served as chairman. Scott retorted that perhaps Reece regretted his mistake in giving up his own House seat. At a special meeting on January 27th, the motion to remove Scott from his position failed by a vote of 50 to 54. As a compromise, Scott agreed to revise the make-up of the executive committee and included Reece as one of the new members. Reece had charged that Dewey failed to give adequate support to senatorial campaigns, including Reece's, in the individual states. Supporters of Scott claimed that the National Committee gave Scott's program too little time to work.[2]

The turmoil over the chairmanship prompted Reece to assure his former constituents of his desire to remain in East Tennessee. At the 100th birthday celebration of Boone, North Carolina, friends of Reece attended with the expectation that during his speech Reece would announce plans to regain his old seat in the House. The celebration turned into a rally as all but one of the attendees belonged to the Republican Party. Reece avowed that living among the people of East Tennessee could not be duplicated in any other part of the world and that no position could induce him to give up living among the people in eastern Tennessee and western North Carolina. When an empty treasury motivated the GOP to remove Scott from his post, Reece refused to let his name be used in connection with the chairmanship. He participated in conferences to discuss Scott's replacement and helped secure the selection of Guy G. Gabrielson—Taft's favorite candidate—as Scott's successor. Reece called Gabrielson "a man of demonstrated capacity who will make a great chairman" and lead the party to victory in 1950.[3]

Reece's lack of public office allowed him to focus more time on civic activities. In August 1949 as a member of the Industrial Committee of the Board of Directors of the Carter County Chamber of Commerce, Reece helped influence the American Lucoflex Company and the E.L. Cournand Company to locate new plants in the county. The Chamber of Commerce sent Reece to New York to keep the E.L. Cournand Company interested in the town of Elizabethton after negotiations with local bankers failed. The E.L. Cournand Company made plexi-glass airplane turrets for the Air Corps, and the American Lucoflex Company manufactured synthetic materials. Together, both plants would employ almost 500 people and make a sizeable economic impact on the area. Reece spoke at a number of civic events and local festivals, and in November 1949 Carson Newman College named him as a trustee. The next month the American Lucoflex Company elected him chairman of its board of directors.[4]

Reece also increased his personal business activity during this time. Between 1939 and 1945, Reece helped found four regional banks: Carter County Bank in Elizabethton, First National Bank of Jonesborough, Farmers Bank of Blountville, and Sullivan County Bank. In late 1949 he announced that the Carter County Bank would expand to Roan Mountain in March 1950. On February 21, 1950, Reece purchased the *Bristol Herald Courier*, an independent Democratic newspaper operated in the city of Bristol on the Tennessee-Virginia border, for the sum of $500,000. Reece promised to keep the current staff and operational policies of the paper. He also purchased half interest in the *Virginia-Tennessean*, which then acquired half interest in the *Bristol Herald Courier* through a special merger arrangement. Each paper owned half of the other paper in a joint operating company. This allowed them to remain competitive editorially, with the *Bristol Herald Courier* printing the morning edition and the *Virginia-Tennessean* printing the evening edition. Reece upheld his promise to allow the paper to remain an independent Democratic publication, and the staff reserved the right to disagree politically while acknowledging his business acumen.[5]

During Reece's absence from political office international events provoked concern over the growth of communism. After the end of World War II the nationalist and communist forces in China resumed their civil war. By mid-1948 the balance favored the communists and the following year the nationalist government under Chiang Kai-Shek sought refuge in Taiwan. Mao Zedong proclaimed the creation of the People's Republic of China under communist control in 1949 and established a relationship with the Soviet Union. In addition, the Soviets exploded their first atomic bomb in August 1949, years before many expected them to be capable of developing the technology. This led some to believe that communists in America gained access to atomic information and funneled it to Soviet scientists. The crisis and blockade in Berlin prompted twelve nations— including the United States—to create the North Atlantic Treaty Organization (NATO) that declared an armed attack against one member would be considered an attack against all and maintained a standing military force in Europe to defend against the threat of Soviet invasion.

Throughout the early months of 1950 residents in the First District anxiously awaited a formal announcement from Reece confirming the long-circulated rumors that he would run in the election for his old House seat. In February, the Carter County GOP split into two sets of Republican Party officers—one supporting Reece and the other supporting the current First District Representative, Dayton Phillips. By March, a number of other counties endorsed Reece for the Republican nomination. When Phillips succeeded Reece as First District Representative Reece gave high commendation of Phillips and called him a man who grew up the same way Reece did and who would not stray from the high road. At the April 21st state GOP meeting, any generosity Reece had shown Phillips during his attempts to be discharged from the army during WWII and Reece's political support disappeared. Reece remained cool towards Phillips because of his refusal to consider two of Reece's nominations for patronage positions. Guy Smith, who had become the head of the state GOP, recognized the Carter County faction that supported Reece, even though Carter County was Phillips' home county.[6]

On May 20th Reece ended speculation and announced his candidacy for the First District Seat in the House of Representatives. Phillips simultaneously declared his intention to run for reelection. In a speech announcing his candidacy, Reece stated that he resigned his seat in 1946 to devote time to leading the party in efforts to regain control of Congress. He noted that at the time he resigned his chairmanship in 1948, "it was not my purpose to run for Congress again, and in no way did I attempt to influence the selection of my successor. But now there appears to be an almost unprecedented demand that I run." He credited the petitions generated in the district with convincing him to enter the campaign. Reece pointed to his experience as congressman and his chairmanship of the GOP as distinct advantages to the district. That February Senator Joseph McCarthy made his infamous speech in Wheeling, West Virginia, in which he declared to posses the names of persons in the State Department loyal to or members of the Communist Party. Reece asserted that as chairman he "led the fight against Communist infiltration in our government" and that the world approached a "showdown" between "freedom under a system of government which protects the liberty of the individual, or serfdom under a system of government in which the individual has no rights except those bestowed by the state." Reece accused Phillips of departing from Republican leadership by voting against the Taft-Hartley Act, and in an indirect slur, pointed out that when he volunteered for WWI he "asked no favors of my Congressman, nor anyone else, and I received none."[7]

Reece's announcement immediately provoked responses from both the conservative and liberal factions of the Republican Party. On May 27th former GOP Chairman Scott criticized the Republican Party in the South and what he described as the "hard-bitten professionals" who ran it. He hinted at deals made with Democratic leaders and accused Reece of maintaining an alliance with Democrat boss E.H. Crump. Scott pointed out that Reece even published a Democratic newspaper. He claimed that actions such as these damaged the Republican Party in the South. Reece attributed Scott's remarks to Reece's involvement in the movement to replace Scott "after he needlessly led the Republican Party to its political Waterloo in 1948." Crump denied making any deals with Republicans as Taft came to the defense of Reece and southern Republicans. "No one with any sense would question Carroll Reece's Republicanism," Taft declared. "In 1948 he put on the most strenuous Republican campaign Tennessee has ever seen." In a letter to Reece, Taft expressed delight that Reece entered the campaign and said he looked "forward to welcoming you again here in Washington. Hugh Scott is and always has been a complete screw-ball."[8]

Reece campaigned on the assertion that a radical element was trying to take control in America. He stated that deficit spending would be the downfall of the nation if it continued and that "destructive taxation will ultimately destroy the principles of government," which would lead some to view capitalism as a failure. He pronounced the concessions at Yalta and Potsdam as causes of the Iron Curtain. Earlier that year Congress defeated the Korean Aid Bill, designed to send economic assistance to South Korea for defense in the event of a North Korean attack, by one vote. Reece asserted that had Phillips been present he could have tied the vote and let the Speaker of the House break the tie in favor of the bill. Before another aid bill managed to pass both houses North Korea invaded the South and captured much of the equipment—assembled near the thirty-eighth parallel—the United States had supplied the South until that point. Reece cited numerous absences of Phillips for three months during important votes and lamented that because of Phillips' lost vote "our boys are over there being shot down with materials sent from the United States." Reece also blamed spies like Alger Hiss and William Remington—people he claimed to have named as subversives when GOP Chairman—for leaking secrets and a soft policy towards Russia for the current crisis. He said that Republicans like him, who opposed a soft policy, faced labels of "reactionaries, conservatives, isolationists, and what-not."[9]

Reece campaigned on the need for a two-party system to defeat the radical element. He declared that his record showed him as "a Republican, first, last, and always." He stressed that he had never and would never run as an independent because the two-party system could not be maintained when candidates failed to "accept the decision of the people as expressed in legalized primaries." Although directed as a comment against his former opponents to confirm his voting record as a Republican, this statement would also indict his current opponent for future actions.[10]

Reece's voting record in Congress and his independent wealth served as Phillips' main political ammunition. He accused Reece of voting against the TVA and defense measures and of getting rich from his pension. Reece attempted to defend his position on the TVA and control damage on this sensitive issue with claims that he foresaw the possibilities of developing the Tennessee Valley and sponsored the movement in the early 1920s to prevent the Federal Power Board from issuing permits to construct private dams on the Tennessee River. Reece stated that he voted for the original TVA Act and appropriations for every TVA dam since. He

Figure 6.1. B. Carroll Reece meeting with his constituents. The date and exact location of this photograph is unknown, but it appears to be a school in Carter County—the newspaper in the gentleman's pocket at the front left is the *Elizabethton Star.* Courtesy of the B. Carroll Reece Papers at the Archives of Appalachia, East Tennessee State University.

asserted that he voted against all measures that did not accomplish the vital purposes of making power available to the military in times of war and to local communities via locally controlled power authorities, while at the same time using the nitrate plants at Muscle Shoals to produce cheap fertilizer for farmers. Reece replied to attacks about his personal wealth with the statement that "I certainly hate to think that I have not attained at least a small measure of success in the past 30 years."[11]

The First District primary race in 1950 overshadowed all other Tennessee races. In 1949 the Tennessee state legislature removed the poll tax requirement, making this election the first vote without this encumbrance. A high number of voters arrived early at the polls, with the final turnout reaching over 56,000. Reece won the First District Republican primary by less than 2,000 votes, and in what had to seem like a bad case of déjà vu, Phillips immediately charged Reece with fraud and spending excessive money in the campaign. He claimed that Reece borrowed $1.5 million from the Republican Finance Committee for the election, a charge that Reece vehemently denied. Phillips asked for an investigation into voting irregularities and called Estes Kefauver, the Democratic senator, to discuss the possibility of running as an independent. The GOP Chairman, Guy Gabrielson, asked Phillips to refrain from entering the November election as an independent. Phillips probably hoped for an outcome similar to the 1930 election, but his hopes faded when Democrats in the First District refused to pledge support for an independent candidate over their own candidate. Phillips would have needed these votes to defeat Reece. In addition, Phillips' former law partner and his Greene County campaign manager pledged support for Reece.[12]

Phillips continued his independent campaign even after a congressional sub-committee conducted a full hearing in Knoxville on Phillips' charges and absolved Reece of any guilt in voting irregularities. A letter to Reece acknowledged "minor irregularities which would be found in any primary election anywhere, and do not in any way reflect on the candidates for office." Phillips continued his barrage against Reece and noted that he had won twice over Reece-backed candidates. His supporters said that Reece made a political blunder by purchasing the newspaper because it made it difficult to explain how the former GOP head published a Democratic newspaper. Phillips drew criticism, however, when he pronounced that he wanted only the votes of the common men, not the millionaires. Phillips forgot that residents of Appalachia resented wealth only when it was flaunted in their faces, not when it was used for good purposes, as Reece had been doing in his recent business ventures.[13]

Once Congress cleared Reece of wrongdoing in the primary, other prominent Republicans came to the First District on his behalf. Reece and the Second District Republican candidate, Howard Baker, attended a GOP reception in Knoxville on Friday, October 13th, for Joseph McCarthy, characterized by local newspapers as the man who had exposed Communist infiltration in the State Department. McCarthy predicted that once more men like Reece and Baker entered Congress, "there will be a general exodus of the present State Department personnel." McCarthy described Reece as a "star-spangled American and one of the first to warn the nation of the Communistic infiltration." With McCarthy at the height of fame, his endorsement proved invaluable to Reece's campaign against subversion. Harold Stassen, the former presidential hopeful, arrived one week later to make his first political speech in the South at Johnson City, Tennessee. He called for support for both Reece and Baker and blamed the administration directly for the Korean War. Guy Gabrielson spoke days before the November election in Kingsport, Tennessee, and echoed Stassen's charges on the Truman administration. Democrats countered by hosting events that featured Speaker Sam Rayburn, Senator Estes Kefauver, and Governor Gordon Browning[14]

The Reece campaign strategy prevailed and returned Reece to his old seat in the House in 1950. In a record off-year vote, he won by more than 12,000 votes over Phillips and the Democratic candidate. The Democratic candidate had hoped to win because of the split among Republicans, but Reece's control of the Republican organization in the First District and party loyalty proved too daunting. He did create a modicum of resentment among Republicans in the Second District, who felt that he "engineered" the primary to the benefit of his friend, Howard Baker. Reece immediately affirmed that he would "advocate a firm policy toward the communists in foreign affairs." He had also taken steps to ensure that he would no longer have to face independent challengers in future campaigns. In late October, Reece and Guy Smith proposed a measure to the state legislature that would prohibit a candidate who lost the primary election from running in the November election on the basis that it made the primary worthless if the loser refused to accept defeat. The measure gained widespread notice even though the state tabled the issue until the following year.[15]

Republicans failed to achieve the same level of success nationwide in the 1950 congressional elections. Democrats maintained a majority in Congress even with losses in both Houses. Republicans campaigned on issues of high inflation and the spread of communism to gain seats in both the House and Senate. Taft faulted the administration for both high taxes and the loss of China to communism. He also blamed Truman for the conflict in Korea. An upswing in Republican support based on these issues threatened Truman's Fair Deal program and focused more attention on subversion in America.[16]

The events of 1950 prompted many in the Senate to take a closer look at the status of internal security. Pat McCarran, senator from Nevada, proposed an omnibus piece of legislation in 1950 to restrict the employment of and help ferret out existing communists in government. Truman worked to convince the public that the communist threat was external, but the outbreak of war in Korea and McCarthy's rants heightened fear among Americans. The arrest of Julius and Ethel Rosenberg in June 1950 on charges of atomic espionage confirmed the suspicion of many that communism posed a dire threat to America. McCarran formed the Senate Internal Security Subcommittee (SISS) in 1951 to examine how the McCarran Act was being executed. J. Edgar

Hoover eventually formed a secret liaison with the SISS to investigate subversion. McCarran tried to make the hearings conducted by the SISS respectable, but McCarthy soon became a major attendee and guided a portion of the inquisition's direction [17]

In Congress Reece continued his focus on legislation to strengthen the nation's defense. In January 1951 he received an appointment to the House Foreign Affairs Committee, which gave him a basis to pursue Communists. In April 1951 he proposed a bi-partisan National Commission of Security and Peace to clarify foreign policy and give Congress access to Truman's files. The measure failed to pass but won support among those fearing the spread of communism. In August Reece proposed an additional $350 million cut to Truman's foreign aid bill. The House passed the bill at $690 million less than Truman had wanted, and Reece reasoned that "America simply cannot carry the rest of the world on its back." In September Reece wrote two letters to the Secretary of Defense asking about money the United States had paid to France in order to build military roads. He questioned why the United States would pay French taxes on supply roads built to defend that country. His letters prompted the House to approve a military spending bill the following month that included a ban on paying taxes to foreign governments. [18]

In his first year back in the House Reece also resumed his efforts to enact legislation that benefited his district. The president of the Great Smoky Mountain Conservation Association presented a plea to Reece to construct a much needed road to Gatlinburg. That May, Reece announced that following a four-year delay, Congress had made funds available for a four-lane road to the Great Smoky Mountain National Park from Banner Bridge to Gatlinburg. In July, he and Estes Kefauver began a three-month campaign to construct a Navy guided-missile plant in East Tennessee. By August, newspapers reported that the region just west of Bristol, Tennessee, would receive a contract for the plant that would employ 1,500 people. [19]

Reece's private life flourished during this time as well. Sullivan County Bank named him Chairman of the Board in early 1951. On April 1st he announced the engagement of his daughter to Lt. Colonel George W. Marthens, II of the United States Air Force. The two married on September 8th in Johnson City in a ceremony that papers described as "marked by great music." The bride looked "exquisite" and the reception "perfectly carried out." With his personal life and local political influence secure, Reece once again involved himself in the national arena. [20]

The Minks, the Pinks, and the Stinks

After the November 1950 elections, attention turned toward the presidential election of 1952. As early as November 24th, newspapers predicted that if Taft won the Republican nomination for president and named Reece as his vice presidential choice that Truman would run with Kefauver to counter the southern vote. The Republican National Executive Committee decided in December to start an immediate campaign to use publicity to gain votes in the South and organized voting drives. Robert Taft remained influential in Congress and in 1951 organized a presidential campaign team. Dwight D. Eisenhower emerged as Taft's Republican opponent for the primary nomination. Eisenhower had evaded many questions about his political affiliation but declared through Senator Henry Cabot Lodge, his recognized chief of staff, that he would be receptive to the Republican nomination "if he did not have to campaign adequately for it" and if he could retain his duties as Supreme Commander. Taft became more cordial on the hill and tried to minimize the differences between himself and Eisenhower to win support. As part of his strategy, Taft named Reece his southern campaign manager on October 25, 1951.[21]

Reece immediately began an arduous crusade to win votes for Taft. He faced more difficulty than in previous elections because many in the area resented what they considered Taft's interference in previous Tennessee campaigns. The *Knoxville News Sentinel* stated that Reece "worships at the Robert Taft Throne, and owes his political life to Taft's influence." Reece asserted Americans would get a voice in politics only if Taft secured the nomination. He felt that Taft had been one of the few politicians who discussed political issues honestly in the 1950 election. Reece believed this led to Taft's reelection "by the greatest majority ever given a candidate for Senator in the State who had real opposition." He expressed great confidence as he traveled over much of the South that Taft would be elected. He predicted that Taft would get at least 200 votes at the convention from southern states and the majority of delegates in all of the southern and border states. Reece declared that the South would stand solid for Taft, and Tennessee complied with this directive in February 1952 when the Republican state convention instructed its delegates to vote for Taft.[22]

Reece drew much of his campaign material from criticisms of the Truman administration and what he perceived as their failure to halt the spread of communism. In early November 1951, Reece added a fifth "C" his platform of the "Four C's" used during the 1946 campaign— confiscation. He argued that "Washington's master planners are floundering in a sea of controls, confusion, corruption, communism, and confiscation" as the South stood helpless while the Democratic Party violated the party system to maintain control in the government. "Our people," Reece declared, referring to conservative Republicans, "have already determined to drive out of Washington all of the minks, the pinks and the stinks who are destroying the moral fiber of our nation . . . Morality must be restored." He blamed the president directly for the Korean War and called it a "Truman war." Reece attempted to justify his comment by tracing the withdrawal of United States troops out of Korea as the instigating factor for communist invasion. He believed this action announced to the world that the United States had no interest in defending Korea. He even went so far as to blame the Roosevelt Administration during the Normandy invasion of World War II, asserting that if the United States had demanded a definite location of Russia's western frontier that the communist threat to Europe would have been erased.[23]

In his condemnation of Truman, Reece managed to disparage Taft's Republican opponent as well. He accused Truman supporters of backing Eisenhower because they believed it would be an easier win than against Taft. He called it a Democratic attempt to name the Republican nominee. Reece also condemned the reduction of the nation's air power between 1946 and 1950, citing Eisenhower's 1949 plans under Truman to reduce military spending. He acknowledged that Eisenhower might have been in favor of air power, but as a member of the military he acted under orders of his commander in chief and refused to fight for air power at the cost of losing the support of the Truman administration. In Reece's mind, the administration "was able to employ General Eisenhower to cover up its fatal gambling with our security." He acknowledged Eisenhower as "a great general, but that doesn't mean he could succeed in other lines of work."[24]

The struggle between Taft and Eisenhower split the Republican Party in the South. In March the Shelby County Republicans scheduled a meeting at 2:00 pm to choose a delegation for the state convention. Eisenhower supporters planned to arrive at noon to fill up the small room, but Taft supporters arrived at 10:00 am and refused to move the meeting to a larger location to house all of the delegates. A similar occurrence happened at the Texas state convention, and Taft supporters accused Eisenhower Republicans of influencing Democrats to enter the primary to manipulate the Republican nominee. Reece later told Taft that Eisenhower supporters had as much right to "take the Texas delegation" as he had "to go in the corncrib at two o'clock in the morning and carry a man's corn off on my back." The Taft Committee declared the actions of Taft supporters at the Texas convention proper and legal and cited other states where Eisenhower supporters supposedly acted dishonestly. Reece characterized the incident as an attempt of Eisenhower forces to "ride rough-shod over all opposition when they are in control in a state but are unwilling to accept the decision of the majority when that majority is against them."[25]

Throughout 1952 Reece remained confident that Taft would secure the number of delegates needed to win the nomination by the time of the convention. In correspondence with Fred McWane, Taft's unofficial campaign manager in Virginia, Reece expressed some concern over the length of time some delegates took to declare their loyalty, but both men remained hopeful that they were slowly making progress. One report in early June noted that Taft had acquired the support of fifty-two delegates to Eisenhower's one. Reece, even though he believed Taft had obtained enough support for the nomination, still emphasized Taft supporters needed to continue to campaign just as hard as Eisenhower's supporters campaigned.[26]

At the Republican National Convention Reece assumed Taft would win on the first ballot. Recent articles predicted that although a number of Eisenhower backers criticized Reece's tactics and rivaled Taft delegates in some states, Reece most likely accomplished his task of getting the South behind Taft. Reece made a critical mistake, however, in assailing the patriotism and integrity of Eisenhower and his role in reducing the nation's air power. This proved to be an unpardonable charge among some Republicans, and one newspaper labeled Reece "one of the obstacles to building a respectable Republican Party in the South." At the national convention in Chicago, Eisenhower won the nomination over Taft.[27]

Most scholars agree that Eisenhower had a distinct advantage over Taft. The General entered the presidential nomination campaign first and "was a military hero whose popularity was almost legendary." In the contest for state delegates to the national convention, Eisenhower's candidates were described as "men of state-wide reputation who could be expected to poll a considerable vote in their own right." Taft's main advantages over his opponent were the willingness to campaign and the support he received from national newspapers and local politicians. Some scholars credit Taft's loss to his appearance as "stiff and humorless," while others believe that he "failed to impress voters looking for positive, constructive reasons" why they should support Taft for president. Taft focused much of his campaign on criticism of the Democratic administration and Eisenhower's work for it. Televised coverage increased the exposure of the candidates and although not a decisive factor in the election, it may have propagated the image of Taft as stiff while voters continued to view Eisenhower as a hero and "father symbol."[28]

Many blamed Reece for Taft's loss at the national convention. Citing convention controversies in Texas, Georgia, and Louisiana, critics blamed Reece for jeopardizing fair play. Rumors circulated that Taft had fired Reece as a top advisor but refused to publicly admit it out of consideration for their friendship. This is unlikely, because Taft wrote to Reece shortly after the convention to thank him for his help in the campaign and for his "extraordinary job" in the South. Taft expressed deep disappointment with the new control of the Republican Party and with the time and money "spent vainly in my behalf." Taft credited his defeat to the "unholy strength of our opponents." In an unpublished memorandum dictated by Taft after his loss, he charged that the influence on "New York circles" and the newspaper support given to Eisenhower contributed to Eisenhower's victory. Taft believed that underlying causes that developed before the convention—such as his inability to afford a "real campaign" in Pennsylvania, New York, and Michigan—explained his defeat. He feared his lieutenants would be blamed wrongfully for the outcome. Although disappointed with his loss, Taft still hoped Eisenhower would adhere to conservative principles. Reece believed that had Taft won the nomination in 1948 or 1952 he would have won the presidency by a huge margin.[29]

Reece set aside his personal disappointment over Taft's loss and hit the campaign trail for the Republican Party. Before Eisenhower's national headquarters could get organized, Reece, Representative Baker, and Guy Smith took over the Republican campaign in Tennessee. One paper noted that all had favored Taft—who if chosen probably would have placed Reece in a cabinet position—but they settled for distributing patronage positions. Eisenhower had little choice but to work with a less than friendly Reece faction. Reece spoke at rallies in Florida and Tennessee on behalf of Eisenhower. In November Eisenhower carried Tennessee. Reece won reelection with little campaigning. Republicans captured only a narrow majority in Congress, but Eisenhower won a sweeping victory over his Democratic opponent, Adlai Stevenson. The discontent over Korea, high prices, and accusations of corruption in the federal government all contributed to the Republican win. Reece pointed out the "tremendous responsibilities" faced by both Eisenhower and the Republican Party to regain the nation's trust. Eisenhower thanked Reece for his support by inviting him to his 1953 inauguration. Vice President Nixon wrote Reece to thank him for the "personal support you extended to me during the campaign—you can be sure that it will never be forgotten."[30]

Eisenhower's win signified a victory for middle-of-the-road Americans.
During his presidency he accepted the social welfare influence of the New
Deal and Fair Deal policies, disappointing many Republicans. Eisenhower
had promised "not to turn the clock back—ever," and scholars assert that
during his presidency social welfare legislation became an "accepted part
of American history." Taft most certainly would have renounced at least a
portion of the Democratic legislation, but Eisenhower managed to
maintain the policies and keep his support. Eisenhower took a middle-of-
the-road stance on most issues, failing to satisfy either liberals or
conservatives. He retained his popularity because Americans wanted to
avoid extremes and maintain security at home and abroad. Fears about the
Korean War and the Cold War created a desire for peace. After a three-
year virtual stalemate, the armistice in Korea gave Eisenhower credit for
ending the war, which he advertised in his 1956 campaign. Scholars
initially criticized the Eisenhower presidency for submerging the problems
arising in the civil rights area, but revisionists are taking a less critical look
at his accomplishments and perceived mediocrity.[31]

Reece lost a degree of his national influence after Taft's defeat for the
party nomination. The *New York Times* predicted a decline of Reece's
influence in shaping national policy, even though it conceded he most
likely would remain prominent in Tennessee politics. Reece attained a
small victory over doubters in July 1953 when the new Republican
National Chairman announced that patronage in Tennessee would be
handled through the Reece organization rather than Eisenhower
supporters. He also secured a position on the House Rules Committee in
1953, a coveted position since the Rules Committee effectively determined
what legislation made it to the House floor.[32]

Increasing division marked Reece's return to Congress and politics.
The split among Republicans intensified after Dewey's loss to Truman in
1948. Reece's political organization and civic activities sustained his
influence among people of the First District and earned their support in his
1950 bid to return to the House. He campaigned against the radical
element of the party and accused his successor of deviating from his
Republican loyalty. Reece received support from both local and national
Republican leaders and overcame his Republican opposition in the
primary to win the election. His political authority grew so strong that he
was able to spend most of his next term in office campaigning for Robert
Taft's presidential bid and still win his own congressional election without
opposition. He based his campaign strategy on the increasing fear of
communist infiltration of the American government and criticism of the
Truman administration. He suffered great disappointment when Taft lost

the Republican primary but rallied to campaign for Eisenhower, the Republican nominee for president, across Tennessee. Eisenhower's win was a victory for the Republican Party, which also won control of Congress, but signaled a loss of Reece's standing in national politics.

CHAPTER SEVEN

UN-AMERICAN AND SUBVERSIVE ACTIVITIES

Not in the Interest or Tradition of the United States

In the midst of Taft's crusade to win the Republican nomination, the fight against communism surged forward. Politicians soon realized that the panic created by the investigations of HUAC and SISS and the unfounded accusations of Senator Joseph McCarthy could be manipulated to accomplish other political goals. Campaigners accused their opponents of being Communists or not working hard enough to fight subversion. Legislators, such as Democratic Representative Eugene Cox, viewed this fear as a path to pursue personal vendettas by incorporating it into bills or proposed inquiries. An anti-Truman Democrat, Cox introduced a resolution on August 2, 1951, to investigate tax exempt organizations for un-American activities. The Rules Committee reported the resolution on August 15th, but it died on the House calendar. On March 10, 1952, Cox again introduced his resolution, reported from the Rules Committee on March 18th. The House passed the measure on April 4, 1952, by a vote of 194 to 158. He requested funding of $100,000 to conduct the study, but the House allocated only $75,000 for the investigation.[1]

Cox asserted that some non-profit foundations and philanthropic organizations had been taking advantage of their tax-exempt status to promote and finance communist activities. The House appointed a bipartisan committee headed by Cox on April 30, 1952, to investigate these charges. The members included Democrats Donald O'Toole of New York, Aime Forand of Rhode Island, and Brooks Hays of Arkansas, along with Republicans Richard Simpson of Pennsylvania, Angier Goodwin of Massachusetts, and Reece of Tennessee. Reece increasingly believed that the spread of communism threatened the nation's safety. One month before the investigation started, Reece accused Dean Acheson, the Secretary of State, with allowing Communists to leave the United States in order to attend an international communist conference in China. This, along with McCarthy's speech, reinforced Reece's belief that Communists ran the State Department. The committee confronted well-placed criticism that it would spread hysteria and fear as it began its official investigation on November 16th.[2]

The Cox Committee had little time to conduct an investigation and prepare a report for Congress. If it did not make its final report by January 1, 1953, the committee would automatically dissolve unless recreated by the new Republican-controlled Congress. The committee felt that questionnaires presented the best method to accomplish its goals in such a short period. It distributed questionnaires to 1,500 foundations, interviewed 200 people, communicated by telephone with others, and solicited statements from fifty additional people. The committee determined from the responses and additional data gathered that 67,000 foundations operated on $7.5 billion of resources within the United States. The questionnaire asserted that the committee would conduct a full investigation of tax-exempt educational and philanthropic foundations and "other comparable organizations" in order to determine which used their resources "for un-American and subversive activities or purposes not in the interest or tradition of the United States."[3]

The questionnaire used by the Cox Committee, while impartial in theory, gathered very little useful information. The committee expected the form to provide data that otherwise would have had to be obtained through subpoenaing witnesses and records. The five-page form contained questions regarding the name of the foundation or organization, its nature, incorporation, and other basic organizational and financial data. It then asked a series of questions about foreign activities, grants made to subversive organizations as defined by the United States Attorney General, and whether governmental regulation of organizations was necessary. It allotted minimal space for each answer with an indication that additional pages could be provided. It served as a quantitative method that could not begin to answer such a complex question, in part because the committee relied on the integrity of the respondents to provide complete and truthful answers.[4]

Cox was determined to stem the flow of foundation money to civil rights organizations in the South. His fellow committeemen did not share the same sentiments, ensuring the hearings proceeded free of Cox's biases. Although some reports insisted Cox experienced "some change of heart," the truth of this remains elusive because Representative Cox died during the investigation on December 24, 1952. Cox's main concern in 1952 involved foundation support of what he viewed as un-American activities. This included grants to programs that investigated abuses of civil rights. The Democratic-controlled House prevented Cox from presenting a significant barrier to foundations, but had he lived he might have been able to intimidate foundations enough to stem the flow of money to organizations in the South that upset the "natural" balance.[5]

The Cox Committee's final report found little fault with existing foundations. In fact, the committee concluded that foundations played a large role in relieving the suffering of many and that America had a growing need for their humanitarianism. It did acknowledge that foundations had made mistakes in the past regarding grants but insisted these organizations were taking steps to correct them. The biggest fault the committee uncovered during the investigation involved trusteeships—since trustees served without pay, it largely limited the position to the very wealthy or retired. George B. de Huszar organized the responses to the questionnaires in a volume with his interpretive observations on the major foundations, including the Ford, Rockefeller, Carnegie, Guggenheim, and Field Foundations. De Huszar concluded that only a small percentage of total grants went to "subversive individuals, causes, and organizations" and an even smaller amount to "pro-American projects, organizations and causes and persons." His most damning conclusion was that foundations had failed to develop a balanced program, which he viewed as a "violation of public trust, for this money ought to be spent on representing the views of all the people and not only the liberal, socialist, and international segment." He considered it a moral obligation to support an equal number of pro-conservative programs to balance against any socialist activities. Despite this condemnation of foundations, the final report of the Cox Committee concluded "little basis for the belief expressed in some quarters that foundation funds are being diverted from their intended use."[6]

Despite his intense political interest, personal matters prevented Reece from attending many of the Cox Committee hearings. His daughter Louise gave birth to his first grandchild on Memorial Day in 1952, and Reece's wife underwent a hip replacement that August because of arthritis that resulted from an injury she experienced in 1922. He noted that her sacrifices for him over the years led him to stay with her during her recovery and a later extended illness, taking Reece away from Washington for much of 1953. Reece signed the final report of the committee with a disclaimer that the committee lacked enough time to complete its job. He strongly believed that the matter warranted further investigation.[7]

A More Comprehensive Study

Shortly after the Cox Committee investigation ended Reece announced his intention to reopen the inquiry through Congress. He first mentioned his dissatisfaction with the committee through the Congressional Record of the House in April 1953. Reece described the findings of the Cox Committee as badly misinterpreted because testimony that disclosed subversive and communist activities had been omitted from the report. He insisted that the evidence indicated at least one case where foundation trustees were communists, as well as some other officers of legitimate foundations. The future "magnitude of the problem," according to Reece, warranted further investigation, especially considering large family fortunes based on corporation stock funded these foundations.[8]

Even though Reece had attended only three of the Cox Committee meetings because of his wife's illness, he criticized the entire proceedings of the committee. A memorandum circulated among the Board of Trustees of The Twentieth Century Fund noted the irony that Reece was the only member who failed to attend regular meetings of the committee and the only one who believed the investigation inadequate. Aaron M. Sargent, an attorney from California whom the Cox Committee had considered for its general counsel, served as Reece's source of information. A former member of the California Un-American Activities Committee, Sargent remained close to the Cox investigation without an official appointment on the committee. On June 21st, Sargent sent Reece the records of the Cox Committee in a locked filing case. Sargent claimed that a cursory investigation of the records proved that the committee lacked sufficient time to fully investigate foundations.[9]

Reece cited faults of the Cox Committee as justification for a renewed investigation into foundations. He noted that he had signed the Cox Committee report with reservations that the inquiry would be continued if Congress desired "a more comprehensive study." Reece believed that the need stemmed from five flaws that he identified with the prior investigation. He reiterated Sargent's claim that the Cox Committee had inadequate time to complete a thorough investigation. In addition, Reece argued that foundation officers excused grants to communist organizations as an unintentional oversight without further examination into these statements. The committee also failed to require those who testified to give their statements under oath, which Reece believed made the statements less valid. He claimed that the committee failed to ask foundation representatives why they supported subversive propaganda through their grants and lastly, that the committee failed to make full use of the documentary evidence it possessed.[10]

At a meeting in July 1953 with Joseph Martin, Jr., the Speaker of the House, Reece broached the subject of a new investigation, and Martin suggested that Reece wait until the middle of July to bring forth a proposal. Reece reported this news to the Cox Committee's research analyst, George de Huszar, with whom he had carried on a correspondence since April regarding the possibility of another investigation into tax-exempt foundations. Reece also received encouragement from Father Edward A. Keller, Director of the Bureau of Economic Research at the University of Notre Dame. Heartened by the support Reece felt he had for his proposal, he introduced a resolution for a new committee in July 1953.[11]

Before the House could vote on his resolution, Reece first had to move his proposal out of the House Rules Committee. Most members felt that the Cox Committee had sufficiently investigated the matter and were unwilling to support another congressional inquiry. A bill to extend the excess-profits tax came before the House Rules Committee at the same time, and Reece saw this as an opportunity to move his resolution to the House floor. President Eisenhower wanted to extend the tax, but the House Ways and Means Committee had delayed action on the proposal. The Rules Committee countered this tactic by introducing its own bill to extend the excess-profits tax. Reece opposed the extension, but he made a bargain with Eisenhower Republicans who wanted their bill to go to the House. He agreed to report the excess-profits bill out of the Rules Committee in return for a vote on his investigation of tax-exempt foundations.[12]

Reece structured his petition to Congress to establish a new investigation with more diplomacy than his earlier plea. He opened by describing the majority of foundations in the United States as honest and efficient entities that had made many contributions to society, even though it cost American taxpayers billions. Congress needed to concern itself, he insisted, only with the minority that had tried to overthrow the government and undermine the "American way of life." Communists accomplished this by taking control of foundations and turning them to finance the destruction of capitalism. Reece supported a new investigation by reiterating the inadequacy of the Cox Committee and relating specific "foundation-financed unscholarly projects" he considered "pro-Communist and pro-Socialist propaganda." The Ford Foundation received specific attention because not only was it the wealthiest and most influential, but it also donated more money to investigate congressional committees than any committee itself received for its own work. Most damning were the comments of the director of the Ford Foundation, Robert Hutchins, about communism not being a threat even during the Berlin airlift.[13]

The proposal generated controversy among the House members during its open discussion. Many members opposed a duplication of the Cox

Committee while others believed HUAC or the Ways and Means
Committee better suited for such an investigation. One of Reece's close
colleagues opposed the resolution because it put the House in the position
of using the power of investigation as a weapon. Another member more
clearly insisted that any money appropriated to the committee would be
"money thrown down the river." Brooks Hays, who served on the Cox
Committee, stated that even though his committee confirmed communists
had tried to take over some foundations, they met resistance where they
tried to infiltrate. Those in favor of the resolution argued that the House
should focus on the needs of America first. They asserted that foundations
spent money on political propaganda and that HUAC's jurisdiction was
not broad enough to cover foundations. One supporter of the proposal
believed the committee better qualified to decide such questions than
individuals "picked at random" and funded with money that could be spent
in any "novel" way. In the end, support for the investigation carried the
resolution, which passed the House by a vote of 209-163.[14]

Reece's success derived in part from the support of Democrats in the
House. Although Republicans maintained a majority, few Republicans or
Democrats normally would have voted for a resolution proposed so soon
after the Cox Committee. The bill received support from southern
Democrats who were upset at the rumor that the Fund for the Republic
planned to use a large part of its funds to study race relations. The
Southern Regional Council (SRC) grew out of the Commission on
Interracial Cooperation established after World War I. Its board requested
grants from the Ford, Rockefeller, and Carnegie foundations for its
programs. In 1954 the Fund for the Republic gave the SRC $150,000 in
support of its educational programs in southern states. These actions
caught the attention of southern Democrats, including Eugene Cox, and
influenced investigations into foundations.[15]

Many southern congressmen used anti-communism and investigations
such as the one Reece proposed to intimidate or destroy what they
considered to be undesirable organizations. The SRC began with the
premise that racial problems of the South could be solved only by looking
at the political, social, educational, and economic problems of the area.
Council members soon realized that race relations stood at the root of all
problems and by 1948 had published documents that urged "abolition of
the white primary, equal educational opportunity, publicly financed low
cost housing, adequate public health agencies, improvement of the courts,
and fair employment practices." In 1951 the SRC publicized its stance
against segregation. Three years prior, the much stronger and more
politically-active Southern Conference for Human Welfare had succumbed

to red-baiting and disbanded. The SRC managed to avoid scrutiny until its brief mention during Reece's investigation. Reece condemned the Fund for the Republic's 1954 grant to the SRC, and in 1955 the committee's general counsel accused the SRC of including twenty-one members with pro-Communist affiliations on its board of directors. Southern Democrats practically jumped at this opportunity to dismantle an organization that had become increasingly active in promoting civil rights for blacks.[16]

The one area in which Reece could herald some independence in thought from many in the Republican Party was in the area of civil rights. He voted for both the anti-lynching and anti-poll tax laws and recognized blacks as a valid part of the American voting population. Reece, a seasoned veteran of Congress in 1954, could hardly have been so naïve as to be oblivious of the motives of Southern Democrats in supporting his committee. They, in fact, had forced Reece to make a choice between his political desire to gain power and recognition through his anti-communist hunt and the advancement of civil rights for blacks. In that moment, Reece chose to pursue foundations. Decisions such as this helped postpone the advance of civil rights for minorities to another decade. Had he lived, it is unlikely that Reece would have proved to be a powerful figure in the civil rights movement—his attachment to the Republican Party and his desire for seniority prevented that—but he could have prevented Southern Democrats from using his committee to destroy the work of the Southern Regional Council.

House Resolution 217 officially created the Special Committee to Investigate Tax Exempt Foundations during the Eighty-third Congress. The resolution closely resembled the one that had created the Cox Committee the prior year. The committee possessed authorization to investigate educational, philanthropic, and any other foundation exempt from federal income taxation in order to determine if these foundations used their resources "for purposes other than the purposes for which they were established" or more specifically for "un-American and subversive activities; for political purposes; propaganda, or attempts to influence legislation." Reece chaired the committee, composed of Republicans Jesse Wolcott of Michigan and Angier Goodwin of Massachusetts and Democrats Wayne Hays of Ohio and Gracie Pfost of Idaho. Representative Goodwin had served on the Cox Committee with Reece. Pfost and Goodwin both voted against the creation of the committee, and Representative Hays, the minority leader, voted against the formation of both the Reece and Cox committees. Reece requested an appropriation of $125,000 to conduct the investigation because he hoped to receive

$75,000, but the House cut his allocation to $50,000, the same amount spent by the Cox investigation.[17]

Representative Hays proved to be the foremost dissenter on the committee. He came from a family of staunch Republicans, with the exception of his grandfather. Disappointed with Hoover and his failed policies, Hays voted for Franklin D. Roosevelt in 1932 and supported the New Deal legislation. He continued his independent nature as a high school history teacher in Flushing, Ohio. A member of the Board of Education reprimanded Hays for failing to put enough emphasis on the accomplishments of the Republican Party, but he refused to change his teaching methods. He later was elected to the Board of Education and served as mayor and state senator within a two-year period before his tenure in the House. The Reece Committee formed before Hays had amassed great influence in the House, but his strong personality still presented an effective opposition. Hays expressed "considerable disgust" to the House minority leader, Sam Rayburn, that "no one was able to stand up to McCarthy," and he felt someone should. Rayburn responded by appointing Hays to the Reece Committee, telling him that "you have been complaining about the McCarthy tactics around here, and here is a chance to see what you can do about it."[18]

A New Kind of Blank Check

Once news of the second investigation reached the public, critics immediately questioned the committee's motives. Many had come to view the Cox Committee as a means for Taft supporters to label Eisenhower and his term as president of Columbia University as internationalist, a dangerous label at a time when anti-communism was at its height. Papers attributed these same motives to Reece's investigation once his targets became apparent. Paul G. Hoffman, former head of the Ford Foundation, took a leave of absence from the foundation to work on a pre-convention campaign for Eisenhower in 1952. Hoffman wrote to Earl Hall, a newspaper editor in Iowa, in September 1953 that he had not seen Reece in years but heard that Reece held him responsible for "having busted up his 'procurement' of southern delegates for Mr. Taft." Hoffman assumed Reece wanted to teach him a "good lesson" and to smear the liberal wing of the Republican Party as a "preparatory step" for the Old Guard to take over after Eisenhower stepped "out of the picture." Henry Ford II and the Rockefeller family, operators of two of the biggest and most high-profile foundations, also supported Eisenhower's campaign. Skeptics reported that Reece harbored bitterness that Taft had been robbed of the nomination because he believed he would have received a cabinet post with Taft's election. Even if this did play a role in Reece's motivation for creating the committee, Taft's sudden death on July 31, 1953, after a short fight with cancer ended any hopes Reece may have held.[19]

Reece insisted that the focus of his investigation differed significantly from the previous one. He believed that the inquiry carried on after Cox's death had been too gentle on foundations. Reece noted that HUAC and the Senate Internal Security Subcommittee (SISS) were confined to the investigation of subversion as defined by the federal government. Reece inferred that the House gave him "a new kind of blank check" by approving his resolution. The Reece Committee, he asserted, would focus less on subversion and more on the extent to which money had been used for propaganda and to "influence public opinion for the support of certain types of ideologies that tend to the left." Reece argued that foundations gave money to liberal institutions promoting internationalism but avoided grants to conservative institutions that promoted nationalism. To secure House funding for his inquiry, he had to assure the congressmen that his committee would avoid an investigation into the tax-free status of foundations, since that fell under the jurisdiction of the House Ways and Means Committee.[20]

Months passed before Reece's committee announced significant progress or direction. The Twentieth Century Fund tracked the development of the committee, which by September had conducted no further meetings or made any staff appointments, perhaps falsely leading it to think the committee less determined. Reece turned to Aaron Sargent for advice on selecting the general counsel for the committee. Sargent had been a consultant to the SISS in 1952. He had represented a number of organizations in public hearings concerning education, and Reece recognized him as having experience in investigations involving education and subversion. He informed Sargent that he hoped to gather some of his friends together to analyze and chart the course of the investigation. Sargent recommended an attorney named Rene Wormser to assist the Reece Committee. Wormser and Arnold T. Koch operated a law firm in New York, but he had few credentials to offer. Reece later described Wormser as "widely recognized in America and Europe as outstanding in the field of estate planning and taxation," a considerable stretch of the truth, considering Wormser admitted never having tried a tax case. He had written Reece in April to offer his observations on foundations. Wormser believed that these organizations violated the law, had unreasonable accumulations of income, and caused a tax loss to the government. Although few instances of direct subversion actually existed, he felt the law governing foundations might need to be strengthened to avoid subversion. These beliefs appealed to Reece, who named Wormser General Counsel to the Reece Committee. In October Reece announced the remaining staff members: Arnold T. Koch as Associate Counsel, Norman Dodd—a Yale graduate and former banker—as Research Director, Kathryn Casey as Legal Analyst, and John Marshall Jr. as Chief Clerk.[21]

The appointment of staff members generated controversy among the committee's members that would prove indicative of all future proceedings. *The Washington Post* reported Hays and Reece clashed over staff that Hays considered "a Republican majority action." Hays insisted he had insufficient time to fully review all the qualifications of those selected. Reece issued a statement at the same time to relieve fears generated by this disagreement. The statement requested suggestions for the investigation and indicated that although little evidence of direct support for communist activities existed, many urged the committee "to confront the fact that there could not be so many developments along collectivist lines unless a great deal had been done indirectly to pave the way."[22]

In November Reece announced the necessity of a preliminary investigation before the committee organized open hearings to determine if legislative action should be taken. Norman Dodd conducted the majority of the research during this period, which entailed gathering information on foundations that Reece considered suspicious. Although Reece announced that the committee would exclude areas of religion, medicine, health, and physical sciences because the Cox Committee indicated subversive activities occurred more in social sciences and humanities, Dodd focused on the Kinsey Report, a study on sexual behavior by Dr. Alfred Kinsey published in two books in 1948 and 1953. A grant from the Rockefeller Foundation made the study possible, but the foundation discontinued funding after the published report generated controversy. Dodd gathered medical opinions, international articles, and statistical information about the Kinsey studies. Dodd's actions caused some to believe that the research staff had converted the investigation into an ideological attack on education. Reece recognized Dodd's motives but did nothing to limit his activities. He wrote to Wormser that Dodd appeared to be convinced of "a conspiratorial influence" that had "a concentration of evil men" who had exploited "foundation funds in the field of education for a number of years." Reece wrote that Dodd's opinion was in accordance with what they believed had been the situation "in most all phases of the activities of the foundations."[23]

The committee staff immediately identified four major foundations of interest to the investigation. All of the foundations—the Rockefeller Foundation, Ford Foundation, Carnegie Foundation, and Fund for the Republic—possessed immense resources, and the list surprised few people. Rockefeller's support of the Institute of Pacific Relations, Carnegie's underwriting of Gunner Myrdal's study of race relations, and Ford's creation of subsidiary foundations to study civil liberties garnered much attention. President Eisenhower made the preliminary investigation easier in February 1954 when he allowed the Reece Committee to look at tax returns filed by charitable, educational, scientific, religious, and other organizations that claimed exemption from income taxes. By law, the Treasury kept these forms secret unless the president authorized their disclosure.[24]

Reece held particular interest in the Fund for the Republic, created through a $15 million grant by the Ford Foundation in 1951. The foundation incorporated in December 1952 and received a temporary certificate of tax-exemption in March 1953 along with $2.8 million of the promised funds. The Fund for the Republic received its permanent tax-exempt status and the remaining $12 million in January 1954. The foundation was established to defend the first ten amendments of the Constitution and to help "roll back the tide of McCarthyism." Its first action, a grant of $25,000 to the American Bar Association (ABA) to study congressional investigations and their possible infringement on civil liberties, raised the indignation of Reece and other congressmen. Many of these congressmen asserted that the ABA intended to investigate Congress and compared this grant to the "meager" amount allocated to committees such as McCarthy's. In his address to Congress Reece stated that Robert M. Hutchins, an associate director of the Ford Foundation and future president of the Fund for the Republic, "consistently expressed" concern for the civil rights of Communists. Since Hutchins' concept of civil rights mirrored that of Communists, Reece argued, this foundation naturally would "aid the communist conspiracy" and discredit any who fought it.[25]

Reece failed to grasp the futility of attacking the character of the men at the head of the Ford Foundation and the Fund for the Republic. Paul Hoffman dropped out of college but worked his way from car salesman to president of the Studebaker Corporation. He was a Rotarian, Mason, Republican, director of the Federal Reserve Bank of Chicago, and member of a number of other civic and charitable organizations. By 1950 he held twenty-seven honorary doctorates. Scholars considered him a "middle-of-the-road conservative and a vigorous anti-communist . . . famous as the man who made the Marshall Plan the economic miracle it was." He requested a three-month leave from the Ford Foundation to campaign for Eisenhower's presidential nomination in 1952. Hoffman, aware of the threats presented by communist witch hunters, advocated creation of the Fund for the Republic to protect civil liberties.[26]

The Fund for the Republic named directors who were prominent in their field of study in hopes of withstanding attacks from McCarthy. The first president, Clifford Case, "vigorously supported" Eisenhower in 1952 and resigned in 1954 to run for the Senate at Eisenhower's behest. Robert Hutchins was an ambulance driver in Italy during World War I, attended Yale Law School, and taught at a boys' school. He became dean of the Yale Law School, and Franklin D. Roosevelt once considered appointing him to the Supreme Court. For twenty-two years he served as head of the University of Chicago, where his ideas on education—eliminating compulsory attendance and abolishing some classes as well as intercollegiate football—raised both controversy and admiration. He informed the Illinois commission investigating subversive activities that he refused to dismiss teachers solely because of their beliefs or associations, and the university trustees agreed with him. While at the Ford Foundation Hutchins' "brilliance was unquestioned. The programs he had created at the Ford Foundation had produced repercussions around the world." He succeeded Case after his resignation and moved the Fund's focus away from investigation of communism into other areas—the federal security program, a study of extremist groups, community relations, legal rights of aliens, blacklisting in entertainment, and an examination of the mass media. At the time of Wormser and Dodd's inquiry the changes in the structure of the foundation had prevented it from moving far on its goals, but its potential remained evident.[27]

Critics of the committee argued that thousands of other foundations escaped scrutiny during Reece's investigation. The investigation focused on larger foundations that had a greater effect on government and politics, and herein lay the main fault of the Reece Committee. Reece specifically targeted certain large foundations for their involvement in politics because of a political grudge he held against them. The Pew family of Philadelphia controlled Sun Oil, along with other mineral and industrial enterprises, and created a foundation that contributed financial support to the Republican Party and identified with the conservative wing of the party. In his study on foundations Waldemar Nielson concluded that the Pew Foundation therefore had "considerable" political influence and directed many of its grants "almost exclusively to anti-communist organizations, some religious and others military in orientation, and to groups advocating *lassiez-faire* economics." The Pew foundation obviously met with Reece's approval, and therefore escaped examination. Reece even later wrote to the Pew family for assistance in publishing books and financing projects.[28]

The focus of the investigation on a few foundations drew criticism from the public. Newspaper editorials accused Reece of perceiving little difference between liberalism and communism. Many recognized the danger inherent in an investigative committee given wide authority through a vague resolution that created it. Reece's committee targeted foundations that contributed money to social science programs and drew sharp disapproval from those outside the conservative camp. One journalist accused Reece of initiating a second investigation because the Cox investigation failed to explain how so many things he disliked could have occurred. The article described Reece as a man who disapproved "of every major social change since 1932." Reece recognized that he might have made a mistake by identifying specific foundations and attempted to control the damage to his investigation. He told the *Washington Post* that it was "usually bad business to name certain things" because it implied the exclusion of all others. Reece wanted to remove the perception of bias and insisted that most of the committee's work would be outside the foundations that received specific mention in the press.[29]

The world of academia presented a promising arena to dispel suspicions of subversion, but this very same reason subjected it to close scrutiny. Most universities depended on public funding and discouraged radical thought to save their reputations and contributions. Once the FBI, HUAC, or SISS noted an employee as a possible subversive, many universities automatically began an investigation. While some survived the purge from teaching, they were often left with high legal expenses. Few came out in defense of those who lost their jobs. In essence, the academic community "administered the economic sanctions" of McCarthyism. The American Association of Universities met in February 1953 to issue a public statement—financed by the Rockefeller Foundation—on the rights and responsibilities of universities, but many faculty refused to support and sign the statement over fear of losing their jobs. Those who signed faced accusations of radicalism and subversion.[30]

An investigation into foundations seemed a better avenue of attack than directly investigating educational facilities. The foundations selected for investigation by Reece were run by Republicans, and his past voting record supported businesses such as the ones that had created these foundations. However, the foundations named supported Eisenhower and advocated that communism was a declining threat. Supporting Eisenhower over Taft eliminated Reece's connection to national power and prominence, and reports that subversion presented little danger threatened to decrease public support that investigations like Reece's depended on for appropriations. Foundation studies challenged the notion that taking the Fifth Amendment was un-American. While politicians did all they could to intensify fears of communism for political gain, foundations worked just as hard to dispel the fears and rumors. Politicians maintained no control over donations to foundations, so the only avenue of attack that seemed available was the use of grants in education.[31]

Reece's committee became one of many Congressional investigations into the threat of subversion. Harold Velde, House Representative from Illinois and ex-FBI agent, headed HUAC in 1953. He directed HUAC to increase identification of subversives and "traveled the country widely, getting banner headlines for its 'exposure' of the Red Menace in education, the church, and the Democratic Party." The SISS, led by Senator William Jenner of Indiana, also held a number of hearings during 1953 on subversion in government. Few were outside the reach of Joe McCarthy, who attacked "liberal, non-communist Johns Hopkins professor Owen Lattimore," Secretary of Defense George Marshall, and Secretary of State Dean Acheson. In 1953 McCarthy managed to obtain a seat on the Committee on Government Operations and its Permanent Subcommittee on Investigations, which gave him broad powers to explore almost any organization he deemed suspicious. The Institute of Pacific Relations had already become a target of both the Senate and the House in 1951, and McCarthy named Paul G. Hoffman, president of the Ford Foundation, as a member of his public list of those "soft on communism."[32]

The Reece Committee commenced at a less opportune time for anticommunist investigations than Reece had realized. By 1954 the United States financially sponsored much of France's struggle against nationalist forces to maintain its colony in Vietnam. The outbreak of the Korean War changed America's attitude on communism from confidence to fear, and Joseph McCarthy rode this fear to new heights of power. Republican strategy had been to support McCarthy quietly while assisting his crusade. Many politicians disapproved of his tactics, but if his accusations proved true, they recognized the political rewards. If the accusations proved false, Republicans could quickly disown him. McCarthy manipulated the press to his advantage and remained on the front pages of newspapers from 1950 to 1954. Two of the staff members on McCarthy's investigative committee—Roy Cohn and David Schine—toured Europe in the summer of 1953 under the guise of collecting information on communism in American locations overseas. Their audacious behavior created a sensation in newspapers both locally and abroad and greatly embarrassed McCarthy. Reports aptly characterized the two as a "Laurel and Hardy" as they traveled to libraries and cultural centers and demanded to be shown collections of communist authors. A plethora of reporters followed the two wherever they went, and one German newspaper reported that Schine chased Cohn around a hotel lobby, "swatting him on the head with a rolled-up magazine." Shortly thereafter, the army drafted Schine, which set into motion a series of events that almost completely overshadowed Reece's investigation.[33]

The Army-McCarthy hearings that began in March 1954 damaged the credibility of anti-communist investigations. Fueled by his perceived power and recent embarrassments, McCarthy attacked General Ralph Zwicker for signing an honorable discharge for a person later accused of holding communist sympathies. This incident culminated a series of events that led Congress to initiate a public investigation into McCarthy's allegations. The death of Robert Taft in July 1953 removed the only Republican powerful enough to temper McCarthy. Republicans had stood silently in the background of McCarthy, but by this time they recognized the folly of letting him proceed unchecked. Network television stations broadcast the Army-McCarthy hearings, which gathered a larger television audience than either the *Brown v. Board of Education* decision or the fall of Dien Bien Phu, which ended France's attempt to regain control of Vietnam. By the time Reece commenced testimony on subversion in foundations, McCarthy had captured the attention of America and gravely injured the cause of anti-communism.[34]

CHAPTER EIGHT

A LABOR OF LOVE

Some Sections of the General Subject of Foundations

Norman Dodd's preliminary report seemed to confirm Reece's suspicion that subversives infiltrated and directed the grants of foundations. Dodd's six-month study recognized that foundations provided numerous public benefits, and he wanted the report to be viewed as constructive criticism. Dodd included a disclaimer that although the results of his study seemed conclusive, they were achieved only from exploratory studies. These results included an insistence that foundations used grants to direct education and steer it away from the "American way of life." Dodd believed a number of "accessory agencies" such as the American Council on Education and National Education Association warranted investigation as well because, aside from depending on foundations for funding, they cooperated to plan and control aspects of life through the federal government and education. He asserted that foundations and the government accepted the conclusions of social scientists as fact although they were founded on empiricism and neglected the public interest. The Ford Foundation deserved close consideration because the foundation set aside separate funds for education, national planning, and political investigations. Dodd concluded that foundations had been permitted to use money to finance ideas in opposition to fundamental ideas in the American Constitution.[1]

The Reece Committee hearings began on May 10, 1954, with a review of Dodd's preliminary investigation. Reece announced that monetary limitations forced the committee to confine itself to "only some sections of the general subject of foundations," such as the work of the Ford, Carnegie, and Rockefeller Foundations in social sciences. Research Director Dodd testified first and provided a summation of the Cox Committee and its methods. All of the committee members attended the first day to hear Wormser question Dodd about the findings, with occasional interruptions by Representative Hays. The first day of testimony adjourned because Dodd failed to provide a hard copy of his data to the committee members. On the second day of hearings, Dodd included Reece's resolution to introduce new hearings into the record. Reece defended his criticisms of the Cox Committee as part of its overall report to the House. Dodd quoted passages out of Gunner Myrdal's book on race relations and the charter of the Carnegie Endowment to provide illustrations of subversive motives. He asserted that Myrdal's book criticized the Constitution and read what he considered the Carnegie Foundation's attempt at a disclaimer, placed in the opening pages. The book acknowledged a grant from the foundation but added that the "corporation is not, however, the author, owner, publisher, or proprietor of this publication and is not intended to be understood as approving by virtue of its grant any of the statements made or views expressed therein." Although the foundation placed this text in all publications it financed, Dodd insisted this provided evidence that the foundation trustees wanted to renounce responsibility for the use of their grants. Representative Hays, the minority committee member, accused Dodd of taking these quotes out of context and thus altering their meaning.[2]

Dodd's testimony marked the beginning of lengthy criticism of the committee's procedure. Newspapers reported that Dodd accused foundations of focusing on social science programs that he felt could influence American thought toward an international viewpoint. Dodd feared that foundation grants allowed schools to become less accountable to the surrounding community, which he considered a natural safeguard, and altered curriculum to the point it denied what he defined as American principles. Representative Hays protested that the group's approach implied that the committee would focus only on foundations that Republicans considered "Red." Dodd provided the committee members with a written copy of his findings before the third day of hearings, but Hays accused Dodd of editing the version of his testimony that he provided to the press. The committee called its legal analyst, Kathryn Casey, to testify about the different versions, which she explained as the result of a clerical error. She said that the staff had prepared stencils for copying too soon and had to edit them for the official version. The staff intended to destroy all copies of the old version because they contained errors, but Hays managed to obtain one. He accused Dodd of tempering his harsh remarks because they suggested that foundations had become dedicated to a new idea of socialism, which very likely would have resulted in a cry for the end of the investigations.[3]

The committee's preliminary report received a similar reception in the press. The *Washington Post* called Dodd's preliminary report a "relatively mild playback of Reece's own charges, coupled with an emphatic comment that they have not by their repetition as yet been proved." While the *New York Herald Tribune* recognized the importance of the investigation, it lamented that Dodd's report left only the "foggiest notion" of the investigation's purpose. It reported that Dodd inferred that unless a foundation could judge in advance that its funds would be used in the best public interest it should not risk giving grants. The paper questioned the investigation as a waste of time and an example of "how mixed up some Americans can get." The *New York Times* agreed that the committee seemed to be headed in a direction to limit free inquiry.[4]

The committee called members of the academic community to give evidence on the nature of research conducted with foundation grants. Dr. A.H. Hobbs, Assistant Professor of Sociology at the University of Pennsylvania, seemed an ideal witness for the committee. Hobbs called himself "the oldest assistant professor east of the Rockies," a condition he attributed to his criticism of methods used in social science research funded by foundations. The committee believed Hobbs' dissidence and independent mind resulted in restraint in his academic freedom. He charged that foundation grants adversely affected morality, politics, and the country's military policy. Citing the Kinsey Reports on sexual behavior of men and women, the volumes written by social scientists on "The American Soldier," and Stuart Chase's "Proper Study of Mankind," Hobbs attacked the foundations that sponsored these studies, the scientists who conducted them, and the methodology behind the studies. When Representative Pfost questioned the relationship of the Kinsey Reports to the investigation, Wormser pointed out that the Rockefeller Foundation sponsored the study through a grant to the National Research Council's committee on sex. He also justified Hobbs' testimony as an example of the effect that such publications have on the public, especially through television and the radio. At this point, Representative Hays announced his concern about foundations having a chance to respond to these accusations.[5]

The next witness before the Reece Committee sparked heated controversy between the Democratic members of the committee and Reece. On May 24th, Aaron Sargent testified before the committee as an "expert" on school textbooks and foundation operations in education. Representative Cox had approached Sargent about serving as counsel to his committee in 1952 but never officially offered him the position. Representative Hays grilled Sargent about his assertion that the Cox Committee had offered him the job and accused Sargent of perjury. Hays then questioned Sargent about both his own definition of socialism and his position on the TVA, which Hays knew would provoke Reece. Reece interrupted the questioning with a summary of how he viewed the development of the TVA. He described how the question arose of who should distribute power generated at the dams and stated he opposed the federal government establishing a "sprawling power distributing system" in favor of local authorities distributing the power. Reece noted that the federal government generated the power and sold it wholesale to the municipalities for distribution. He pointed out that although the government owned all of the facilities, they could be privately owned if desired. Hays commented that the TVA had provided much for East Tennessee, including food on the tables and shoes on the feet of many. Reece interjected that that "some of them wore shoes down there before TVA."[6]

Sargent intimated that the research he conducted on radicalism in education qualified him to judge the influence of foundations on schools. He accused foundations of sponsoring subversive teaching and charged Senator Paul Douglas with spreading socialism while Douglas attended college. Sargent also charged Cordell Hull, the former Secretary of State, with sponsoring the 1913 income tax law, which Sargent considered a plot to socialize America through taxing and spending. Representative Hays objected to Sargent's testimony because he read from a prepared statement that had been distributed to the press but not to the committee members. Reece took responsibility for having Sargent prepare a written statement, but Representatives Hays moved for a closed hearing so that the committee could be informed of Sargent's testimony. Minority committee member Representative Pfost agreed with the motion for a closed hearing, but Reece had the proxies of the other two Republicans on the committee, who were absent, and voted against the motion. Hays and Pfost then walked out of the investigation in protest over the conduct of the inquiry. The two accused the committee of allowing witnesses to charge foundations without the committee having prior knowledge of the content of the testimony and of allowing witnesses to drop names that cast a derogatory implication at public figures. Their actions forced the committee to adjourn hearings because House rules required a quorum with at least one Democrat in the absence of all Republican members.[7]

The hostility continued into the next day's hearings. All Republican members of the committee attended in order to prevent the Democrats from forcing an end to the hearings. Hays reiterated his objection that Sargent had failed to prepare a written statement for the entire committee, as directed by the rules of the committee. Reece ignored Hays' objection and wanted to move forward with testimony. Hays observed that Reece refused to uphold any point of order with which he disagreed, regardless of the rules. He warned Reece against interrupting him and expressed fears of a "Republican dictatorship." Hays then called for another point of order that the committee had failed to appoint a staff member for the minority members of the committee. Reece noted that Hays had recommended the stenographer hired by the committee. The official record deleted the next exchange between Reece and Hays at the request of Reece, who later recounted that Hays accused him of breaking his word and of double-crossing Hays. When Reece refused to respond, Hays taunted Reece that he "thought they had more guts in East Tennessee." In an interview that August, Reece stated with a laugh that Hays called him names that he was "not accustomed to being called, but I took no exception to it." Representative Wolcott tried to resume the hearings and Sargent's testimony as a visibly angered Hays informed Wolcott that he would interrupt at any point he wanted, so Wolcott should save his breath.[8]

Reece faced accusations of tailoring the hearings to target specific foundations. The *New York Times* reported that Congress conducted so many investigations that the Reece Committee had met in virtually every room except the boiler room. Sargent testified for two more days amid countless interruptions by Hays. He emphasized that foundation grants influenced education, textbooks, and authors. Hays accused Reece of directing the hearings against foundations and of omitting witnesses for foundations. Hays asserted that Reece knew that the House would refuse further funds for the committee and intentionally delayed calling rebuttal witnesses for the foundations. Reece expressed his belief that there would be enough funds for the entire hearings and agreed to Hays' request that Dean Rusk, president of the Rockefeller Foundation, be called to testify. Reece stipulated, though, that the committee needed to hear all criticism against foundations before allowing them to respond. He then announced a one-week "cooling off recess" for the committee before the next hearing.[9]

Three of the next four witnesses called by the committee proved to be less enthusiastic about denouncing foundations. The assistant commissioner of the Internal Revenue Service informed the committee that only a fraction of one percent of the 32,000 educational foundations had strayed from the regulations that allowed them to maintain tax-exempt status. He added that from 1952-1954 the government had withdrawn tax-exempt status from fifty-five organizations in a thorough review. Since the government granted tax-exempt status without legal definitions of "educational" and "propaganda," the Reece Committee faced making conclusions without established guidelines. David Nelson Row, from the department of political science at Yale University, testified as an expert on the Far East. The recipient of several foundation grants, Row believed that foundations erred only when they deviated from established methods of reviewing grants. Professor Kenneth Colegrove, a retired political science professor from Northwestern University, professed his hesitancy to appear. He feared that much of the public received the impression that witnesses desired to smear foundations and their officers because he believed that newspapers misquoted testimony. Colegrove announced his respect for foundations and gave a balanced overview of their operation. His only criticism pertained to the fact that grants may have leaned more towards internationalism and globalism than would be desired.[10]

The testimony of Thomas M. McNiece, the committee's assistant research director, inflicted untold damage to Reece's crusade. On June 3rd, McNiece read from an initial staff report given to all committee members and quoted excerpts from books regarding the relationship between foundations and education. He linked grant money used by educational foundations to "a movement to socialize" the country into a "collectivist state." Hays contended that some of the evidence the staff used was twenty years old and that the problems McNiece mentioned had been rectified by the New Deal. McNiece continued reading excerpts when he resumed his testimony on June 9th. Tired of what he viewed as a Republican tactic of quoting passages out of context to prove subversion, Hays took action that made front-page news. Hays read three passages to McNiece and asked his opinion on them. McNiece likened the passages to some communist literature he had read, and Hays then revealed the source of the writings— a papal encyclical of Pope Leo XIII in 1891 and Pope Pius XI in 1931. McNiece realized immediately the enormity of his mistake. He wrote to Reece less than two weeks later that Hays' misuse of quotes had little effect on the evidence he had submitted and assured Reece that Hays' failure to further examine the quotes "established no weakness or error" in his testimony. McNiece's attempt at an explanation proved futile, as newspapers and magazines widely circulated the incident to the detriment of the committee.[11]

Only two other witnesses appeared before the Reece Committee during the open hearings. Kathryn Casey testified again to summarize the activities of the Carnegie Corporation, the Carnegie Foundation, the Rockefeller Foundation, and the Rockefeller General Education Board. She stated that a number of foundations, including Carnegie and Rockefeller, overrode state control of education by using grants to force their own views into curriculum. The president of the Social Science Research Council of New York came as a witness in favor of foundations and accused the hearings of attempting to characterize the educational and scientific progress of the last fifty years as a socialist or communist conspiracy.[12]

The animosity between the Democratic and Republican members brought the committee to a virtual impasse. Representative Pfost argued that the Republicans treated the Democrats like visitors to the committee. The Americans for Democratic Action called for the committee to disband because of its members' ignorance about foundations. Representative Hays described the proceedings as an "Alice in Wonderland investigation" because he felt the other members of the committee had come to a verdict about foundations before hearing any evidence. Quarrelling between members of the committee progressed to the point that witnesses had little time to testify. On June 17th Reece called for another cooling-off period in what he described as an attempt to maintain the dignity of the committee.[13]

The tempers of the committee members calmed during the two weeks, but that of the public became incensed. Many found the tactics of the Reece Committee unfair and its accusations against foundations absurd. *Business Week* agreed that the growing number of foundations presented a need for closer monitoring and analysis of their financial power. It warned, however, that regulation of intellectual activities fell outside the government's authority. The magazine predicted that the investigation would yield little value other than some mistakes made by foundations in granting money to a few people who later turned out to be communist sympathizers. It applauded Representative Hays for trapping McNiece in his own device of reading selective excerpts from books. *The New Republic* concurred with this evaluation of Hays, calling him the stabilizing factor in the committee. It praised Hays' legislative record and hailed him as a man who challenged Reece's direction of the committee and the predetermined conclusions of the staff.[14]

The growing discontent with the conduct and the investigation of the committee prompted Reece to offer a request that altered the committee's procedure. On June 2nd Representative Pfost had made a motion to suspend the investigation until all the committee members felt fully informed on the nature and projected length of the hearings. Reece denied any attempt to keep the Democratic members uninformed about the progression of the investigation and voted against her motion. Representative Goodwin and Representative Wolcott—through proxies given to Reece—also voted against Pfost. At the end of the recess, Reece recognized the increasing animosity against his committee and proposed to end open hearings. With a vote of three to two, the Republican members decided that foundations could present their cases through sworn statements or briefs that would be made public at a later date. The committee denied foundation representatives the opportunity to testify in public about the charges brought against them.[15]

A Very Unpleasant and Distasteful Duty

Foundations immediately denounced Reece's actions to close public hearings. They protested that Reece ended the hearings just as they had begun to make their rebuttals. Dean Rusk, president of the Rockefeller Foundation and Rockefeller General Education Board, wanted the opportunity to defend his foundation. Rusk complained that the foundation had refrained from commenting on the allegations because they expected to be able to attend the public hearings. Charles Dollard, president of the Carnegie Foundation, criticized the end of the hearings for the same reason. Dollard claimed that the committee questioned the corporation's "Americanism" and made unfounded charges with factual errors. He argued that the tax-exempt status of the foundation did not give Congress the right to censor the recipients of research and educational grants. Dollard defended the actions of the Carnegie Foundation and asserted that putting education in the hands of the government was more akin to Russia than America.[16]

Reece justified his motion to close the hearings based on Representative Hays' actions towards the witnesses. He reasoned that Hays' continual interruptions, his treatment of witnesses, and his constant vilifying of the staff and other members of the committee made it impossible to continue the testimony. During the initial days of testimony Hays' interruptions seemed to have come from a genuine desire to add balance to the hearings. As Reece overruled Hays' objections and continued an obviously one-sided investigation, Hays felt forced to adopt obstructionist tactics. His objections and interruptions became extreme in an attempt to prevent Wormser and Reece from railroading the committee and press to accept their foregone conclusions.[17]

Reece and Hays appeared on NBC's "American Forum of the Air" on August 8th to discuss the investigation. Reece described the problem as 7,000 foundations within the United States with $315 million of tax-exempt funds and a responsibility to the public. Steven McCormic, the moderator, questioned why Hays served as a member on a committee that he felt unnecessary. Hays replied that since Reece favored the committee and became the head of it, he served to prevent the committee from being biased in one direction. When questioned how foundations violated public trust, Reece reiterated his belief that economic support given to foundations like the Institute of Pacific Relations channeled information to Russia and thus led to the breakdown of policy in the Pacific and the rise of communism to power in China. Even though foundations may have later realized their mistakes, the damage had already been done. McCormic questioned Hays about his frequent interruption of Aaron Sargent's testimony. Hays replied he was unsure as to the exact number of times he interrupted but was certain that it was insufficient. Hays explained that he read the papal quotes to demonstrate the danger of lifting passages out of context rather than to embarrass the Reece Committee. He knew it was unfair but believed it no more unfair than what the committee witnesses were doing by insinuating guilt by association.[18]

Both Reece and Hays criticized each other's actions as being responsible for the hostility present among committee members. Reece reproached Hays for calling him various names during the hearings, and Hays explained that he only made assertions about Reece's actions. Hays insisted he "called a spade a spade" and interrupted witnesses only when necessary. He professed respect for Reece and agreed that some of the smaller foundations did need to be investigated. Hays' main contention with the investigation was that he believed the committee focused only on Ford, Carnegie, and Rockefeller and omitted all other foundations. When questioned about the money given by the Rockefeller Foundation to the Kinsey study, Hays admitted the money was probably a waste but it had "box-office appeal." He believed the staff was probably trying to get newspaper space since the committee competed with the McCarthy hearings. Reece denied a vendetta against foundations that supported Eisenhower, stating his focus was the large amount of money in foundations exempt from taxation. Reece targeted the most powerful foundations perhaps as an effort to dissuade smaller organizations from allowing communist infiltration. The fact that they favored Eisenhower simply provided an additional perk.[19]

Reece spoke before the House on a "Point of Personal Privilege" to defend himself against Hays' accusations. He explained that the initial study of foundations caused the delay in starting the hearings and criticized Hays' "ungentlemanly behavior" towards himself and witnesses. Reece insisted that "great provocation and a sense of patriot duty" forced him to speak against Hays. He considered it "a very unpleasant and distasteful duty" because of his friendships with both Democrats and Republicans but felt he needed to express his feelings on the matter.[20]

Reece continued to defend the investigation against the mounting criticism. In response to Hays' accusation that the committee only looked at large foundations, Reece stated that the committee looked at small foundations as well, some of which would be investigated by the government. He described many smaller foundations as "tax dodgers" and recommended that the IRS remove the tax-exempt status from a number of them. He considered the investigation a fair and objective vehicle used to determine if foundations promoted socialism through their grant money. Reece maintained that the only federal control of foundations advocated by the committee was in respect to compliance with tax-exempt statutes. When newspapers called the committee "a disgrace to Congress" and accused Reece of only trying to obtain publicity, he attacked the press for being overly critical of his inquiry and stated the press misrepresented the actions of the committee to the public in a "smear campaign against a Congressional committee." He explained the conduct of the press as a ploy by large foundations to prevent any further inquiry into their social and political activities. Citing Hays' "rude, unreasoning and ruthless attitude" as the reason for halting testimony, Reece described him as having "the personality of a kid in a schoolyard who yearns to fight but can't find anybody he can lick."[21]

The written responses submitted by the foundations lashed out against the committee's decision to close the hearings. Charles Dollard defended five specific studies funded by the Carnegie Foundation, asserting that texts presented during the hearings had been taken out of context. Reece reasoned that the Carnegie Foundation simply feared an investigation because it had allowed Alger Hiss—"a proved traitor"—to serve as president of the foundation. Hiss served a brief term as president of the Carnegie Endowment for International Peace in 1947, but this organization existed apart from the actual foundation. The League for Industrial Democracy criticized the committee's tactics as unfair and un-American. Paul Hoffman accused Reece of slander for a speech made before the House in which he implied that the Fund for the Republic was subversive because it granted money to an inquiry into congressional investigations. Hoffman described the research as an expression of freedom of thought.[22]

The most severe condemnation of the Reece Committee came from the Ford Foundation and the Rockefeller Foundation. H. Rowan Gaither, Jr., president of the Ford Foundation, denounced the end of the hearings as an act of injustice. He asserted that all Ford Foundation money had been spent to ensure a stronger American society and free world and that most foundations worked to ensure freedom in many areas as an alternative to communism. Gaither believed that the conspiracy theory propagated by the committee could harm the usefulness of the foundations. He urged the committee to dispel the irresponsible testimony from the final report and show the good done by foundations. Dean Rusk responded directly to Reece to express his disappointment with the committee. Rusk telegrammed Reece that since the committee prevented the foundations from replying he assumed no adverse opinion would be given to Congress. He submitted a written statement that he expected to be made public.

Reece replied to Rusk that the Rockefeller Foundation would be given the same opportunity to submit statements for the record as they would have been given in open hearings. The Rockefeller statement defended its grants and announced its goal to fight any attempt to use taxation as a means to curb intellectual freedom.[23]

One of America's most influential men also criticized Reece's decision to close the open hearings. John J. McCloy served as assistant Secretary of War during World War II and president of Chase Manhattan Bank from 1953 to 1960. He served as trustee of the Rockefeller Foundation for a number of years and later as chairman of the Ford Foundation. McCloy had known Reece for a number of years and wrote him that he found the conduct of the committee during the investigations depressing and hoped that the report would do justice to the foundations. He complained that the committee failed to give foundations the opportunity to refute the "nonsense" that had been presented and advised against the staff preparing the report. McCloy agreed that some of Hays' comments had been extreme but allowed that the staff's conduct gave Hays a "barn door opening." Reece replied that McCloy failed to understand the staff's approach because of biased newspaper reports. He defended the staff and Dodd's initial report and credited Hays with a suspicious attitude and distrust of the Republican members of the committee from the start of the hearings. Reece pointed out that the initial report acknowledged the studies were exploratory rather than factual. McCloy considered this disclaimer proof against the procedures employed by the staff.[24]

The Reece Committee created such a disturbance that some members of Congress feared the final report would be tainted. Reece wrote to George B. de Huszar that the closed hearings would prevent anyone from impeding the development of the final report, as "worrying with Hays" had become too much bother. Representative Jacob K. Javits, a liberal Republican from New York, recognized the potential danger of allowing the staff to pronounce a verdict against foundations and submitted a resolution to establish a legislative oversight committee over the Reece Committee and its upcoming report. Reece reasoned that Javits' request stemmed from the mention of his name during the investigation of the League for Industrial Democracy and apologized to Javits for any embarrassment this caused. Javits assured Reece that the mention of his name had nothing to do with his resolution. He explained that he felt obligated to take action because the committee had created such dissatisfaction that it threatened the prestige of all congressional investigations and foundations. Javits declared his motives were to serve the public interest. The House failed to take action on the resolution, but it revealed the Reece Committee's loss of credibility among the House.[25]

The Reece Committee's hearings fell directly during the months when the 1954 campaigns began in full force. In the summer of 1954 the House and Senate conducted three other separate investigations into education, including one in the House and one in the Senate that looked at alleged Communists on teaching staffs and one headed by Representative Ralph W. Gwinn on trends in teaching and possible harmful influences on the government. The conduct and procedures of the Reece Committee generated much more publicity and criticism than these other investigations. Some newspapers chalked the increased number of congressional inquiries to raw politics. The *New York Times* anticipated negative responses from the public and predicted that the Reece Committee would wait to issue its final report until after the November elections to avoid damage to Republican candidates.[26]

Reece's preoccupation with his investigation prevented him from actively campaigning for reelection to the House in 1954. Talk of opposition to Reece in the Republican primary circulated as early as February 1954, but few were willing to "stick their own necks out" or give support to another candidate. Rumors circulated that since Reece bought a house in Florida to help his wife recuperate from an illness that he would resign in 1954 because of his extended absences from the House to care for her. Local papers gave little credit to the rumors since, as they noted, Reece had missed a number of quorum calls in the House in his previous terms and remained a congressman. Republican Hassell Evans, superintendent of Unicoi County Schools, announced his candidacy against Reece in the primary. He described Reece as an enemy of the TVA and claimed Reece's "dictatorial methods" of the last thirty-four years exceeded those of Crump's machine. On June 5th Reece revealed his intention to run for reelection because his wife's health had improved, and he desired to continue serving his district. He also claimed to be in a better position to accomplish things for the district with the Eisenhower administration, to which he professed a "strong sense of obligation."[27]

Reece's absence from the First District became the focal point of the primary campaign. Evans accused Reece of residing in Florida and only coming to the district every two years right before the election. He questioned Reece's loyalty to the Eisenhower administration and his legislative record. Reece's campaign manager, C.L. Marshall, noted that if Congress' session continued through the primary election Reece most likely would have to remain in Washington. The Reece campaign attributed his absence from Tennessee before the primary to the "demanding pressure of the legislative program" in the final days of the congressional session. Reece lauded the accomplishments of that session in ridding Washington of Communists. He called for another Republican Congress to purge the government entirely of Communists. Reece's domination of local politics once again proved effective, and he won the primary, carrying all but one county.[28]

Meager Democratic opposition in the First District assured Reece of his reelection in November. Reece failed to return to his district during the campaign because he felt he needed to ensure the Republican Congress continued to drive "the minks, the pinks, and the stinks" out of Washington. He expressed little concern about his Democratic opposition in the November election, even though President Eisenhower telegrammed that his schedule prevented him from making a campaign stop in Tennessee. Criticism of Reece's investigation did not hurt him in Tennessee, and he won the November election easily over the Democratic candidate, Arthur Bright. Republicans failed to mirror his success, and Democrats once again claimed control of Congress[29]

An Anchor to the Windward

As predicted, the Reece Committee waited to publish its report until after the fall elections. The Senate also delayed voting on a censure of Joseph McCarthy until early December in order to avoid harming Republican chances in the elections. After the vote, McCarthy lost all measure of support and suffered virtual exile under the Senate's censure. He vowed to return to his fight against communism, although it had lost much of its public after the hearings damaged his credibility. Neither delay benefited Republicans as Democrats won control of the House and the Senate in 1954, which created an even more hostile atmosphere for the Reece Committee report. Republicans on the committee made it obvious that they agreed with the initial staff findings on foundation grants, so Democratic members, anticipating an unfavorable final report, requested time to prepare a minority report of the committee.[30]

The Majority Report of the Special Committee to Investigate Tax-Exempt Foundations turned into an ordeal almost as large as the actual hearings. The committee released the report on December 20, 1954. It included two sections on the committee and investigation, a minority report written by Democratic members of the committee, and a supplemental statement by Representative Angier Goodwin. Goodwin had reservations about the majority report after he signed it and requested permission to include a side report. The entire report consisted of over

1,500 pages, and its enormity forced most media to print only excerpts and summations of the official texts. Representative Hays became indignant over the content of the report and protested that the minority members received only a few copies. He also became angered that someone outside the committee had reviewed Part Two before he had an opportunity to look at it. Wormser worried about Goodwin's "mysterious separate statement," but he realized omitting or altering it would have turned the report into an even greater debacle. Goodwin's report arrived too late to be included in the initial report so the committee added it as a supplemental statement.[31]

Part One of the official report offered an explanation of the committee's procedures and the need for a subsequent investigation. Its authors—the staff members of the committee—began with a summary of House Resolution 217 that created the Reece Committee and a review of the Cox Committee and its shortcomings. The staff explained the discontinuation of hearings "with deep regret and only through necessity." They acknowledged the negative effect that witnesses created about foundations but argued that the situation permitted no other recourse but to close the hearings. In an attempt to defend the committee's actions, the staff asserted that closing the hearings had little effect on the inquiry because oral testimony held "far less importance than research." They claimed that the committee had full knowledge of the good rendered by foundations to many fields of research but asserted that certain dangers necessitated an investigation. The authors lamented the lack of funds that forced the committee to focus on the social science area and justified the inquiry because of the federal laws related to tax-exemption. They cited specific examples of unfair business activities by foundations, most notably the creation of the Ford Foundation. The authors insisted that the family could have donated money directly to charitable organizations, but the family wanted to retain voting control over the stock and avoid taxes on a large inheritance.[32]

The second part of the report, published in a separate volume, established fourteen main conclusions drawn by the committee. The staff considered the investigation more of a "pilot study" because of the time and money limitations placed on the committee and encouraged further investigation based on these findings. Half of these conclusions closely resembled the findings of the Cox Committee and revealed little new information. The report detailed the dramatic increase in the number of foundations within the United States, the positive impact of foundations when they operated in natural sciences, the enormous power wielded by large foundations and their influence on national politics, and the necessity of monitoring the professional class of administrators and public funds used by foundations. The remaining conclusions identified criticisms that conservative members held against large foundations. These criticisms, unproved by the hearings, included: foundations had influenced the media and government to the point that objective criticism of the organizations had become nearly impossible; foundations controlled the direction of research and emphasized empirical over theoretical research; this new research supported theories slanted to the left that were detrimental to the religious and moral fiber of America; and foundations worked in tandem to exercise control over America's foreign policy. The final conclusion of the report noted that foundations avoided directly supporting communist organizations "with several tragically outstanding exceptions."[33]

Reece added a supplemental statement to the majority report to offer a rebuttal to criticisms of the committee. Reece felt it necessary to excuse the committee in closing the hearings by demonstrating how the minority leader tried to disrupt the hearings. Reece denounced Hays' interruptions and his use of the papal readings and explained the preliminary investigation as the fairest way to let foundations know what evidence would be brought against them in order to let them reply appropriately. The amount of justification presented in the lengthy report immediately alerted any reader that some grain of truth had to be present in the many criticisms of the investigation.[34]

The final pages of the report contained Representative Goodwin's dissenting views and the minority report. Goodwin explained his position that the Cox Committee had fully answered any questions regarding the tax-exempt status and activities of foundations. He pointed out his disagreements with the Reece Report and cited the Cox final report as evidence. The minority report condemned the Reece report as a "complete waste of public money" in five specific areas: prejudgment of foundations, a lack of factual basis, denying a fair hearing to foundations, the nature of the public hearings, and the report itself. It criticized Reece for attacking newspapers and described the report and proceedings as having a "monstrous nature."[35]

The Reece Committee placed responses from foundations at the end of Part Two. The Ford Foundation called the investigation "biased from start to finish." The Rockefeller Foundation considered the study "discredited in advance" because of the biased nature of the preliminary investigation. The Reid Foundation offered similar criticism of the committee, and the Meyer Foundation described Reece as a "classic, if minor, illustration of men who believe in operating congressional committees according to personal whim and arbitrary prejudice." The foundations asserted that they operated within the limitations of the law and encouraged growth and research in many fields of education.[36]

Condemnation of the Reece Report began in earnest immediately following its publication. Dean Rusk and H. Rowan Gaither, Jr. charged in a joint statement to the press that the committee failed to print their rebuttals to testimony given against foundations, even though the final report contained almost all of the accusations. They reiterated their belief that the committee conducted a biased investigation with unfair methods that resulted in false findings.[37]

The media echoed the sentiments of the major foundations regarding the Reece Committee. The *New York Times* announced that the report received more attention than it deserved because of its outright charge that foundations supported subversion and considered it best if the report was soon forgotten. It claimed that if this charge were true, Reece would have recommended that the tax-exempt status of foundations be revoked, not that tax laws be changed. The paper labeled the findings as the "Reece-Wolcott report" and pointed out that the majority members applied new definitions to terms such as "subversion" to prove that foundations failed to fund research that supported their isolationist views. One newspaper noted that the Reece investigation and report would prevent foundations from being regulated in the public interest, which they should be considering their growing power. It compared Reece with McCarthy and concluded that the "superficial emotion" inherent in the investigation allowed the real problem to "escape study."[38]

Criticism of the report and Reece continued well into the next year. *Time* attributed Reece's resentment against foundations to the 1952 campaign when Henry Ford II and Paul Hoffman supported Eisenhower over Taft. It asserted that Reece suffered "from a delusion that he would have been Secretary of State if Bob Taft had been elected President." It criticized the excessive cost of the investigation and report as well as Reece's assumption that he was qualified to distinguish between good and bad research. Referring to Representative Goodwin's side report, Paul Blanshard, writing for *The Nation,* considered the committee to be divided two and a half to two and a half. Blanshard agreed with the minority report and described Reece as a "bitter-end Taft Republican." He characterized the staff as unsuitable because they lacked experience in education and social science and criticized the choice of "professional" witnesses for the committee. A writer for *Harper's Magazine* pointed out that the committee failed to present any new witnesses, but rather used witnesses from the Cox Committee hearings who supported the staff's theory of subversion. He asserted that the committee operated under a theme of conspiracy among foundations and scholars. The writer commended Hays for trying to bring out facts during the hearing and credited Reece with not only convicting based on guilt by association, but also "guilt by distinction and guilt by advanced education."[39]

Reece maintained his defense of both the Committee's procedures and its final report. He responded to the editorials and articles condemning the investigation in a letter to the *New York Times*. Reece felt that the press failed to explain why he decided to close the hearings and again cited Hays' interruptions and abuse of witnesses as the mitigating factor. He referred to two undisclosed letters he received from two "professors of standing" that complained about Hays' conduct toward the witnesses. Reece felt the final report stood on its own merits and pointed out that foundations made statements that appeared in the Congressional Record and most likely received more attention in the papers than anything published against them. He considered attacks directed against him for having a "personal plot against the foundations" unfounded since the House had passed the resolution authorizing the investigation.[40]

Hays maintained his position that the Reece Committee failed to provide an adequate forum for foundations to be heard. In a letter to the *New York Times*, Hays contended that Reece stopped the public hearings when a witness for the foundations attacked the facts presented by the committee. Hays defended his actions and his interruptions as an attempt to balance the obviously biased proceedings. Reece responded to Hays' letter to defend his position, but the editor of the *New York Times* felt that publishing a second letter from Reece would simply prolong the controversy. Rene Wormser had actually written the letter for Reece. Wormser accused Hays of creating an atmosphere of fear for witnesses and added "a plug" for himself at the end of the letter. The letter called Wormser a "respected attorney of national reputation, a man of high character and unquestioned integrity." Wormser wrote that this characterization gave him publicity for his law practice and helped the cause in general because he felt himself "difficult to attack." His encouragement of Reece to respond to Hays' letter had as much to do with personal gain as defending the investigation.[41]

Reece stood by the veracity of his committee's report. He wrote to Norman Dodd that although the committee had been confronted with numerous obstructions he was determined to do a good job and reach his objectives. He conceded that little good would result immediately from the report but felt that over the coming years it would "furnish an anchor to the windward" and "the many sound Americans" who desired to "keep this country on an even keel." He later acknowledged that the report had several faults but maintained that it was a "competent one" and would stand as the first effort to alert the nation to the possible threat of some forces within foundations. By July 1955 Reece had forgotten enough of the criticism to relate that the committee received "a very good reaction to the report." He admitted that the report received some negative responses but maintained that its influence would endure.[42]

Reece believed that he had truly served the American public in his investigation of foundations. Speaking before the Commonwealth Club of California and the National Press Club luncheon, Reece admitted that the committee erred only in making known the nature of the inquiry before the hearings, which allowed foundations to smear the investigation before it began. He maintained that foundations favored socialist and leftist ideals and prevented professors who refused to "follow the liberal lead" from receiving foundation grants. Reece described his efforts as "purely a labor of love." Confident in his committee, Reece reported that he had become "pretty much immune to criticism" following the disparagement of the Reece Report. He insisted that his actions followed his conscience and reinforced his patriotism and objectivity in the investigation.[43]

Reece's motivations in proposing a new investigation into the tax-exempt status of foundations most likely included a desire to vindicate Taft's loss to Eisenhower at the 1952 Republican convention and a personal vendetta against what he viewed as an attack against conservatism within foundations. When Taft died, Reece turned to his hatred of communism to justify another congressional inquiry and used his position on the Rules Committee to ensure its vote before the House. The staff of the Reece Committee reinforced the campaign against large foundations under the guise of violating rules that governed tax-exempt organizations. The nature of the preliminary report and the hearings supported claims that the committee was biased against foundations from the start. The Reece Report read like a diatribe against foundations rather than an objective summary of findings. Faced with intense national criticism and minimal support for the report, Reece once again held firm to his beliefs and his conservative Republican viewpoints. Reece believed that one day his findings would be appreciated as a warning against the communist threat to America, but they served only as reinforcement to the lesson learned from McCarthy against unfounded accusations and investigations. In the end, most reports characterized the committee as a debacle and one of the most poorly conducted inquiries in Congress.

CHAPTER NINE

OUR ENEMY, THE COMMUNIST

Blastings [of] Half-Truth

Although the Reece Committee officially ended its investigation with the final report in 1954, Reece continued to express interest in the crusade against communism for a number of years. Many considered him to be a relative "expert" on the subject of foundations and continued to seek his advice. While the Reece investigation failed to garner any concrete evidence of subversion among foundations, it managed to increase the caution of Americans about receiving their funds. Supporters of Reece brought to his attention acts they felt qualified as subversive. He thanked all of the writers for their information, but he kept his responses brief to individuals who held extreme opposition to all foundations. Physicians even wrote to Reece about foundation grants to hospitals and their programs, questioning the advisability of accepting the money. In these situations Reece or an assistant responded with a general form letter approving these types of grants. General R.E. Wood, Chairman of the Finance Committee at Sears, Roebuck and Company, forwarded Reece a copy of a letter he received from Dean Rusk regarding the work of the Rockefeller Foundation. In the letter Rusk emphasized that the fund refused to support communist agendas because of the United States government's opposition and because communism prevented free investigation in research. He stressed that Rockefeller grants supported true investigation and research. Reece had to believe that this letter resulted from his committee's work in exposing subversion. In late 1955 Reece diverted some of the information he received to HUAC, which he felt might serve as a better vehicle for investigation.[1]

The Reece investigation increased caution among educational institutions receiving and foundations giving grant money. Newspapers sought Reece's reactions on new grants, validating his belief that the committee had served a valuable purpose. In December 1955 the Ford Foundation gave half a billion dollars in grants to schools and hospitals. Reece approved of the foundation's gift to deserving institutions, particularly those in Tennessee, for research outside the social science field. Carson-Newman College received a portion of these funds, which Reece deemed appropriate. He insisted that only some of the actions of the Ford Foundation seemed tainted, whereas the grants given to educational institutions were acceptable. The SRC noticed the Ford Foundation's grant. George Mitchell, the executive director of the SRC, copied an editorial from the *Atlanta Journal and Constitution* in which the author criticized politicians for labeling foundations communist. The author insisted that this resulted when a "shyster politician" came upon a "large amount of money in a foundation" and realized he was unable "to graft, steal, appropriate, or take any of it for his own profit." Mitchell called the editorial a "pleasant letter," indicating his opinion of Reece and his investigation.[2]

Although many of Reece's remarks regarding foundations became tempered, the hostility between Reece and the Fund for the Republic persisted. Robert M. Hutchins, president of the Fund for the Republic, spoke at a National Press Club luncheon on January 26, 1955, attended by Representatives Wayne Hayes and Gracie Pfost—the Reece Committee's minority members—and Reece. Hutchins opened with a disclaimer that his remarks represented his views only and not those of the Fund for the Republic or the Ford Foundation. The Reece Committee's methods, he declared, exploited public concern about Communists in order to further political ambitions. He charged Reece and Wolcott with being opposed to empiricism and charging schools for sponsoring it. Hutchins stated that Reece had managed to harass foundations and subdue any courage to forage new research "without firing a single serious shot, without saying a single intelligent word." Hutchins accused the Reece Committee of achieving "some of its gaudiest effects by the simple process of giving old words new definitions and then pinning the old words on the foundations." He asserted that the committee defined subversion as "a promotion of tendencies that may lead to results that the committee will not like." Thus, supporting the New Deal and many other reform efforts became labeled communistic. Hutchins called the appendix of the majority report "an endless carnival of good clean fun" and insisted the committee held no more "than symbolic or symptomatic importance. Its wild and squalid presentation affords a picture of the state of our culture that is most depressing." In short, Hutchins concluded, "the Reece investigation in its inception and execution was a fraud."[3]

Reece responded to Hutchins' charges at the February National Press Club luncheon and before Congress. He announced that he had received so many letters about the Fund for the Republic's grant to investigate congressional committees that he felt compelled to make a public statement. The content of the remarks given at the luncheon and before Congress on July 21st was much the same. Reece accused Hutchins' foundation of participating in political propaganda and attacking the security system of the United States government by distributing copies of Edward R. Murrow's interview with Dr. Robert Oppenheimer, who had been dropped from the atomic energy program as a security risk. Reece asserted this gave Oppenheimer a chance to defend his associations with Communists. He also stated that Robert Hutchins' dual position as president of the foundation and chairman of the editorial board of the Encyclopedia Britannica gave him too wide of an influence and mixed politics with private gains in the management of a tax-exempt organization. Reece claimed that an "intellectual cartel" existed and that it tried to influence public opinion by directing foundation grants. He complained that the Ford family had avoided paying income tax on ninety percent of the profits it received through the Ford Foundation, yet no one challenged this grossly inaccurate statement. He reiterated that the investigation was directed not against foundations but their use of resources.[4]

Reece maintained deep animosity toward the Fund for the Republic and its president. In October 1955 the Harvard Law School requested that Reece appear with Hutchins at its forum. Reece agreed but informed the program coordinator that Hutchins probably would hesitate to appear. In January 1956 the program coordinator announced that Harvard had to cancel the forum because Hutchins would be unable to appear and because they had failed to find another speaker of Reece's "stature." Reece replied with regrets for the cancellation but noted that he expected Hutchins to decline to appear after Reece's recent speech at the National Press Club, which he claimed "contributed considerably to the widespread comment of an unfavorable nature about the Fund for the Republic in the magazines and news columns."[5]

Reece and Hutchins continued their public debate in private correspondence. In March 1956 Reece responded to a comment made by Hutchins that communism had failed in the United States. Reece requested clarification on Hutchins' definition of communism—whether he meant the overthrow of the American government or the rise of socialism and Marxism. Hutchins responded with a brief note that he meant communist political organizations had failed to achieve their goals. The letters seemed to be a continuation of Reece's interest in foundations, but accompanying letters from Richard Rimanoczy, the educational director of the American Economic Foundation, proved otherwise. Rimanoczy advised Reece on how to phrase his responses in order to elicit an answer from Hutchins and possibly entrap him.[6]

Although the press labeled the Reece Committee inefficient, the investigation prompted action among the public and foundations. Reece received countless requests for copies of his speech on the Fund for the Republic. Many even contributed money to help with the cost of printing additional copies. The head of the American Legion asked for a boycott of the Fund for the Republic and its programs after Reece's speech. The Rockefeller Foundation responded to public disapproval by announcing it would support legislation that required tax-exempt foundations to report to the public. In November 1955 the Ford Foundation yielded sixty percent of its voting power so that Ford stock could qualify for listing on the New York Stock Exchange. The Ford family claimed that they had been working on the idea for the last five years, although it had become a "prime objective" within the last year. This action made the foundation responsible to public scrutiny, a perceived victory for Reece, who believed his observation on the tax savings of the family prompted the move. Going public, however, raised the price of Ford stock and made the foundation the first to possess over one billion dollars in assets.[7]

Despite the continued criticism, Reece maintained his stance that foundations posed a threat. In a radio broadcast on March 28, 1955, Reece responded to the assertion of Adlai Stevenson that his investigation warned against developing new ideas by describing Stevenson and foundation presidents as "egg heads" who refused to give support to conservative ideas or theories. Reece encouraged freedom of action among foundations as long as they promoted projects the general public—meaning conservatives—wanted. Reece inserted an article from the June 1955 issue of the American Legion magazine in the Congressional Record that praised the work of the Reece Committee and its staff. The author insisted that opponents, especially Representative Hays, deliberately tried to hinder the investigation and that even though the Reece investigation produced solid evidence, its reward had been "the smear" of its name and the "blastings [of] half-truth" regarding its findings. Speaking at the Association of American Physicians and Surgeons meeting in Columbus, Ohio, Reece insisted that the "intellectual aristocracy" desired an "America governed by social scientists." He believed his investigation "incontrovertibly established" that Moscow directed Communists to infiltrate foundations in order to use their funds for the promotion of communism in the United States. He pleaded with trustees of foundations to monitor their own organizations in lieu of legislation.[8]

Figure 9.1. B. Carroll and Louise Reece. This photograph was taken late in the Reece's life at their Johnson City home, Bois d'Ormont. They are standing in front of a portrait of their daughter. Courtesy of the B. Carroll Reece Papers at the Archives of Appalachia, East Tennessee State University.

American Way of Life

Reece and Rene Wormser hoped to disseminate the findings of the Reece Committee in a more accessible format than the voluminous final report. Reece mentioned in March and May 1955 that he hoped funds would be allocated for a follow-up study of his inquiry. He urged further investigation and even proposed speaking with the Pew family to ask for financing, but he also recognized the heavy pressure against such a continuation. As an alternative, Reece sought to foster publication of a book detailing the committee and its results. In late 1955 Rene Wormser reported to Reece that he had already begun making notes for a book about the Reece Committee and requested information on the Cox Committee to include in his book. Wormser originally planned to write the book in collaboration with another writer but decided to finish the book on his own. Reece received a draft of the book in February 1956 for review. Wormser secured a publisher for his book but feared marketing the title would become a challenge. He asked Reece for assistance in advertising the book, and Reece agreed to do whatever he could to help.[9]

Reece and Wormser developed a close friendship as they collaborated in promotion of Wormser's book. Throughout 1957 Wormser continued work on his analysis of the Reece Committee and invited Reece to visit him to discuss the book. Reece remained steadfast that foundations had failed to fund research in natural sciences to the detriment of young scholars. The Devin-Adair Company published Wormser's book in 1958, and Reece wrote numerous letters trying to publicize it and obtain reviews. He expected bad reviews of the book but concluded that bad reviews were better than none at all since they created a sensation that could sell more books. Reece wrote to the publisher and related his disappointment that "intellectual liberals" had conspired to discourage reviews of this important book. Wormser hoped that his book would tell the "true story" of the Reece Committee and questioned why few congressmen expressed indignation at the treatment of Reece. Wormser felt Reece had received "one of the dirtiest deals in Congressional history."[10]

Foundations: Their Power and Influence echoed much of the information detailed in the Reece Committee's controversial final report. Reece wrote an introduction to the book, recapping the reasons behind a second congressional investigation into foundations. Wormser began the book with an explanation that a liberal movement had "captured" foundations and led them to use public funds to finance political goals, resulting in increased power in social science research and education. He described the growing activity of foundations in foreign affairs and lamented that responsible and well-meaning boards of trustees failed to realize the effect grants could have "in the world of men's minds." The book argued against the right of a foundation to discriminate among certain groups on the basis of their philosophies or religious persuasions, meaning those with a conservative viewpoint. Wormser specifically identified the Ford Foundation and the Fund for the Republic as examples of foundations that had become liberal, which he believed had come to interfere with government programs, and practiced "international dogooding." Wormser ended with an assertion that the operation of foundations created problems that could cause further injury to society.[11]

Wormser's book received little recognition when it appeared in bookstores. He expressed dismay with sales of the book and blamed the publisher for poor sales. Reece understood the plight of the publisher as a result of the resistance made against the book and the investigation and believed they should have prepared for low sales. His friendship with Wormser led him to continue his efforts at promoting the book as "an accurate and dispassionate review of that hectic episode, which was probably the most maligned, misrepresented, and malreported [sic] investigation ever conducted by a Congressional committee."[12]

Since Reece's efforts to curb the influence of foundations in education failed, he turned to other avenues during his last years in office to balance what he viewed as a liberal influence. In 1955 he began a three year campaign to produce a textbook used in schools that outlined the differences between democracy and communism. Professor Kenneth Colegrove—the same man who testified before the Reece Committee— began writing such a book, and Reece publicized it in Congress. Reece was unable to persuade Congress to mandate the insertion of *Democracy versus Communism* into school curriculum, but he maintained his support of Colegrove and his efforts to reform education. In 1956 Reece also began supporting a book written by Father Edward A. Keller, the director of the Bureau of Economic Research at Notre Dame University. He agreed to look for funding in order to finance distribution of the book, which he viewed as an aide to help maintain the "American way of life."[13]

Reece feared that intense focus on social sciences would eventually threaten the safety of the nation. In a speech titled "American Crisis in Education," he lamented that in the last twenty-five years educators had been preoccupied with social sciences to the point that Americans had been "unequipped" for the problems "of national survival and constructive citizenship." He insisted that "our enemy, the communist" had taken advantage of this preoccupation to focus on other areas that could threaten national security. Reece asserted that foundations contributed inadvertently through their grants to educators who wanted to "reshape the social and economic structure of the United States into a semi-Socialist welfare-state pattern" that they felt was superior to capitalism. He reasoned that changing human behavior prevented social sciences from becoming an exact science. Russia's launch of the first earth-orbiting satellite in October 1957 created fear that American research fell behind that of the Soviet Union. Reece insisted that the United States remained in a strong defensive position and that foundations could aid by granting scholarships for the study of "pure science" rather than social science.[14]

Reece's investigation marked the third time Congress probed the activities of foundations. None of these investigations resulted in new legislation. The 1934 change in the requirements for income tax exemption that prohibited propaganda or influence in legislation can be traced to the Walsh Committee Hearings of the Progressive Era, but even this required interpretation by the courts as to what constituted propaganda and influence. The politically-motivated Cox and Reece Committees had little to no bearing on public support of foundations or their treatment under the law. A Gallup poll conducted shortly after the Reece hearings revealed that "if anything, [the hearings] increased the popularity of the Ford Foundation."[15]

Although most foundations refused to be intimidated by men like Cox and Reece, they became wary of supporting unpopular ideas. By the early 1960s foundations had become more organized and professional. An analysis conducted in 1962 revealed that few projects sponsored by foundations failed, which suggested that little to no risky grants had been allotted. One scholar pointed to unadvisable trends among foundations, including an aversion to the interdisciplinary studies that had been favored a few years before, "a penchant for the safe bets," and a reluctance to deal with controversial issues. The press recognized the Reece Committee as "the most totally mismanaged Congressional investigation of the McCarthy period," but it contributed to the retreat of foundations from "risk zones."[16]

Representative Wright Patman presented the next major challenge to foundations. A Democrat from Texas, Patman used a small business subcommittee to look into the tax-exempt status of foundations beginning in 1961. He accused foundations of "being vast concentrations of wealth controlled largely by easterners, and of being guilty of abusing the sanctuary of tax exemption at the expense of the common man." The eight-year investigation garnered little notice until the late 1960s, when the House Ways and Means Committee began an inquiry into foundations. Patman, who was quite unpopular in Congress, attacked any large concentration of wealth and wanted a "25-year death sentence" placed on foundations. A study of his inquiry pronounced it misleading and "rabble-rousing," but it did reveal a number of abuses of the tax-exempt laws that forced the IRS to investigate. Patman uncovered foundations illegally lending money for speculation in the stock market and the use of foundations as fronts for the Central Intelligence Agency to channel funds to other organizations. These irregularities appeared almost entirely in smaller foundations, however, rather than the larger foundations attacked by Cox and Reece.[17]

Although the Reece Committee failed to produce any credible evidence against foundations, Reece maintained that his investigation hindered Communists from infiltrating foundations and directing funds toward socialist ideas. The investigation assuredly left a bitter memory with directors and trustees of foundations, evidenced by interactions between Reece and Fund for the Republic president Robert Hutchins. The strength of both the foundations and their leaders prevented any permanent damage to the operation of foundations, but after the Cox and Reece hearings foundations significantly curbed grants to organizations that could have been perceived to have a questionable purpose. The committee report and Wormser's book soon became difficult to find, not because of their huge demand but because of a lack of their credibility.

The hostile reaction to the Reece Committee Report marked the end of Reece's strong presence within the Republican Party and the House. Party members sought his favor but recognized that with the death of Taft, new figures such as Eisenhower and Nixon sustained the majority of the power within the party. Nevertheless, Reece continued his vendetta against foundations, proving that his animosity stemmed from something deeper than a desire to punish those who supported Eisenhower over his beloved Taft. Reece observed that Old Guard conservative Republicans were losing ground to liberal Republicans, and he fought desperately to prevent this loss of power by any means possible. He believed that he could reinforce conservative Republicans by preventing foundations from funding programs he viewed as slanted to the left. Reece's local prominence ensured his reelection to Congress, and he remained faithful to the Republican Party in presidential campaigns until his death. The social and political backlash from Senator McCarthy's unfounded accusations, the investigations of HUAC and SISS, and congressional inquiries such as Reece's damaged the public's perception of red-baiting as an acceptable basis for a political agenda. This contributed to Eisenhower and Nixon's reluctance to rely on communism as the cornerstone of their national agenda. Civil rights problems had been overshadowed for a number of years by anti-communist rhetoric. These problems increased during the Eisenhower Administration and forced civil rights to the forefront of politics. Communism became relegated to a Cold War with Russia—an external threat associated with the escalating involvement in Vietnam.

CHAPTER TEN

TENNESSEE'S MISTER REPUBLICAN

Honored to Have Been Selected

At the same time he scrutinized foundations for possible subversion, Reece himself became president of a newly established foundation. After Taft's death in 1953 left the Republican Party without one of its most powerful members, supporters began raising funds for a memorial foundation in Taft's name. In August 1954 the Robert A. Taft Memorial Foundation, Inc. named Reece president of the non-profit organization formed to "perpetuate the ideals" of Taft. While the Reece Committee prepared its final report, Reece contemplated how best to honor the former senator. The foundation considered a physical memorial, an institute to study policy, and grant money for scholarships and research activities as possible benefactors of foundation funds.[1]

The obvious contradiction in Reece's actions and his investigation raised probing questions among the public. Reporters asked Reece how he planned to avoid the "socialistic matters" in the work of the Taft Foundation that he had criticized in other larger foundations. Reece responded that the Taft Foundation would avoid promoting propaganda and any efforts to influence legislation and would concentrate on matters acceptable to both political parties. He insisted that he directed his criticism of foundations toward their administration and their use of their funds rather than the organizations themselves. He wanted the Taft Foundation to preserve the "American way of life as exemplified by Senator Taft." Reece declared that he felt "honored to have been selected" as president of the foundation, which would "always be open to inquiry" as long as he maintained his connection with it. The growing bipartisan feeling toward Taft—John F. Kennedy included him in his 1956 *Profiles in Courage*—indicated the increasing respect for the late senator and support for the organization. The Taft Foundation decided in October 1957 to build a bell tower in Washington, D.C., and to establish the Taft Institute for Government in New York to provide lectures, publish books, and conduct research in line with Taft's ideals.[2]

Reece declared that the Taft Memorial would stand as a lasting monument to his name and the principles for which he stood. He lauded that the Taft-Hartley Act had withstood attempts to change or abolish it and credited this to Taft's prominence. By April 1959 the foundation completed work on the Taft Memorial Bell Tower, and Presidents Hoover and Eisenhower attended the dedication ceremony. In his dedication speech, Reece commended Taft as one of the noblest Americans of all time. He stated that Taft possessed "the three infallible signs of greatness—generosity in design, humanity in execution, and humility in success." One newspaper called the monument a tribute to those "who never quite made it." The Taft Institute opened two years later in 1961.[3]

A second memorial project also captured Reece's attention shortly after the Reece Committee published its final report. Reece had long admired former President Andrew Johnson. In 1955 two barefoot Tennessee residents visited Reece in Washington to propose a bust of Andrew Johnson to be located in Washington, and the visit prompted Reece to renew his efforts to erect a memorial to Johnson. Reece had spoken to Congress in March 1941 on a motion to appoint a commission that would formulate plans for a suitable memorial, but involvement in World War II postponed action on the bill. In April 1958 his efforts came to fruition when the city of Greeneville, Tennessee—Johnson's home town—opened Johnson's restored home and tailor shop and unveiled a statue to stand in the city. Reece spoke at the dedication ceremony, calling Johnson "the greatest martyr and unsung hero in American history."[4]

Reece had long been considered an avid researcher of Andrew Johnson. Shortly after the dedication ceremony, Reece discovered the fourth of only four pictures made of Abraham Lincoln at his second inauguration ceremony. Reece found this by accident when a bookstore owner who knew of his interest in Johnson gave him the photograph. Reece sent the negative to the National Archives but kept the original picture, which showed Johnson, covering his face with his hat, a blurry Lincoln in motion, and just above Lincoln's head, John Wilkes Booth. Reece continued to collect information to write a book on Johnson. Although Reece died before he could find a publisher, his wife followed through with his intent in 1962. *The Courageous Commoner: A Biography of Andrew Johnson* perhaps reflects how Reece hoped critics would view his own political career. Reece wanted readers to understand Johnson's motivations. Reece portrays his rise from poor tailor to state representative to governor, and eventually president, as a heroic feat against surprising odds. He describes Johnson's battles against the aristocracy and believed radicals attacked Johnson for his compassion. Reece informally refers to the former president as "Andy" throughout the work, perhaps suggesting a familiarity between the two and hinting at the similarities of both careers. It is likely that Reece greatly admired Johnson and hoped to model his political career on the former president—rising from poverty to a position of influence in the nation. Though misunderstood by many critics, Johnson—and thereby Reece—remained strong and courageous and stood by their convictions.[5]

Private War on Communism

The negative response Reece received from his committee investigation had little effect on local elections. Speculation circulated that Reece would retire from Congress in 1956, but he announced that he had "no alternative" but to run after an expression of confidence from those who knew him. He asked for a sixteenth term because of his devotion to his constituents and because he felt that he could better serve the people in office during what he described as the "troubled days" of the nation. Reece announced that his wife agreed to his candidacy but lamented that his duties in Washington prevented him from returning to the district to campaign. He offered his legislative record as evidence of his devotion to the interests of his district and won the Republican primary without any opposition. Arthur Bright won the Democratic primary to challenge Reece in the November elections.[6]

Just before the election Reece committed an act of kindness that demonstrated his true concern for the citizens of his district. In October one of his constituents gave birth to conjoined twins. Her husband died unexpectedly just before the birth, leaving her alone to care for the twins as well as her two other children. Reece arranged for the twins to be admitted to the National Institute of Health for observation and later separation. Local papers gave ample space to the story and the successful separation surgery. No paper interpreted Reece's act as an election ploy, most likely because Reece held little concern about his opponent. Bright ran as the Democratic nominee against Reece in 1952 and 1954 and lost. Reece's victories gave him confidence that he would defeat Bright once again, which allowed him time to focus on the national campaign.[7]

Reece faced a much tougher challenge in securing Tennessee's vote for the national Republican ticket. He admitted that although he loved Eisenhower, he disliked many of his policies. He assured voters, however, that he supported Eisenhower through his first four years in office and pledged his support in the next four years after his reelection. Reece praised Eisenhower for ending the Korean War and organized the

Republican Party in Tennessee to support the Eisenhower-Nixon ticket. Democrats mounted a strong campaign in Tennessee because Estes Kefauver ran as the vice presidential candidate on the Democratic ticket with Adlai Stevenson. The state Democratic machine had declined with the death of Crump in 1952, leaving Democrats free to decide their own vote. Many disliked Kefauver but voted Democratic because they felt the Republican Party had failed to do enough for the state. Republicans triumphed, however, and returned both Eisenhower and Reece to Washington.[8]

Reece's adept political maneuverings helped maintain his popularity within his district. In 1957, the city of Johnson City dedicated their newest government building, the Carroll Reece Post Office. In April 1958 Reece announced his candidacy for another term in office. He invited Vice-President Nixon to visit the Rhododendron Festival at Roan Mountain that June, proving his ability to bring attention to his district. The following month John B. Waters, Jr., an attorney who lived in Sevierville, announced that he would challenge Reece in the Republican primary. Waters expressed his concern of what he viewed as the deterioration of the Republican Party and Reece's bossism of the First District. Waters conducted an elaborate campaign. He paraded through towns with three elephants to advertise his dedication to the Republican Party and his platform of higher teacher salaries, road improvement, and attracting tourists to the area. He charged Reece with being an absentee congressman who spent more time at his home in Florida, his hotel in West Virginia, and traveling in Europe than in his district. Waters ran an advertisement in the *Knoxville Journal* the day before the primary that recalled Reece's 1920 campaign slogan: "Ten Years in Congress is a long time. It is long enough for a good Congressman and too long for a poor one." He reminded voters that Reece had served for almost forty years and asserted that Reece had lost touch with the people. He asked for support from the thousands of people he met during his campaign in the district.[9]

Reece placed little emphasis on Waters' challenge and informed his constituents that the Middle East crisis in Lebanon prevented him from returning home to campaign in his district. Egypt and Syria united in March 1958 under the United Arab Republic (UAR) and resented Lebanon maintaining ties with western nations that refused to support Egypt during the 1956 Suez Canal crisis. Muslims in Lebanon wanted the nation to join the UAR, threatening civil war with Christians that wanted to maintain pro-western ties. Reece described the situation as very serious and potentially dangerous to the free world. Although he believed military action justified, he doubted all-out war would result. A local newspaper ran an article that supported Reece and justified his absence from the district. The article asserted that for Reece, Tennessee came first. It related that after his rise from "Tennessee hill boy" to chairman of the Republican National Committee, he made the decision to "hold back a bit" and represent the people of his district rather than rise higher in the GOP. The article declared that Reece had successfully combined national party interests with "day-to-day details" of his constituents, revealing the key to holding long tenure in office in the First District. Residents wanted their politicians to remain faithful to their hometowns as Reece did by attending numerous local festivals and proposing legislation to directly benefit his district. Reece defeated Waters in the primary by more than a two-to-one majority.[10]

Although Reece won the 1958 primary without an official campaign, the November election forced him to modify his strategy. He had been able to write only a few letters asking for support to win over Waters, but the Democratic candidate, Mayne Miller, used Reece's legislative record as political ammunition. In October Reece announced that he would return to the district in the coming weeks to campaign. Miller attacked Reece for his 1954 investigation, his isolationism, and his opposition to Eisenhower. Miller pointed out that Reece had failed to sponsor any important national legislation and only concerned himself with legislation for his district. He considered Reece to have a complacent attitude on national defense and claimed Reece had called the TVA "un-American." Miller attacked Reece's personal character by calling him selfish and cynical and insinuated that he used his influence to transfer federal funds to his own banks and get a post office named after him.[11]

Reece recognized Miller's candidacy as the first serious attack in years and understood the need to return to his district to defend his record. Reece's supporters ran an article that claimed Reece was responsible for TVA electricity being distributed by locally-owned organizations. It asserted that Norris had intended for the federal government to distribute power, which they believed challenged his legacy as the father of the TVA. Reece wanted the power to be available to municipalities for local boards to distribute and thus deserved credit for the existing format of the TVA. It alleged that Norris agreed with this sentiment. The fact that the city of Norris and Norris Dam were named after the senator disputes this assertion. In an attempt to combat negative publicity, Reece and Representative Howard Baker from the Second District proposed a bill that would allow for self-financing of the TVA, but it failed to make it to the House floor. Days before the November election, Reece called their plan a sound business venture and believed it would have passed. He

Figure 10.1. B. Carroll Reece. This photograph served as Reece's political photograph later in his career. Courtesy of the B. Carroll Reece Papers at the Archives of Appalachia, East Tennessee State University.

promised to reintroduce his proposal at the next congressional session if elected. Reece remained confident that he would defeat Miller, and he won the election with more than a 12,000 vote majority.[12]

Reece began his seventeenth term in Congress with a continued focus on the dangers of communism but expanded his concern to its international implications. He credited hostility and violence in Latin American nations during Nixon's 1958 good will tour to a "communist menace" present in those countries and stated that the United States had been a good neighbor, even if it had made a few regrettable mistakes. He specifically pointed to Cuba and the Fidel Castro regime as a menace to the world. Reece threatened that the United States could remove the

United States sugar quota, cut off aid to the nation, and impound Cuban funds as incentives for Cuba to return to a democracy so that the "cancer" of communism would not spread to other nations. Reece warned fellow Congressmen to be careful during heated debates so that they avoided words or actions that "Iron Curtain countries" could use to embarrass representatives to the United Nations.[13]

The fight against communism, according to Reece, began with every individual and their own actions. In a 1959 article Reece wrote for *The American Mercury*—an extreme right-wing publication that described itself as "a militant, 100 percent American magazine"—he reviewed the recent seizure of power by Communists in Czechoslovakia and warned that American citizens needed to do more than just oppose communism if they wanted to help save America from the same fate. Reece detailed a list of activities that Americans could follow in order to actively fight communism that included: read more to understand the subject; take an active interest in local and national affairs; refuse to agree with communist opinions; supply evidence to lead others to identify Communists; attend and support church; examine schools; and advocate the principles of Americanism, including free speech, religious freedom, and free enterprise. Reece insisted these steps would help Americans fight the "private war on communism." For many politicians, the unsuccessful public attacks against communism left little alternative than encouraging Americans that individuals alone remained the only way to stop its spread.[14]

Reece argued that the lack of public responsibility explained much of what had gone wrong in America. At the May 1959 commencement ceremony at Virginia Intermont College in Bristol, Reece spoke on the problems of American citizens. He felt comfortable speaking on this controversial subject because he declared he had built up immunity to criticism during his lifetime. Bad government, asserted Reece, came from the bad judgment of people. He laid the blame for inflation on the desire of people who wanted the government to do things that could be accomplished only with inflationary spending, and he attributed unemployment to a low customer base of companies, which prevented them from hiring more employees. Reece condemned what he viewed as a lack of patriotism when compared to prior generations and criticized the "beat generation" for complaining about hard work and the responsibilities of freedom. He equated communism with "mama-ism"—an emotional dependency on another with security through obedience—and asserted that Christianity could combat communism because it advocated self-reliance.

Good government, insisted Reece, depended on the good character of its citizens.[15]

Reece maintained that America had become better equipped to withstand the increased threat of communism. While serving on the Armed Services Committee, he stated that although the Soviets had made "some disturbing progress," the United States had a strong defense and great retaliation powers, which would deter large-scale war. He hoped that foundations, which had amassed millions though tax-exempt exceptions, would aid in the study of pure science rather than social science. Reece believed that communist governments lagged behind America in military equipment and in economic security and that this ensured America's defensive position.[16]

A Man of Great Courage and Dignity

As the immediate threat of communism subsided, Americans focused on other issues they perceived to have a significant bearing on their lives. The importance of education to his home district forced Reece's hand on a bill brought before the Rules Committee. The Thompson Education Bill came before the House in May 1960 with provisions to appropriate $975 million for school construction. Reece opposed the bill because it excluded Catholic schools, but he pledged to Tennessee educators that he would not be the person to obstruct its passage in the Rules Committee. The twelve members of the committee split over the decision, and Reece broke the deadlock by joining the six Democrats voting for the bill to reach the House floor. He noted that his vote did not signal support of the bill, but he felt that the committee should not stand in the way of the full House voting on it. The next month, the House and Senate presented very different bills, forcing a joint conference to work out a compromise. Reece and Representative William M. Colmer, a Democrat from Michigan, switched their earlier vote in favor of the bill to vote against a Senate-House conference, effectively blocking the bill from going to the House. Reece successfully kept his promise to his district while preventing the Thompson Bill from passing.[17]

This relaxation in the perceived threat of communism brought to light the one area where Reece advocated international involvement. After World War II a number of German citizens found themselves displaced from their home after the post-war agreements redrew boundaries. Reece's interest in the plight of East Germans intensified after Prince Louis Ferdinand, grandson of Kaiser Wilhelm II, visited Johnson City, Tennessee, in 1956 and discussed the matter with Reece. Reece considered the expulsion of Germans from Poland "one of the great wrongs committed in the wake of the Second World War" and even took his friend, John McCloy, to task for suggesting that claims to reunify Germany might have to be renounced. Reece believed the only avenue for genuine peace involved American intervention. He introduced a series of speeches into the Congressional Record that his wife later published as *Peace Through Law: A Basis for an East-West Settlement in Europe.* These speeches, dated from 1956-1960, described what he considered the economic, historical, legal, and political aspects of the division of Germany and displacement of its citizens. Much of Reece's evidence stemmed from the writings of Jedrzej Giertych, a war veteran and journalist who lived in London and worked in a bookshop. Giertych later accused Reece of taking his writings out of context regarding lands given to Poland and wanting to partition Poland to make Germany more powerful. He insisted that although Reece possessed knowledge of some of the problems, he failed to firmly grasp European politics, which allowed Germans who wanted to destroy Poland with the help of Russia to influence him.[18]

During his penultimate term in office Reece finally received recognition for work on the TVA. In May 1960 President Eisenhower signed the TVA self-financing bill passed by Congress the prior year. The measure allowed the TVA to issue bonds to pay for new projects, but it established limits on its territorial expansion and required TVA to begin repayment of money that the United States government had invested in it over the last twenty-five years. Eisenhower credited both Reece and Baker with their "behind-the scenes" work on behalf of the bill for easing his doubt about it. He had worried that the measure allowed the TVA to by-pass him and the Budget Bureau in submitting programs to Congress. After years of struggling to prove that he supported the TVA project, Reece finally had a tangible law as evidence of his endorsement.[19]

That same month, Reece announced his candidacy for the fall election and what would be his last term in Congress. He again issued a statement that expressed his devotion to the district and the benefit of his service in Congress. As in the previous campaigns, Reece insisted that the nation's business prevented him from leaving Washington to return home for an extended campaign. This bothered his constituents little, as the town of Roan Mountain declared June 25th "Carroll Reece Day" that year as part of their annual Rhododendron Festival. Any potential challengers most likely realized the strength Reece held in a district where he could win Republican primaries without even campaigning. No candidate came forth in the 1960 primary to oppose Reece, who considered this friendship and confidence in his ability "the highest compensation a man in public life" could receive.[20]

Tension between the United States and Soviet Union enveloped the 1960 presidential and local campaigns. The tense peace established by visits between the nations shattered when Soviets shot down an American spy plane over Russian territory in May 1960. The U-2 incident heightened distrust between the two nations. Reece justified the flight with the argument that had the United States had a similar flight over Japan before Pearl Harbor, the outcome would have been drastically different. Reece argued that Richard Nixon, the Republican candidate for president, was better equipped to deal with the threat of Russia than John F. Kennedy, the Democratic candidate. He believed few could imagine "young Jack Kennedy" in vital negotiations with Khrushchev, especially after Kennedy remarked after the collapse of the Summit Conference that Eisenhower should have apologized or expressed some regret for the U-2 incident. He felt peace could be achieved through economic and military strength and a firm policy towards Russia.[21]

Reece placed all his efforts into campaigning for Nixon in Tennessee. He predicted a Republican president and Congress would be elected because he believed Eisenhower had strengthened America's military prowess and thus "insured the peace of the world." Reece pointed out that Lyndon B. Johnson, Kennedy's running mate, had voted against Kennedy in the Senate 238 times since 1953. In an attempt to divide Democrats, he argued that if Kennedy were elected he would overrule Johnson when their opinions differed, leaving Johnson without a voice. Since Eisenhower officially recognized Reece's work on the TVA, he utilized a tactic that had been successful against him and accused Kennedy of voting against the TVA and then changing his opinion. Reece asserted that Kennedy thought it took industry away from the New England area. He introduced Nixon at a rally in Memphis, where he declared that Nixon would carry the state. His predictions proved correct, and Nixon won over Kennedy in Tennessee by a large margin, marking the third successive presidential election that Tennessee voted Republican. His win suggested that Tennessee was becoming a two-party state, but others credited the win to the large number of Protestants in the state who refused to vote for a Catholic. Nixon failed to achieve the same success across the nation, and Kennedy became America's first Catholic president. The first district unsurprisingly returned Reece to the House.[22]

Illness prevented Reece from becoming involved in the new session of Congress early in 1961. Reece's wife saved a newspaper article that claimed British researchers had related exposure to gas attacks in World

War I to lung cancer, tuberculosis, and bronchitis. A study conducted in the United States concluded that the study could not be proven, although World War I veterans did have higher incidents of lung cancer. Mrs. Reece most likely kept this article because Reece experienced increased lung problems in January 1961, when he entered the hospital for treatment. Reece tried to maintain an appearance of health, leaving the hospital on January 31st to vote against a measure before Congress that proposed adding more people to the House Rules Committee. He left a back row seat after casting his vote to return to the hospital. In early February 1961 Reece's wife reported that he had undergone surgery for a lung condition after having been hospitalized for pleurisy. Press releases stated that the surgery had been for physicians to examine his lungs and determine the exact cause of his illness.[23]

Reece's condition seemed to improve, and his family kept optimistic regarding his recovery. He left the hospital in late February and returned to his temporary home in Washington at the Mayflower Hotel. Reece received continued treatment but wrote a letter to the publisher of the Johnson City *Press-Chronicle* that stated the doctors were confident of curing his illness within a short time. On March 9th, however, Reece returned to Bethesda Naval Hospital, where x-rays revealed malignancies in his lung. He underwent radiation and cobalt treatments, but he continued to lose strength as his condition worsened with each passing day. Reports to the media omitted details of his treatment and maintained hope that Reece would improve. Because of this, Reece's death from cancer on March 19, 1961, seemed sudden to many who were unaware of the seriousness of his illness.[24]

The following day, papers all over the nation reported the news of Reece's death and paid tribute to his distinguished career. Editorials commended his service to the nation and to his district and tried to pinpoint the reason for his success. One article attributed it to his "astute opportunism, a sixth sense of sorts . . . his boundless energy and tireless pursuit of a goal . . . his ability to organize and direct men . . . his wealth" and "his resolute and full use of power available to him." The *Knoxville News-Sentinel* called Reece "a man of great courage and dignity" both in war and in his adherence to his principles. Another local paper described him as "Tennessee's 'Mr. Republican,'" a reference to the popular nickname given to his longtime friend, Robert Taft. Even those opposed to Reece and his political maneuvers related their respect for him as a citizen. George McCanless, Tennessee's Attorney General, gave a somewhat humorous but accurate portrayal of Reece when he declared that "a sixth grade student could make a better speech than Carroll. But Carroll could get things done." Senator Kefauver announced Reece's death in the Senate by describing Reece as "a man who always kept his word, and a man of exemplary character." Other Congressmen described Reece as a "man of conviction," "an honest conservative," and a "sturdy oak."[25]

Shortly after his death, residents of East Tennessee formed the B. Carroll Reece Memorial Committee to pay tribute to the legislator. The twelve-member committee solicited donations to build a section of a library to house Reece's memorabilia on the campus of East Tennessee State University (ETSU) in Johnson City, Tennessee. Although the committee considered Reece the leader of the Republican Party in the South and one of "its top leaders in the nation," the committee found it very difficult to raise the desired $150,000. Some believed Reece failed to make enough of a broad national impact to deserve a foundation, though they admired him personally. Others, however, called Reece a "life-long friend" and "undoubtedly one of the outstanding Americans in Congress." Robert Taft, Jr., wrote to Louise Reece that "Carroll was always one of my idols, and in serving in the House, I have come to admire his dedication even more." Though the committee was unable to raise enough to build a new space, it raised enough to renovate an existing area into a museum. On October 10, 1965, ETSU dedicated the Carroll Reece Museum, which housed Reece's private papers, public documents, and his collection of elephants.[26]

The death of B. Carroll Reece ended the reign of an Old Guard conservative, but Republicans continued to dominate East Tennessee politics. Less than a week after the funeral, papers printed editorials calling for Mrs. Reece to run in the special election to fill her husband's vacant seat. Louise won by a two-to-one margin in a race reminiscent of those run by her late husband and carried all counties in the district. The newspaper headlines once again, and for the last time, proclaimed a Reece victory. Louise finished her husband's term and announced in 1962 that she would resign from office at the end of her term. She endorsed James H. Quillen, a good friend of the family and Tennessee state representative, as her replacement. Quillen easily won election to Congress and served in the House for thirty consecutive years. He credited Reece with his success, recalling that as a young man Reece told him that if he ever ran for public office to remember that if it was important enough for a constituent to write or visit about a matter, then it was important enough to do something to help.[27]

EPILOGUE

B. Carroll Reece's life contained seemingly unexplainable contradictions. He came from one of the poorest and most obscure areas in Tennessee, but he became the national leader of the Republican Party and won election to eighteen terms in Congress. He placed emphasis on the importance of family but opposed his father-in-law during his bid to win the nomination for president. Reece lost his seat in the House because of his support for private ownership over government operation of Muscle Shoals, yet he attacked foundations funded by large businesses—including Ford, who earned Reece's support for operation of Muscle Shoals—for what he considered grants to subversive organizations. He identified himself as a southerner, but he often voted against other southern congressmen in favor of civil rights for blacks.

Reece's devotion became a defining characteristic of his personality and his political career. His sense of loyalty defined the actions he took, even when he faced mounting criticism and hostility. The Reece family supported the Republican Party, and he continued this tradition when he decided to run for political office. His commitment to his district and their individual needs allowed him to maintain his seat in Congress for most of his adult life. His background in economics and finance shaped his ideas regarding America's capitalist system, and he centered his career on protecting that system against external and internal threats. He rarely deviated from the Republican Party platform, and when Robert A. Taft decided to run for national office Reece found a leader to whom he could devote his support. Regardless of his somewhat liberal views regarding civil rights, Reece still held an overall conservative political philosophy that opposed big government interference in everyday life. His actions in the Muscle Shoals controversy, as chairman of the Republican National Committee, and during the Reece Committee investigation evidence his dogged determination to protect capitalism against the threat of socialism and communism. Reece united what he defined as liberalism with anti-communism and the Republican Party. The gains Republicans made in 1946 under Reece's guidance allowed men like Joseph McCarthy to become powerful. The predecessor of HUAC had long been investigating subversion, but it was not until after the 1946 elections that it, along with the SISS, became widely known, publicized, and feared. Reece's fierce devotion to the Republican Party, to Taft, and to the fight against the spread of communism merged at a time when America's fears began to overcome its confidence.

The continued animosity toward large foundations has often prevented American society from wholly accepting the philanthropic deeds of such organizations. Jealousy, greed, and political motivations often thwart the well-intentioned foundations from providing aid in areas such as education, immigration, and international politics. The Reece Committee, whether deliberate or not, played a large role in the persistent suspicion against large foundations. Following so closely on the heels of the Cox Committee, the Reece Committee ensured a long-lasting animosity toward large sums of money "hoarded" by eastern foundations.

B. Carroll Reece's career suffers from one of the worst fates to befall a politician. His legacy resides in that political never-land of failing to achieve lasting national recognition but maintaining enough for those in his home district to recognize his name many years later, if not the man himself. Reece provides an alternate view on the different avenues utilized to gain political prominence and attack the perceived threat of communism. Because of his inability to become a national political figure and his perceived bias, his warnings about the economic destruction sought by socialists and communists went unheeded. While some may classify him among southern demagogues, Reece truly felt he had an obligation to protect his district and the nation from what he believed to be one of the most menacing threats in history. In a time of economic growth and technological advancements, however, his fears seemed antiquated and improbable. Few believed communists could infiltrate the government or foundations to the point that it threatened American security. Reece held firm to his convictions even when his intentions seemed misguided. He considered himself immune to criticism, a trait which he believed all politicians developed after a time. Reece remained, as he once described himself, Republican, first, last, and always.

BIBLIOGRAPHY

Primary Sources

Articles

Reece, B. Carroll. "The High Cost of Illiteracy." *School Life* 34 (May 1952): 115-116, 123.
—. "Tax Exempt Subversion." *American Mercury* 85 (July 1957): 56-64.
—. "Your Private War on Communism." *American Mercury* 88 (March 1959): 65-69.

Audio / Visual

Granik, Theodore, prod. *The American Form: Should Foundations Remain Tax-Exempt?* 29 min. NBC Television Network, 8 August 1954. Videocassette.

Books

Adams, John G. *Without Precedent: The Story of the Death of McCarthyism.* New York: W.W. Norton & Company, 1983.
Dies, Martin. *Martin Dies' Story.* New York: Bookmailer, 1963.
Giertych, Jedrzej. *Poland and Germany: A Reply to Congressman B. Carroll Reece of Tennessee.* London: Jedrzej Giertych, 1958.
Hartley, Jr., Fred A. *Our New National Labor Policy: The Taft-Hartley Act and the Next Steps.* New York: Funk & Wagnalls Company, 1948.
Reece, B. Carroll. *The Courageous Commoner: A Biography of Andrew Johnson.* Charleston: Education Foundation, Inc., 1962.
—. *Peace through Law: A Basis for an East-West Settlement in Europe.* Louise Goff Reece, Ed. New Canaan: Long House, 1965.

Government Publications

Congressional Elections 1946-1996. Washington: Congressional Quarterly Inc. 1998.

United States Congress House of Representatives. *The Communist Party's Cold War Against Congressional Investigation of Subversion: Report and Testimony of Robert Carrillo Ronstadt.* Washington, D.C.: Committee on Un-American Activities, U.S. House of Representatives, 1962.

—. *Muscle Shoals Report No. 2564.* Washington, D.C.: Committee on Military Affairs, U.S. Government Print Office, 1929.

—. *Muscle Shoals Report No. 1430.* Washington, D.C.: Committee on Military Affairs, U.S. Government Print Office, 1930

—. *This is Your House Committee on Un-American Activities.* Washington, D.C.: Committee on Un-American Activities, U.S. House of Representatives, 1954.

United States Congress. *Memorial Services Held in the Senate and House of Representatives of the United States, Together with Remarks Presented in Eulogy of Carey Estes Kefauver.* 88th Congress, 1st Session. U.S. Government Printing Office: Washington, 1964.

Manuscripts

B. Carroll Reece Papers, 1889-1961. Archives of Appalachia, East Tennessee State University, Johnson City, Tennessee.

The B. Carroll Reece Papers, 1921-1944. The University of Tennessee Special Collections Library, Knoxville, Tennessee.

The Burgin E. Dossett Collection, Papers, 1949 1960. Archives of Appalachia, East Tennessee State University, Johnson City, Tennessee.

Butler (Tenn.) Papers. Archives of Appalachia, East Tennessee State University, Johnson City, Tennessee.

Charles Andrew Jonas Papers. Southern Historical Collection, University of North Carolina at Chapel Hill, Chapel Hill, North Carolina.

Divine Family Papers, 1871-1989. The University of Tennessee Special Collections Library, Knoxville, Tennessee.

Estes Kefauver Collection. The University of Tennessee Special Collections Library, Knoxville, Tennessee.

J. Robert Oppenheimer Papers. Manuscript Division, Library of Congress, Washington, D.C.

James H. Quillen Papers, 1918-1999. Archives of Appalachia, East Tennessee State University, Johnson City, Tennessee.

Lawrence J. Spivak Papers. Manuscript Division, Library of Congress, Washington, D.C.

Lemuel Lafayette Maples Reece Papers, 1919-1969. Archives of Appalachia, East Tennessee State University, Johnson City, Tennessee.

Papers of Frederick William McWane, 1912-1961. Special Collections Library, University of Virginia, Charlottesville, Virginia.

The Papers of George V. H. Moseley. Manuscript Division, Library of Congress, Washington, D.C.

Robert Taft, Jr. Papers. Manuscript Division, Library of Congress, Washington, D.C.

Southern Regional Council Papers, Series I. Microfilm.

Wilbur and Orville Wright Papers. Manuscript Division, Library of Congress, Washington, D.C.

Wunderlin, Clarence E., ed. *The Papers of Robert A. Taft, Volume I, 1889-1939*. Kent: The Kent State University Press, 1997.

—. *The Papers of Robert A. Taft, Volume 3, 1945-1948*. Kent: The Kent State University Press, 2003.

—. *The Papers of Robert A. Taft, Volume 4, 1949-1953*. Kent: The Kent State University Press, 2006.

Newspapers

Knoxville Journal, 1956-1958.

Nashville Banner, 1933-1935.

The New York Times, 1925-1961, 1976.

The Reece Scrapbooks contain countless articles from newspapers all over the world. When identified in the scrapbooks, these are noted in the footnotes.

Secondary Sources

Articles

"Are Today's Public Schools Failing to Serve the Best Interests of the Nation?" *The Congressional Digest* 37 (August 1958): 204-210.

Blanshard, Paul. "Malice in Blunderland, Report on the Foundations." *The Nation* 180 (15 January 1955): 51-53.

Bowen, Michael. "Communism vs. Republicanism: B. Carroll Reece and the Congressional Elections of 1946." *The Journal of East Tennessee History* 73 (2001): 39-52.

"Champions of Democracy." *Time*, 13 September 1937.

"Dangers to Labor in the Conscription of Industry Amendment to the Conscription Bill." *The Congressional Digest* 19 (November 1940): 287-8.

Dauer, Manning J. "Recent Southern Political Thought." *The Journal of Politics* 10 (May 1948): 327-353.

DeSantis, Vincent P. "Eisenhower Revisionism." *The Review of Politics* 38 (April 1976): 190-207.

—. "The Presidential Election of 1952." *The Review of Politics* 15 (April 1953): 131-150.

DeVoto, Bernard. "Guilt by Distinction." *Harper's Magazine* 210 (April 1955): 14-15, 18-21.

Dishman, Robert B. "How It All Began: The Eisenhower Pre-Convention Campaign in New Hampshire, 1952." *The New England Quarterly* 26 (March 1953): 3-26.

Dunbar, Leslie W. "The Southern Regional Council." *Annals of the American Academy of Political and Social Science* 357 (January 1965): 108-112.

"Fighting Bob." *Time* 59 (2 June 1952): 17-20.

"GOP: Safe Haven." *Newsweek* 27 (8 April 1946): 25.

"House Foreign Aid Debate." *The Congressional Digest* 30 (November 1951): 286.

"Is This How we Fight Subversion?" *American Mercury* 83 (July 1956): 149-150.

"Investigating the Foundations." *Business Week* 1294 (19 June 1954): 180.

Lee, R. Alton. "The Truman – 80th Congress Struggle Over Tax Policy." *Historian* 33 (November 1970): 68-82.

"The Lesson." *Time* 63 (21 June 1954): 55-56.

"The Man Who Talks Back." *The New Republic* 130 (28 June 1954): 12-13.

Miller, Helen Hill. "Investigating the Foundations." *The Reporter* 9 (24 November 1953): 37-40.

"New Chairman." *Time* 47 (8 April 1946): 23.

"Politics and the Power Issue." *The Nation* 131 (17 December 1930): 666.

'The Price Gamble," *Time* 48 (8 July 1946): 19-20.

"Propose New Probe of Foundations." *The Christian Century* 70 (12 August 1953): 908-909.

"Reading the Record on Reece." *The New Republic* 114 (15 April 1946): 493.

"Reece Election Triumph for Conservatives." *Business Week* 866 (6 April 1946): 7.

Rosenbloom, David H. "'Whose Bureaucracy Is This, Anyway?' Congress' 1946 Answer," *PS: Political Science and Politics* 34 (December 2001): 773-777.

"Should Uncle Sam Operate Muscle Shoals?" *The Congressional Digest* 9 (May 1930): 129-50.

"The Show's the Thing." *Newsweek* 31 (21 June 1948): 21-23.

"They Work Together." *The New Republic* 130 (24 May 1954): 4-5.

"Those Men in That Anti-Trust Quiz." *Business Week* 461 (2 July 1938): 15-17.

"Those Other Hearings." *The Reporter* 10 (8 June 1954): 2-3.

"Thought Control." *Time* 65 (3 January 1955): 15-16.

"The Un-Tory Activities Probe." *The New Republic* 129 (10 August 1953): 3.

Books

American Battle Monuments Commission. *26th Division Summary of Operations in the World War*. Washington: United States Government Printing Office, 1944.

Avrich, Paul. *Sacco and Vanzetti: The Anarchist Background*. Princeton: Princeton University Press, 1991.

Blum, John Morton. *V Was For Victory: Politics and American Culture during World War II*. San Diego: Harcourt Brace & Company, 1976.

Braim, Paul F. *The Test of Battle: The American Expeditionary Forces in the Meuse-Argonne Campaign*. Newark: University of Delaware Press, 1987.

Carr, Robert K. *The House Committee on Un-American Activities, 1945-1950*. Ithaca: Cornell University Press, 1952.

Cherny, Robert W., et al., eds. *American Labor and the Cold War: Grassroots Politics and Postwar Political Culture*. New Brunswick: Rutgers University Press, 2004.

Coben, Stanley. *A. Mitchell Palmer: Politician*. New York: Columbia University Press, 1963.

Coffman, Edward M. *The War to End All Wars: The American Military Experience in World War I*. New York: Oxford University Press, 1968.

Culver, John C. and John Hyde. *American Dreamer: The Life and Times of Henry A. Wallace*. New York: W.W. Norton & Company, 2000.

Davies, Norman. *Europe: A History*. Oxford: Oxford University Press, 1996.

Dickson, Paul and Thomas B. Allen. *The Bonus Army: An American Epic*. New York: Walker & Company, 2004.

Doherty, Thomas. *Cold War, Cool Medium: Television, McCarthyism, and American Culture*. New York: Columbia University Press, 2003.

Donovan, Robert J. *Conflict and Crisis: The Presidency of Harry S. Truman, 1945-1948.* New York: W.W. Norton & Company, 1977.

Edwards, Jerome E. *Pat McCarran: Political Boss of Nevada.* Reno: University of Nevada Press, 1982.

Elving, Ronald D., Ed. *Congress and the Great Issues 1945-1995.* Washington: Congressional Quarterly, Inc., 1996.

Fontenay, Charles L. *Estes Kefauver: A Biography.* Knoxville: The University of Tennessee Press, 1980.

Fraser, Steve and Gary Gerstle, eds. *The Rise and Fall of the New Deal Order: 1930-1980.* Princeton: Princeton University Press, 1989.

Goodman, Walter. *The Committee: The Extraordinary Career of the House Committee on Un-American Activities.* New York: Farrar, Straus, and Giroux. 1968.

Griffith, Robert. *The Politics of Fear: Joseph R. McCarthy and the Senate.* Lexington: The University of Kentucky Press, 1970.

Griffith, Robert and Athan Theoharis, eds. *The Specter: Original Essays on the Cold War and the Origins of McCarthyism.* New York: New Viewpoints (Franklin Watts, Inc.), 1974.

Harnsberger, Caroline Thomas. *A Man of Courage: Robert A. Taft.* Chicago: Wilcox and Follett Company, 1952.

Havard, William C. *The Changing Politics of the South.* Baton Rouge: Louisiana State University Press, 1972.

Heinrichs, Waldo. *Threshold of War: Franklin D. Roosevelt and American Entry into World War II.* New York: Oxford University Press, 1998.

Hoffmann, Stanley and Charles Maier, eds. *The Marshall Plan: A Retrospective.* Boulder: Westview Press, 1984.

Hubbard, Preston J. *Origins of the TVA: The Muscle Shoals Controversy, 1920-1932.* New York: The Norton Library, 1961.

Huston, James A. *Outposts and Allies: U.S. Army Logistics in the Cold War, 1945-1953.* Cranbury: Associated University Presses, 1988.

Johnson, Haynes. *The Age of Anxiety: McCarthyism to Terrorism.* Orlando: Harcourt, Inc., 2005.

Kelly, Frank K. *Court of Reason: Robert Hutchins and the Fund for the Republic.* New York: The Free Press, 1981.

Kennedy, John F. *Profiles in Courage.* New York: Harper Perennial, 1956, 1964.

Key, Jr. V.O. *Southern Politics in State and Nation.* Knoxville: The University of Tennessee Press, 1949, 1984.

Kingseed, Cole C. *Eisenhower and the Suez Crisis of 1956.* Baton Rouge: Louisiana State University Press, 1956.

Lacey, Jim. *Pershing.* New York: Palgrave MacMillan, 2008.

Leffler, Melvyn P. *The Specter of Communism: The United States and the Origins of the Cold War, 1917-1953*. Eric Foner, consulting editor. New York: Hill and Wang, 1994.

Lengel, Edward G. *To Conquer Hell: The Meuse-Argonne, 1918*. New York: Henry Holt and Company, 2008.

Leuchtenburg, William E. *Franklin D. Roosevelt and the New Deal, 1932-1940*. New York: Harper & Row, 1963

Macdonald, Dwight. *The Ford Foundation: The Men and the Millions*. New York: Reynal & Company, 1956.

Majors, William R. *The End of Arcadia: Gordon Browning and Tennessee Politics*. Memphis: Memphis State University Press, 1982.

McCraw, Thomas K. *TVA and the Power Fight, 1933-1939*. Philadelphia: J.B. Lippincott Company, 1971.

McDonald, Forrest. *Insull*. Chicago: The University of Chicago Press, 1962.

McKinney, Gordon B. *Southern Mountain Republicans, 1865-1900: Politics and the Appalachian Community*. Chapel Hill: The University of North Carolina Press, 1978.

Michie, Allan A. and Frank Ryhlick. *Dixie Demagogues*. New York: The Vanguard Press, 1939.

Millett, Allan R. and Peter Maslowski. *For the Common Defense: A Military History of the United States of America*. New York: The Free Press, 1994.

Nielsen, Waldemar A. *The Big Foundations*. New York: Columbia University Press, 1972.

Ogden, August Raymond. *The Dies Committee: A Study of the Special House Committee for the Investigation of Un-American Activities, 1938-1944*. Washington: The Catholic University of America Press, 1945.

O'Reilly, Kenneth. *Hoover and the Un-Americans: The FBI, HUAC, and the Red Menace*. Philadelphia: Temple University Press, 1983.

Oshinsky, David M. *A Conspiracy So Immense: The World of Joe McCarthy*. New York: The Free Press (Macmillian, Inc.), 1983.

Pach, Jr., Chester J. and Elmo Richardson. *The Presidency of Dwight D. Eisenhower*. Lawrence: University Press of Kansas, 1991.

Patterson, James T. *Mr. Republican: A Biography of Robert A. Taft*. Boston: Houghton Mifflin Company, 1972.

Pipes, Richard. *A Concise History of the Russian Revolution*. New York: Alfred A. Knopf, 1995.

Plaut, Thomas. *People, Politics, and Economic Life: Exploring Appalachia with Quantitative Methods, with an Overview of the Appalachian*

Region by Susan Emley Keefe. Dubuque: Kendall / Hunt Publishing Company, 1999, 1996.

Price, David H. *Threatening Anthropology: McCarthyism and the FBI's Surveillance of Activist Anthropologists*. Durham: Duke University Press, 2004.

Powers, Richard Gid. *Not Without Honor: The History of American Anticommunism*. New York: The Free Press, 1995.

Reeves, Thomas C. ed. *Foundations Under Fire*. Ithaca: Cornell University Press, 1970.

—. *Freedom and the Foundation: The Fund for the Republic in the Era of McCarthyism*. New York: Alfred A. Knopf, 1969.

—. *The Life and Times of Joe McCarthy: A Biography*. New York: Stein and Day, 1982.

Richter, Donald. *Chemical Soldiers: British Gas Warfare in World War I*. Lawrence: University Press of Kansas, 1992.

Riggs, Joseph Howard. *A Calendar of Political and Occasional Speeches by Senator Kenneth D. McKellar, 1928-1940, with Summaries and Subject Index*. Memphis: Memphis Public Library, 1962.

Schrecker, Ellen. *Many Are the Crimes: McCarthyism in America*. Boston: Little, Brown and Company, 1998.

—. *No Ivory Tower: McCarthyism and the Universities*. New York: Oxford University Press, 1986.

Smith, A. Robert. *The Tiger in the Senate: The Biography of Wayne Morse*. New York: Doubleday & Company, Inc. 1962.

Smith, G. Wayne. *Nathan Goff, Jr.: A Biography with Some Account of Guy Despard Goff and Brazilla Carroll Reece*. Charleston: Education Foundation, Inc., 1959.

Smith, John Chabot. *Alger Hiss: The True Story*. New York: Holt, Rinehart, and Winston, 1976.

Stoler, Mark A. *Allies and Adversaries: The Joint Chiefs of Staff, The Grand Alliance, and U.S. Strategy in World War II*. Chapel Hill: The University of North Carolina Press, 2000.

Theoharis, Athan. *Chasing Spies: How the FBI Failed in Counterintelligence But Promoted the Politics of McCarthyism in the Cold War Years*. Chicago: Ivan R. Dee, 2002.

—. *Seeds of Repression: Harry S. Truman and the Origins of McCarthyism*. Chicago: Quadrangle Books, 1971.

Thomas, John N. *The Institute of Pacific Relations: Asian Scholars and American Politics*. Seattle: University of Washington Press, 1974.

Vilensky, Joel A. *Dew of Death: The Story of Lewisite, America's World War I Weapon of Mass Destruction.* Bloomington: Indiana University Press, 2005.

Wilkins, Lee. *Wayne Morse: A Bio-Bibliography.* Westport: Greenwood Press. 1985.

Wormser, Rene A. *Foundations: Their Power and Influence.* New York: The Devin-Adair Company, 1958.

Ybarra, Michael J. *Washington Gone Crazy: Senator Pat McCarran and the Great American Communist Hunt.* Hanover: Steerforth Press, 2004.

Unpublished Material

Alexander, Helen Roth. "Congress and Muscle Shoals." Master's Thesis, The University of Tennessee, 1935.

Bowen, Michael D. "A Politician of Principle: Three Events in the Congressional Career of B. Carroll Reece." Master's Thesis. East Tennessee State University, 1999.

Hicks, John H. "The Congressional Career of B. Carroll Reece, 1920-1948." Master's Thesis, East Tennessee State University, 1968.

Norrell, Robert J. "Triangles of Change: The Southern Regional Council in the Civil Rights Movement." Undated. Unpublished paper.

NOTES

Introduction

[1] B. Carroll Reece letter to the editor dated 1952 in Scrapbook 34, Box 43, B. Carroll Reece Papers, 1889-1961, Archives of Appalachia, East Tennessee State University, Johnson City, Tennessee (Hereafter designated BCR Papers).

[2] Gordon B. McKinney, *Southern Mountain Republicans, 1865-1900: Politics and the Appalachian Community* (Chapel Hill: The University of North Carolina Press, 1978), 5-7.

[3] Two Articles in the Reece scrapbooks clearly stated that Reece stuttered, but taped interviews of Reece show no evidence of this. Reece took numerous speaking and debating classes in school, and this may explain his method of speaking slowly—in order to hide his stutter—and probably led to the conclusion that he was simply a poor speaker. "Reece Turns His Stutter to Good Use in Winning Confidence of Midwest Leaders," *Des Moines, Iowa, Morning Register* dated 16 June 1946 in Scrapbook 16, Box 34, BCR Papers.

[4] One limitation to the study of Reece's life is the absence of some of his personal papers. After his sudden death, his wife was forced to vacate his Congressional office within one week, resulting in the destruction of many of the documents before she had a chance to review them. Letter from Louise Goff Reece to ETSU dated 1961 in Dossett Papers, Archives of Appalachia, East Tennessee State University, Johnson City, Tennessee, Box 23:19. Louise Reece made over 60 scrapbooks with newspaper Articles, photographs, and other memorabilia from his career. The newspaper Articles originate from various parts of the United States, but many of them do not include the name of the paper or the specific date of the Article. These are part of the B. Carroll Reece Papers.

Chapter 1

[1] Newspaper Articles in Butler (Tenn.) Loose Folder, Archives of Appalachia, East Tennessee State University, Johnson City, Tennessee (Hereafter Butler Folder).

[2] Newspaper Article in B. Carroll Reece Loose Folder, Archives of Appalachia, East Tennessee State University, Johnson City, Tennessee (Hereafter BCR Folder); Press Release titled "Story of Carroll Reece" published 1948 in BCR Papers, Box 13:5; Newspaper Article in Scrapbook 34, BCR Papers, Box 43.

[3] Newspaper Articles in Butler Folder; Thomas Plaut, *People, Politics, and Economic Life: Explaining Appalachia with Quantitative Methods, with an overview of the Appalachian Region by Susan Emley Keefe* (Dubuque: Kendall / Hunt Publishing Company, 1999, 1996), 14-15.

[4] Special Edition of *The Elizabethton Star* on Butler dated 2 December 1983 in Butler Folder.

---

[5] Newspaper Articles in BCR Loose Folder, Archives of Appalachia, East Tennessee State University, Johnson City, Tennessee; Newspaper Article in Scrapbook 24, BCR Papers, Box 37.

[6] II Samuel 17:27, 19:32-39.

[7] Butler Folder; Newspaper Article in Scrapbook 1, BCR Papers, Box 24.

[8] Reece essays and speeches in BCR Papers, Box 1:7 and 1:8.

[9] Reece essays and speeches in BCR Papers, Box 1:7 and 1:8.

[10] Reece essays and speeches in BCR Papers, Box 1:7 and 1:8.

[11] Recommendations letters from Watauga Academy and Carson Newman College faculty in BCR Papers, Box 1:2.

[12] Although many of the sources credit Reece with having a Doctor of Laws degree, this was actually an honorary degree conferred upon him by Cumberland University in 1928. He also received honorary degrees from Lincoln Memorial University in 1946 (Doctor of Humanities) and from Tusculum College in 1955 (Doctor of Laws). Incidentally, Tusculum College misspelled Reece's name in a letter commending his military and Congressional record.

[13] Edward M. Coffman, *The War to End All Wars: The American Military Experience in World War I* (New York: Oxford University Press, 1968), 55-60.

[14] Paul F. Braim, *The Test of Battle: The American Expeditionary Forces in the Meuse-Argonne Campaign* (Newark: University of Delaware Press, 1987), chapter 7.

[15] Army Certificates in BCR Papers, Box 61:3.

[16] Army issued booklets and personal notebook of Reece in BCR Papers, Box 1:12.

[17] Allan R. Millet and Peter Maslowski. *For the Common Defense: A Military History of the United States of America* (New York: The Free Press, 1984, 1994), 372; Jim Lacey, *Pershing* (New York: Palgrave MacMillan, 2008), 151-156, 160-164.

[18] Newspaper Articles, army orders, and army memos in BCR Papers, Box 1:14 and BCR Loose Folder.

[19] Coffman, *The War to End All Wars,* 298; Newspaper Articles in BCR Papers, Box 1:14; Newspaper Articles in Scrapbook 1, BCR Papers, Box 24; Lacey, *Pershing*, 160-177; Edward G. Lengel, *To Conquer Hell: The Meuse-Argonne, 1918* (New York: Henry Hold and Company, 2008), 363.

[20] Newspaper Articles, army orders, and Distinguished Service Cross citation in BCR Papers, Box 1:14; Newspaper Articles in Scrapbook 1, BCR Papers, Box 24; Donald Richter, *Chemical Soldiers: British Gas Warfare in World War I* (Lawrence: University Press of Kansas, 1992), 8-10; Joel A. Vilensky, *Dew of Death: The Story of Lewisite, America's World War I Weapon of Mass Destruction* (Bloomington: Indiana University Press, 2005), 14-15; American Battle Monuments Commission, *26th Division Summary of Operations in the World War* (Washington: United States Government Printing Office, 1944), 55-57.

[21] Commendations in BCR Papers, Box 1:14; Certificate from The Yankee Division to Reece in BCR Papers, Box 61:4.

[22] 1938 Newspaper Article in Scrapbook 3, BCR Papers, Box 25.

[23] Copy of Excerpt of a letter from Sergeant Ramsay to his brother Jack, undated, in BCR Papers, Box 1:14.

[24] Newspaper advertisement in Scrapbook 1, BCR Papers, Box 24.

[25] Newspaper Article in Scrapbook 1, BCR Papers, Box 24.

[26] Newspaper Articles in Scrapbook 1, BCR Papers, Box 24.

[27] Coffman, *The War to End All Wars,* 358.

[28] Handwritten memo from Reece to Board on Claims and Lost Personal Property dated 30 April 1919 in BCR Papers, Box 1:14.

[29] Letter from E.E. Lewis directed "To Whom it May Concern" dated 4 May 1919 in BCR Papers, Box 1:14.

[30] Special Orders dated 23 June, 1919 in BCR Papers, Box 1:14; Memos from Reece to army officials dated 9 and 26 July, 1919 in BCR Papers, Box 1:14; Official Discharge in BCR Papers, Box 61:3; Officers Record Book of 2nd Lieutenant B. Carroll Reece in BCR Papers, Box 61:11

[31] Richard Pipes, *A Concise History of the Russian Revolution* (New York: Alfred A. Knopf, 1995), 307-308; Paul Avrich, *Sacco and Vanzetti: The Anarchist Background* (Princeton: Princeton University Press, 1991), 140-144, 165; Stanley Coben, *A. Mitchell Palmer: Politician* (New York: Columbia University Press, 1963), 196-200, 203-207.

[32] Avrich, *Sacco and* Vanzetti, 166-168, 211; Army certificates in BCR Papers, Box 61:3; Coben, *A. Mitchell Palmer*, 209-228.

[33] V.O. Key, Jr., *Southern Politics in State and Nation* (Knoxville: The University of Tennessee Press, 1949), 11; Allan A. Michie and Frank Ryhlick, *Dixie Demagogues* (New York: The Vanguard Press, 1939), 4.

[34] Key, Jr., *Southern Politics in State and Nation,* 78; William C. Havard, *The Changing Politics of the South* (Baton Rouge: Louisiana State University Press, 1972), 173.

[35] Reece Letter to Alvin York dated 30 March 1920, Reece Letter to Sells dated 13 March 1920, and Reece Letter to Lewis dated 15 April 1920 in BCR Papers, Box 1:14; Newspaper Articles in Scrapbook 1, BCR Papers, Box 24.

[36] Newspaper Articles in Scrapbook 1, BCR Papers, Box 24; Newspaper Article in Scrapbook 44, BCR Papers, Box 49; Letter to Reece from Charles J. Furlong dated 15 April 1920 in BCR Papers, Box 1:3.

[37] Newspaper Articles in Scrapbook 1, BCR Papers, Box 24.

[38] Reece speech dated 18 April 1920 in BCR Papers, Box 22:5; Newspaper Articles in Scrapbook 1, BCR Papers, Box 24.

[39] Reece political circular and pamphlet in Scrapbook 1, BCR Papers, Box 24.

[40] Campaign flyers and newspaper Articles in BCR Papers, Box 24.

[41] Newspaper Articles and advertisements in Scrapbook 1, BCR Papers, Box 24.

[42] Newspaper Articles in Scrapbook 2, BCR Papers, Box 25; "Reece-Goff Nuptials," *Washington Post*, 31 October 1923, p. 7.

[43] McKinney, *Southern Mountain Republicans,* 63-88.

[44] McKinney, *Southern Mountain Republicans, 112-122;* G. Wayne Smith, *Nathan Goff, Jr.: A Biography with Some Account of Guy Despard Goff and Brazilla Carroll Reece* (Charleston: Education Foundation, Inc., 1959), 207-8, 225, 277-8.

[45] Smith, *Nathan Goff, Jr.,* 304-309.

[46] Smith, *Nathan Goff, Jr.*, 312-319.

[47] Letters in bound book dated 23 February 1919 – 11 October 1920 in BCR Papers, Box 2:14.

Chapter 2

[1] Newspaper Articles and campaign flyer in Scrapbook 1, BCR Papers, Box 24.

[2] Newspaper Articles in Scrapbook 1, BCR Papers, Box 24.

[3] Newspaper Articles in Scrapbook 1, BCR Papers, Box 24; Newspaper Articles in Scrapbook 5, BCR Papers, Box 27.

[4] Newspaper Articles in Scrapbook 5, BCR Papers, Box 27.

[5] Newspaper Articles in Scrapbook 1, BCR Papers, Box 24; Paul Dickson and Thomas B. Allen, *The Bonus Army: An American Epic* (New York: Walker & Company, 2004), 28-29.

[6] Reece Letter to constituents dated 1930 in Scrapbook 5, BCR Papers, Box 27.

[7] Letters between Reece and Slagle dated 6 October 1924 – 22 June 1944 in The B. Carroll Reece Papers, The University of Tennessee Special Collections Library, Knoxville, Tennessee.

[8] Letters from Reece and Divine dated 7 March 1935 in Divine Family Papers, 1871-1989, The University of Tennessee Special Collections Library, Knoxville, Tennessee.

[9] Newspaper Articles in Scrapbook 1, BCR Papers, Box 24; Newspaper Articles in Scrapbook 2, BCR Papers, Box 25.

[10] Reece named his Johnson City home "Bois d'Ormont" as a tribute to the battle that won him military recognition. It also signified the importance of this event in his life.

[11] Newspaper Articles in Scrapbook 1, BCR Papers, Box 24

[12] Newspaper Articles in Scrapbook 1, BCR Papers, Box 24; Newspaper Articles in Scrapbook 2, BCR Papers, Box 25.

[13] Newspaper Articles in Scrapbook 1, BCR Papers, Box 24.

[14] Newspaper Articles in Scrapbook 2, BCR Papers, Box 25; "Scope's Place Given to Anti-Evolutionist," *New York Times*, 17 August 1925, p. 7; "Scope's Successor Quits," *New York Times*, 2 February 1926, p. 26.

[15] Reece political pamphlet and newspaper Articles in Scrapbook 1, BCR Papers, Box 24.

[16] "Bill to Name Citizen Soldiers to West Point Will Be Offered by War Veteran in Congress," *The New York Times,* 5 September 1927, p. 7; Newspaper Articles in Scrapbook 1, BCR Papers, Box 24; Newspaper Articles in Scrapbook 5, BCR Papers, Box 27.

[17] Newspaper Articles in Scrapbook 1, BCR Papers, Boxes 24; Newspaper Articles in Scrapbook 5, BCR Papers, Box 27.

[18] "Should Uncle Sam Operate Muscle Shoals?" *The Congressional Digest,* May 1930, 130-131, 133.

[19] Preston J. Hubbard, *Origins of the TVA: The Muscle Shoals Controversy, 1920-1932* (New York: The Norton Library, 1961), 1; Helen Roth Alexander, "Congress and Muscle Shoals" (Master's Thesis, The University of Tennessee, 1935), 16;

"Should Uncle Sam Operate Muscle Shoals?" *The Congressional Digest* (May 1930): 130-131, 133.

[20] Hubbard, *Origins of the TVA*, vii, 9; "Should Uncle Sam Operate Muscle Shoals?" 131.

[21] Thomas K. McCraw, *TVA and the Power Fight, 1933-1939* (Philadelphia: J.B. Lippincott Company, 1971), 19; Hubbard, *Origins of the TVA*, 29, 39; "Should Uncle Sam Operate Muscle Shoals?" 131.

[22] Hubbard, *Origins of the TVA*, 108; "Should Uncle Sam Operate Muscle Shoals?" 131.

[23] "Should Uncle Sam Operate Muscle Shoals?" 131; Hubbard, *Origins of the TVA*, 150-156.

[24] McCraw, *TVA and the Power Fight*, 17; Forrest McDonald, *Insull* (Chicago: The University of Chicago Press, 1962), 180.

[25] Alexander, "Congress and Muscle Shoals," 70; Hubbard, *Origins of the TVA*, 193, 200-201; McDonald, *Insull*, 180, 184-185, 266-267; Newspaper Articles in Scrapbook 1, BCR Papers, Box 24.

[26] Hubbard, *Origins of the TVA*, 217, 226; "Should Uncle Sam Operate Muscle Shoals?" 132-133.

[27] Michie, *Dixie Demagogues*, 243-244; Joseph Howard Riggs, *A Calendar of Political and Occasional speeches by Senator Kenneth D. McKellar, 1928-1940, with Summaries and Subject Index* (Memphis: Memphis Public Library, 1962), 15-16.

[28] Hubbard, *Origins of the TVA*, 217, 226; Congressional Record dated 24 May, 1928 in BCR Papers, Box 22:34.

[29] Smith, *Nathan Goff, Jr.*, 325-327; Newspaper Articles in Scrapbook 2, BCR Papers, Box 25.

[30] Newspaper Articles in Scrapbook 1, BCR Papers, Box 24; Newspaper Articles in Scrapbook 5, BCR Papers, Box 27.

[31] Hubbard, *Origins of the TVA*, 246-9; United States Congress House of Representatives, *Muscle Shoals Report No. 2564* (Washington, D.C.: Committee on Military Affairs, 1929), 1, 10, 14, 15, 21.

[32] Hubbard, *Origins of the TVA*, 272-3; United States Congress House of Representatives, *Muscle Shoals Report No. 1430* (Washington, D.C.: Committee on Military Affairs, 1930), 7, 9, 25.

[33] Hubbard, *Origins of the TVA*, 280; Newspaper Articles in Scrapbook 5, BCR Papers, Box 27; McCraw, *TVA and the Power Fight*, 22.

[34] Newspaper Articles in Scrapbook 1, BCR Papers, Box 24; Newspaper Articles in Scrapbook 5, BCR Papers, Box 27.

[35] Hubbard, *Origins of the TVA*, 281-282; William R. Majors, *The End of Arcadia: Gordon Browning and Tennessee Politics* (Memphis: Memphis State University Press, 1982), 6; McCraw, *TVA and the Power Fight*, 159; Newspaper Articles in Scrapbook 5, BCR Papers, Box 27; "East Tennessee Has Hot Election Ahead," *New York Times,* 20 July 1930, p. E6.

[36] "East Tennessee Has Hot Election Ahead," p. E6.

[37] Tilson letter to Reece dated 7 July 1930 and Newspaper Articles in Scrapbook 5, BCR Papers, Box 27; "Tennessee letter by Hoover Resented," *New York Times*, 27 July 1930, p. 2.

[38] Newspaper Articles in Scrapbook 5, BCR Papers, Box 27; "This Week in America: Economics Dominant," *New York Times*, 3 August 1930, p. 49.

[39] Newspaper Articles in Scrapbook 5, BCR Papers, Box 27.

[40] Newspaper Articles in Scrapbook 5, BCR Papers, Box 27.

[41] Newspaper Articles in Scrapbook 5, BCR Papers, Box 27; "This Week in America: We Had an Election," *New York Times*, 9 November 1930, p. E5; "Unlucky Endorsements," *New York Times*, 6 November 1930, p. 24; "Muscle Shoals: Symbol of the Nation's Power Issue," *New York Times*, 7 December 1930, p. 145.

[42] Newspaper Articles in Scrapbook 5, BCR Papers, Box 27.

[43] Newspaper Articles in Scrapbook 5, BCR Papers, Box 27.

[44] Newspaper Articles in Scrapbook 5, BCR Papers, Box 27; Hubbard, *Origins of the TVA*, 288.

[45] Remarks of Harry C. Ransley in *Congressional Record*, 71st Congress, 3rd Session dated 2 March 1931 in BCR Papers, Box 23:7; Newspaper Articles in Scrapbook 5, BCR Papers, Box 27.

[46] Newspaper Articles in Scrapbooks 2 and 3, BCR Papers, Box 25; Photograph in BCR Papers, Box 61:8; White House invitations to Mr. & Mrs. B. Carroll Reece in BCR Papers, Box 61:11; Reece letter to Orville Wright dated 29 May 1926 in Container 54, Wilbur and Orville Wright Papers, Manuscript Division, Library of Congress, Washington, D.C.

Chapter 3

[1] Letter from Guy D. Goff to John Q. Tilson dated 14 November 1930 in BCR Papers, Box 2:4.

[2] Newspaper Articles in Scrapbook 1, BCR Papers, Box 24

[3] Newspaper Articles in Scrapbook 5, BCR Papers, Box 27.

[4] "Confusion Added to House-Control Problem; Lovette Dubious as Republicans Lead 214-212," *New York Times,* 8 August 1931, p. 28; Newspaper Articles in Scrapbook 5, BCR Papers, Box 27.

[5] *Contested-Election Case of O.B. Lovette v. B. Carroll Reece from the First Congressional District of Tennessee* in The B. Carroll Reece Papers, 1921-1944, The University of Tennessee Special Collections Library, Knoxville, Tennessee; Newspaper Articles in Scrapbook 5, BCR Papers, Box 27.

[6] Newspaper Articles in Scrapbook 5, BCR Papers, Box 27.

[7] Newspaper Articles in Scrapbook 3, BCR Papers, Box 25; Smith, *Nathan Goff, Jr.*, 336-339.

[8] "State Politics Enters Tennessee Bond Case," *New York Times* 24 February 1933, p. 18; "$22,000 in L.L. Reece Box," *New York Times*, 25 February 1933, p, 13l; "Reece Files Injunction Suit Answer," *Nashville Banner*, 24 February 1933, p. 1; "4 Tennesseans Accused," *New York Times,* 31 December 1933, p. 16.

[9] "Bond Theft Trial Stirs Tennessee," *New York Times*, 4 March 1934, p. E1; "Reece Files Injunction Suit Answer," *Nashville Banner*, 24 February 1933, p. 1; "Reece Claims Theft Charge is Frame-Up," *Nashville Banner*, 1 March 1933, p. 1; "State Politics Enters Tennessee Bond Case," *New York Times*, 24 February 1933, p. 18; "Reece Suffers Attack on Stand," *Nashville Banner*, 7 March 1934, p. 1; "Walker Asks Maximum Penalty," *Nashville Banner*, 21 March 1934, p. 1; "New Trial Denied to Reece," *New York Times*, 20 May 1934, p. N2; "Tennessee Official Guilty in Shortage," *New York Times*, 16 November 1934, p. 8; "Ex-Official Begins Term," *New York Times*, 7 July 1935, p. 12.

[10] "Muscle Shoals: Roosevelt Yardstick May Go to Work," *Newsweek*, 22 April 1933, 5-6.

[11] William E. Leuchtenburg, *Franklin D. Roosevelt and the New Deal, 1932-1940* (New York: Harper & Row, 1963), 42-59, 118-126, 144-149.

[12] Newspaper Articles in Scrapbook 6, BCR Papers, Box 28; Leuchtenburg, *Franklin D. Roosevelt and the New Deal*, 231-238.

[13] Reece Lincoln Day Address dated 10 February 1940 in BCR Papers, Box 22:31; Newspaper Articles in Scrapbook 5, BCR Papers, Box 27; Newspaper Articles in Scrapbook 6, BCR Papers, Box 28.

[14] Newspaper Articles in Scrapbook 6, BCR Papers, Box 28.

[15] Newspaper Articles in Scrapbook 6, BCR Papers, Box 28.

[16] Newspaper Articles in Scrapbook 6, BCR Papers, Box 28.

[17] Newspaper Articles in Scrapbook 5, BCR Papers, Box 27; Newspaper Articles in Scrapbook 6, BCR Papers, Box 28.

[18] Newspaper Articles in Scrapbook 5, BCR Papers, Box 27; Newspaper Articles in Scrapbook 6, BCR Papers, Box 28; "Tennessee Still a Battleground," *New York Times*, 3 May 1940, p. 10.

[19] Congressional Record, 75th Congress, 1st Session in BCR Papers, Box 22:26; Newspaper Article in Scrapbook 3, BCR Papers, Box 25; "Ocean Travelers," *New York Time*, 25 August 1937, p. 19; "Congress-Group Sails," *New York Times*, 26 August 1937, p. 23; "Champions of Democracy," *Time*, 13 September 1937, 14.

[20] One other Republican also served on the committee, but his anti-monopolist views caused most other Republicans not to consider him a true Republican.

[21] "Those Men in That Anti-Trust Quiz," *Business Week*, 2 July 1938, 15-16; Newspaper Articles in Scrapbook 5, BCR Papers, Box 27; John Morton Blum, *V Was for Victory: Politics and American Culture during World War II*, (San Diego: Harcourt Brace & Company, 1976), 132; Alan Brinkley, "The New Deal and the Idea of the State," in *The Rise and Fall of the New Deal Order: 1930-1980*, Steve Fraser and Gary Gerstle, eds. (Princeton: Princeton University Press, 1989), 91-92.

[22] Newspaper Articles in Scrapbook 6, BCR Papers, Box 28; "Tennessee Still a Battleground," *New York Times*, 3 May 1940, p. 10; John M. Mull letter to Charles Andrew Jonas dated 26 April 1946 in Folder 35, Charles Andrew Jonas Papers, Folder 35, Southern Historical Collection, University of North Carolina, Chapel Hill.

[23] "Seek Curb on Drunken Drivers," *New York Times*, 26 May 1940, p. 10; "House Body Splits on Aviation Set-Up," *New York Times*, 22 October 1943, p. 13;

"Bipartisan House Bill Sets Soft-Coal Price; Operators and Miners Union Back Plan," *New York Times,* 14 April 1944, p. 13.

[24] Newspaper Articles in Scrapbook 16, BCR Papers, Box 34; Newspaper Articles in Butler Folder.

[25] Newspaper Articles in Scrapbook 6, BCR Papers, Box 28; Newspaper Articles in Scrapbook 14, BCR Papers, Box 33; Newspaper Articles in Butler Folder.

[26] Congressional Record, 76th Congress, 3rd Session in BCR Papers, Box 23:17.

[27] Newspaper Articles in Scrapbook 6, BCR Papers, Box 28.

[28] Newspaper Articles in Scrapbook 5, BCR Papers, Box 27; Newspaper Articles in Scrapbook 6, BCR Papers, Box 28; Newspaper Articles in Scrapbook 13, BCR Papers, Box 32; "Reece Was Non-Interventionist," *New York Times*, 3 April 1946, p. 22; "Dangers to Labor in the Conscription of Industry Amendment to the Conscription Bill," *The Congressional Digest* 19 (November 1940): 287-8.

[29] Congressional Record, 77th Congress, 1st Session in BCR Papers, Box 22:33.

[30] Newspaper Articles in Scrapbook 5, BCR Papers, Box 27; Waldo Heinrichs, *Threshold of War: Franklin D. Roosevelt and American Entry into World War II* (New York: Oxford University Press, 1998), 118-122, 180-186.

[31] Newspaper Articles in Scrapbook 6, BCR Papers, Box 28; Mark A. Stoler, *Allies and Adversaries: The Joint Chiefs of Staff, The Grand Alliance, and U.S. Strategy in World War II* (Chapel Hill: The University of North Carolina Press, 2000), 67-83.

[32] Letters between Reece and Phillips dated 9 September 1942 through 18 October 1945 in BCR Papers, Box 1:15.

[33] Letters between Reece and Phillips dated 9 September 1942 through 18 October 1945 in BCR Papers, Box 1:15; Letters from Phillips to Reece dated 1 October 1942 through October 1944 in BCR Papers, Box 2:15.

[34] "House Group Named for Postwar Study," *New York Times,* 27 January 1944, p. 11; "Asks Cities to List Public Works Aims," *New York Times,* 24 July 1944, p. 16; Congressional Record, 78th Congress, 1st Session in BCR Papers, Box 23:10.

[35] Newspaper Articles in Scrapbook 6, BCR Papers, Box 28.

[36] Norman Davies, *Europe: A History* (Oxford; Oxford University Press, 1996), 1044, 1047, 1109.

[37] Newspaper Articles in Scrapbook 3, BCR Papers, Box 25; Newspaper Articles in Scrapbook 6, BCR Papers, Box 28; Newspaper Articles in BCR Loose Folder.

Chapter 4

[1] James A. Hagerty, "Republicans Back Party Policy Draft," *New York Times,* 9 December 1945, p.1.

[2] "Brownell Hinted as Dewey Manager," *New York Times*, 5 March 1946, p. 44.

[3] "Republicans Split on New Chairman," *New York Times*, 18 March 1946, p. 38; "Brownell 'Favors' New Stassen Plan," *New York Times*, 31 March 1946, p. 31.

[4] Smith, *Nathan Goff,* p. 341-2.

[5] Reece letter to Professor Kenneth Colegrove dated 1 July 1958 in BCR Papers, Box 16:20; Republican National Convention Delegates book in BCR Papers, Box 5:5; Undated Newspaper Article from *Virginia*-Tennessean in Scrapbook 47, BCR

Papers, Box 50; Smith, *Nathan Goff,* p. 341-2; Letter from Louise Reece to Robert Taft, Jr. dated 29 November 1963 in Container 7, Robert Taft, Jr. Papers, Manuscript Division, Library of Congress, Washington, D.C..

[6] "The Nation," *New York Times*, 7 April 1946, p. 75; Newspaper Article in Scrapbook 2, BCR Papers, Box 25; "Republicans Elect Reece as Chairman; Stassen is Critical," *New York Times*, 2 April 1946, p. 1.

[7] "Republicans Elect Reece as Chairman; Stassen is Critical," *New York Times*, 2 April 1946, p. 1.

[8] Newspaper Article in Scrapbook 16, BCR Papers, Box 34; "New Chairman," *Time*, 8 April 1946, 23.

[9] Newspaper Articles in Scrapbook 13, BCR Papers, Box 32; John M. Mull Letter to Charles Andrew Jonas dated 12 April 1946 in Folder 35, Charles Andrew Jonas Papers, Southern Historical Collection, University of North Carolina, Chapel Hill, North Carolina.

[10] *The Republican* News dated May 1946 in Scrapbook 7, BCR Papers, Box 28; Newspaper Articles in Scrapbook 13, BCR Papers, Box 32; Article in *The Chicago Sunday Tribune* dated 6 October 1946 in Sub-Series II-B, Folder 5, BCR Papers, Box 10; "Mr. Reece's Job of Holding G.O.P. Liberals," *United States News,* 12 April 1946, 65; "Republicans Elect Reece as Chairman; Stassen is Critical," *New York Times*, 2 April 1946, p. 1.

[11] "Mr. Reece's Job of Holding G.O.P. Liberals," *United States News*, 12 April 1946, 65; "Reece Election Triumph for Conservatives," *Business Week*, 6 April 1946, 7; "Republicans Elect Reece as Chairman; Stassen is Critical," *New York Times*, 2 April 1946, p. 1; Newspaper Article in Scrapbook 14, BCR Papers, Box 33.

[12] Newspaper Articles in Scrapbook 13, BCR Papers, Box 32; Newspaper Articles in Scrapbook 14, BCR Papers, Box 33.

[13] Newspaper Article in Scrapbook 13, BCR Papers, Box 32; "Republican Rift is Denied by Reece," *New York Times*, 3 April 1946, p. 22; Newspaper Article in Scrapbook 14, BCR Papers, Box 33.

[14] Charles Andrew Jonas Letter to John M. Mull dated 24 April 1946 in Folder 35, Charles Andrew Jonas Papers, Southern Historical Collection, University of North Carolina, Chapel Hill, North Carolina; Newspaper Articles in Scrapbook 13, BCR Papers, Box 32; Newspaper Article in Scrapbook 16, BCR Papers, Box 34; Newspaper Article in Scrapbook 14, BCR Papers, Box 33.

[15] Newspaper Articles in Scrapbook 13, BCR Papers, Box 32; Newspaper Article in Scrapbook 14, BCR Papers, Box 33; Danaher letter to Reece dated 2 April 1946 in Charles Andrew Jonas Papers, Folder 35, Southern Historical Collection, University of North Carolina, Chapel Hill, North Carolina; Taft letter to Lester J. Bradshaw dated 11 April 1946 in Charles Wunderlin, *The Papers of Robert A. Taft, Vol. 3, 1945-1948* (Kent: The Kent State University Press, 2003), 141-2.

[16] Newspaper Articles in Scrapbook 14, BCR Papers, Box 33.

[17] Michael Bowen, "Communism vs. Republicanism: B. Carroll Reece and the Congressional Elections of 1946," *The Journal of East Tennessee History* 73 (2001): 43-45; Reece letter in Folder 18, BCR Papers, Box 7.

---

[18] *Chairman's Letter* dated 15 April 1946 and 1 May 1946 in BCR Papers, Box 4; Newspaper Article in Scrapbook 2, BCR Papers, Box 25; Edward L. Bacher letter to Fred W. McWane dated 9 May 1946 and Fred W. McWane Letter to Reece dated 7 May 1946 in Box 3, Papers of Frederick William McWane, Special Collections Library, University of Virginia, Charlottesville, Virginia.

[19] Martin Dies, *Martin Dies' Story* (New York: Bookmailer, 1963), 40; Melvyn P. Leffler, *The Specter of Communism: The United States and the Origins of the Cold War, 1917-1953* (New York: Hill and Wang, 1994), 1-20; Newspaper Articles in Scrapbook 6, BCR Papers, Box 28; Walter Goodman, *The Committee: The Extraordinary Career of the House Committee on Un-American Activities* (New York: Farrar, Straus, and Giroux, 1968), 1-20.

[20] Newspaper Articles in Scrapbook 6, BCR Papers, Box 28; Newspaper Article in Scrapbook 13, BCR Papers, Box 32.

[21] "Democrats' Rule Scored by Reece," *New York Times*, 12 April 1946, p. 17.

[22] *Chairman's Letter* dated 1 May 1946 in BCR Papers, Box 4; *The Republican News* dated June 1946 in Scrapbook 7, BCR Papers, Box 28; Robert J. Donovan, *Conflict and Crisis: The Presidency of Harry S. Truman, 1945-1948* (New York: W.W. Norton & Company, 1977), 232-234.

[23] Newspaper Article in Scrapbook 18, BCR Papers, Box 35; Reece speech dated 1 June 1946 in BCR Papers, Box 29.

[24] Newspaper Article in Scrapbook 20, BCR Papers, Box 36; *Chairman's Letter* dated 1 October 1946, BCR Papers, Box 4; John C. Culver and John Hyde, *American Dreamer: The Life and Times of Henry A. Wallace* (New York: W. W. Norton & Company, 2000), 339-366, 419-437.

[25] Speech dated 28 May 1946 in BCR Papers, Box 29.

[26] Newspaper Article in Scrapbook 14, BCR Papers, Box 33; Newspaper Article in Scrapbook 19, BCR Papers, Box 35; Newspaper Article in Scrapbook 20, BCR Papers, Box 36.

[27] Reece speech in Scrapbook 8, BCR Papers, Box 29; "G.O.P. Sure it Can Win the House," *New York Times*, 16 June 1946, p. E7; *The Republican News* dated June 1946 in Scrapbook 7, BCR Papers, Box 28; Newspaper Article in Scrapbook 18, BCR Papers, Box 35.

[28] Reece Letters to Charles Andrew Jonas dated 29 August 1946 and 22 October 1946, Folder 35, Charles Andrew Jonas Papers, Southern Historical Collection, University of North Carolina, Chapel Hill, North Carolina.

[29] Reece speech dated 27 August 1946 in Scrapbook 8, BCR Papers, Box 29; Newspaper Article in Scrapbook 18, BCR Papers, Box 35; "Reece Assails Racial Bias," *New York Times*, 28 August 1946, p. 36.

[30] *Chicago Times* and *Chicago Sun* Article in Scrapbook 9, BCR Papers, Box 30.

[31] "The Price Gamble," *Time,* 8 July 1946, 19-20.

[32] "The Price Gamble," *Time,* 8 July 1946, 19-20; Newspaper Article in Scrapbook 11, BCR Papers, Box 31.

[33] Newspaper Article in Scrapbook 11, BCR Papers, Box 31; Newspaper Articles in Scrapbook 18, BCR Papers, Box 35.

[34] Newspaper Article in Scrapbook 18, BCR Papers, Box 35.

[35] Newspaper Articles in Scrapbook 18, BCR Papers, Box 35; Newspaper Articles in Scrapbook 20, BCR Papers, Box 36; "GOP Will Retort," *New York Times*, 15 October 1946, p. 1; "'Politics' Laid to Truman By Reece in Meat Action," *New York Times*, 16 October 1946, p. 1; "Text of Republican Reply to Truman's Address on Lifting of Meat Price Controls," *New York Times*, 15 October 1946, p. 4.

[36] Newspaper Article in Scrapbook 18, BCR Papers, Box 35; Speech dated 23 October 1946 at Patterson, New Jersey, in Scrapbook 8, BCR Papers, Box 29.

[37] Newspaper Articles in Scrapbook 18, BCR Papers, Box 35; *Chairman's Letter* dated 15 September 1946 in BCR Papers, Box 4.

[38] Article in June 1946 *Nation's Business* in Scrapbook 2, BCR Papers, Box 25; Newspaper Articles in Scrapbook 14, BCR Papers, Box 33.

[39] "AFL Shares Radio with Party Chiefs," *New York Times*, 27 October 1946, p. 3; "Election Test," *New York Times*, 3 November 1946, p. 91; Newspaper Article in Scrapbook 9, BCR Papers, Box 30.

[40] "Struggle of Rival National Chairmen for Votes in 1946 and Later," *United States News* 21 (25 October 1946), 58; "The Show's the Thing," *Newsweek*, 21 June 1948, 23; "Reece's Area Democratic First Time in 80 Years," *New York Times*, 6 November 1946, 6.

[41] David H. Rosenbloom, whose Bureaucracy Is This, Anyway?' Congress' 1946 Answer," *PS: Political Science and Politics* 34 (December 2001): 773; *Congressional Elections, 1946-1996* (Washington: Congressional Quarterly, Inc.): 3; Newspaper article dated August 1946 in Scrapbook 18, BCR Papers, Box 35.

Chapter 5

[1] *The Republican News* dated December 1946 in Scrapbook 7, BCR Papers, Box 28; Newspaper Article in Scrapbook 22, BCR Papers, Box 37; *The Chairman's Letter* dated 15 November 1946 and 1 December 1946 in Folder 2, BCR Papers, Box 4; Newspaper Article in Scrapbook 21, BCR Papers, Box 36.

[2] "Change Accepted by Party Leaders," *The New York Times*, 7 November 1946, p. 5; Newspaper Article in Scrapbook 18, BCR Papers, Box 35; "Reece Issues Call for Party Session," *The New York Times*, 11 February 1946, p. 22.

[3] Newspaper Article in Scrapbook 29, BCR Papers, Box 40; Newspaper Article in Scrapbook 21, BCR Papers, Box 37; *The Republican News* dated February 1947 in Scrapbook 7, BCR Papers, Box 28; Newspaper Article in Scrapbook 24, BCR Papers, Box 37; Newspaper Article in Scrapbook 28, BCR Papers, Box 39.

[4] *Chairman's Letter* dated 15 January 1947 in BCR Papers, Box 4; Oklahoma City Speech dated 4 January 1947 in BCR Papers, Box 23.

[5] Newspaper Article in Scrapbook 24, BCR Papers, Box 37; *Chairman's Letter* dated 1 February 1947 and 15 February 1947 in Folder 2, BCR Papers, Box 4; "Parties' Chiefs Hit at Other's Efforts," *New York Times*, 9 January 1947, p. 12; R. Alton Lee, "The Truman-80th Congress Struggle Over Tax Policy," *Historian* 33 (November 1970): 68.

[6] Transcript of Robert A. Taft interview with *Meet the Press* dated 31 January 1947 in Lawrence J. Spivak Papers, Manuscript Division, Library of Congress, Washington, D.C.

[7] "Reece Urges GOP in Congress to End Discord, Use Team-Work," *New York Times*, 3 March 1947, p. 1; Newspaper Article in Scrapbook 22, BCR Papers, Box 37.

[8] Newspaper Article in Scrapbook 24, BCR Papers, Box 37; "Morse Raps Reece on GOP Team-Play," *New York Times,* 4 March 1947, p. 19; Newspaper Article in Scrapbook 27, BCR Papers, Box 39; Lee Wilkens, *Wayne Morse: A Bio-Bibliography* (Westport: Greenwood Press, 1985), 19-22; Robert A. Smith, *The Tiger in the Senate: The Biography of Wayne Morse* (New York: Doubleday Company, Inc., 1962), 111-112.

[9] "Texts of Vandenberg's Speech and Reece's Letter on Democratic Policy Proposal," *New York Times*, 19 March 1947, p. 6.

[10] "Texts of Vandenberg's Speech and Reece's Letter on Democratic Policy Proposal," *New York Times*, 19 March 1947, p. 6; Newspaper Article in Scrapbook 24, BCR Papers, Box 37; Newspaper Article in Scrapbook 28, BCR Papers, Box 39; Newspaper Article in Scrapbook 11, BCR Papers, Box 31.

[11] "President's Order on Loyalty Hailed," *New York Times*, 23 March 1947, p. 48; Richard Gid Powers, *Not Without Honor: The History of American Anticommunism* (New York: The Free Press, 1995), 197.

[12] Newspaper Article on Reece Interview dated 20 April 1947 in Scrapbook 29, BCR Papers, Box 40; "Bi-Partisan Purge of Reds Seen by GOP," *New York Times*, 21 April 1947, p. 4.

[13] *The Republican News* dated April 1947 in Scrapbook 7, BCR Papers, Box 28; Newspaper Article in Scrapbook 25, BCR Papers, Box 38.

[14] *The Republican News* dated June 1947 in Scrapbook 7, BCR Papers, Box 28; "Fears a Recession," *New York Times,* 17 June 1947, p. 1; Newspaper Articles in Scrapbook 27, BCR Papers, Box 39; R. Alton Lee, "The Truman – 80th Congress Struggle Over Tax Policy," *Historian* 33 (November 1970): 75-76.

[15] Norman Davies, *Europe: A History* (Oxford; Oxford University Press, 1996), 1063-1064; Donovan, *Conflict and Crisis*, 287-291; Charles S. Maier, "Supranational Concepts and National Continuity in the Framework of the Marshall Plan" in *The Marshall Plan: A Retrospective*, Stanley Hoffmann & Charles Maier, eds. (Boulder: Westview Press, 1984), 29-36; "Secretary of State George C. Marshall's Address at Harvard Commencement, June 5, 1947" in *The Marshall Plan: A Retrospective*, Stanley Hoffmann & Charles Maier, eds. (Boulder: Westview Press, 1984), 99-102.

[16] Transcript of Robert A. Taft interview with *Meet the Press* dated 31 January 1947 in Lawrence J. Spivak Papers, Manuscript Division, Library of Congress, Washington, D.C.

[17] R. Alton Lee, "The Truman – 80th Congress Struggle Over Tax Policy," *Historian* 33 (November 1970): 78; Newspaper Article in Scrapbook 26, BCR Papers, Box 38; "Truman Supported by 71 Democrats," *New York Times*, 21 June

1947, p.3; "Right Not to Strike Demanded by Reece," *New York Times*, 10 May 1947, p. 11.

[18] Newspaper Article in Scrapbook 27, BCR Papers, Box 39; R. Alton Lee, "The Truman – 80th Congress Struggle Over Tax Policy," *Historian* 33 (November 1970): 78.

[19] Fred A. Hartley, Jr., *Our New National Labor Policy: The Taft-Hartley Act and the Next Steps* (New York: Funk & Wagnalls Company, 1948), xii, xv, 1-3.

[20] Letters to and from Reece in Folders 13-15, BCR Papers, Box 7; Newspaper Article in Scrapbook 25, BCR Papers, Box 38; "Reece Empowered to Pick Committees," *New York Times*, 23 April 1947, p. 15.

[21] George Van Horn Moseley letter to Reece dated 25 January 1947 and Reece letter to Moseley dated 28 January 1947 in Container 31, The Papers of George Van Horn Moseley, Manuscript Division, Library of Congress, Washington, D.C.; Letter from Marion E. Martin to Reece dated 11 April 1947 and Letter from Reece to Charles Andrew Jonas dated 26 April 1947, Folder 35, Charles Andrew Jonas Papers, Folder 35, Southern Historical Collection, University of North Carolina, Chapel Hill.

[22] Reece letter to Charles Andrew Jonas dated 23 September 1947 and Postcard from Reece to Charles Andrew Jonas postmarked 2 September 1947, Folder 35, Charles Andrew Jonas Papers, Southern Historical Collection, University of North Carolina, Chapel Hill; Letter from Reece to Mrs. Martin dated 20 July 1947 in Folder 5, BCR Papers, Box 7.

[23] Newspaper Articles in Scrapbook 27, BCR Papers, Box 39; Newspaper Articles in Scrapbook 29, BCR Papers, Box 40; "Says Price Control Means Wage Curbs," *New York Times*, 4 October 1947, p. 2.

[24] Newspaper Article dated 12 May 1947 in Scrapbook 29, BCR Papers, Box 40; Newspaper Article in Scrapbook 27, BCR Papers, Box 39.

[25] Letters to and from Reece and his constituents in Folder 5, BCR Papers, Box 2.

[26] Guy L. Smith letter to Reece dated 2 June 1947 in Folder 5, BCR Papers, Box 2; Newspaper Article in Scrapbook 25, BCR Papers, Box 38; Newspaper Article in Scrapbook 24, BCR Papers, Box 37.

[27] Newspaper Article in Scrapbook 24, BCR Papers, Box 37; Newspaper Articles in Scrapbook 25, BCR Papers, Box 38.

[28] "Republican Albatross," *New York Times*, 4 November 1947, p. C24; "Aiken Asks Reece to Quit GOP Helm," *New York Times*, 27 November 1947, p. 36; ""Reece is Expected to Retain His Post," *New York Times*, 2 December 1947, p. 33; "Futility in Aiken's Call," *New York Times*, 3 December 1947, p. 33; Newspaper Article in Scrapbook 26, BCR Papers, Box 38.

[29] James T. Patterson, *Mr. Republican: A Biography of Robert A. Taft* (Boston: Houghton Mifflin Company, 1972), 367-399; *The Chairman's Letter* dated 1 July 1947 in Folder 2, BCR Papers, Box 4; "GOP Seen Keeping Congress Control," *New York Times*, 31 December 1947, p. 2; Newspaper Article in Scrapbook 37, BCR Papers, Box 45.

[30] Newspaper Article in Scrapbook 36, BCR Papers, Box 45; Newspaper Article in Scrapbook 37, BCR Papers, Box 46.

[31] United States Congress House of Representatives, *This is Your House Committee on Un-American Activities* (Washington, D.C.: Committee on Un-American Activities, U.S. House of Representatives, 1954), 8; Kenneth O'Reilly, *Hoover and the Un-Americans: The FBI, HUAC, and the Red Menace* (Philadelphia: Temple University Press, 1983), Chapter 6; Robert K. Carr, *The House Committee on Un-American Activities, 1945-1950* (Ithaca: Cornell University Press, 1952), 60-85; Powers, *Not Without Honor*, 216-225.

[32] *Chairman's Letters* dated 1 February 1948 and 1 March 1948 in Folder 2, BCR Papers, Box 4.

[33] Undated Speech in Folder 2, BCR Papers, Box 22; "Reece Urges Purge of Communists in U.S.," *New York Times,* 1 February 1948, p. 49.

[34] Carr, 60-85; *The Republican News* dated May 1948 in Scrapbook 7, BCR Papers, Box 28; Newspaper Article in Scrapbook 40, BCR Papers, Box 47; "Condon Data Issue Pushed by Reece," *New York Times,* 2 May 1948, p. 32.

[35] Letter from Charles S. Bolster to Reece dated 2 February 1948 in Folder 8, BCR Papers, Box 3; *Chairman's Letter* dated 15 March 1948 in Folder 2, BCR Papers, Box 4; "Reece Says Issue is 'Pendergastism,'" *New York Times*, 15 March 1948, p. 15.

[36] *Chairman's Letter* dated 1 June 1948 in Folder 2, BCR Papers, Box 4; "Reece Hits Using Public Funds for Truman's 'Campaign Tour,'" *New York Times*, 6 June 1948, p. 1.

[37] Fred W. McWane letter to Edward L. Bacher dated 4 March 1948 and Form Letter from Reece, undated in Box 3, Papers of Frederick William McWane, Special Collections Library, University of Virginia, Charlottesville, Virginia.

[38] Taft letter to Reece dated 9 February 1948 and Reece letter to Taft dated 16 February 1948 in Folder 5, BCR Papers, Box 5; Newspaper Article dated May 1948 in Scrapbook 32, BCR Papers, Box 42; Newspaper Article dated 19 June 1948 in Scrapbook 33, BCR Papers, Box 43.

[39] 1948 Republican National Convention transcript in Folder 11, BCR Papers, Box 14; "Chairman's Address to Opening Session," Folder 8, BCR Papers, Box 22.

[40] Newspaper Article in Scrapbook 21, BCR Papers, Box 36; Newspaper Article in Scrapbook 25, BCR Papers, Box 38; Newspaper Article in Scrapbook 26, BCR Papers, Box 38; Newspaper Article dated April 1948 in Scrapbook 32, BCR Papers, Box 42; E.A. Graham letter to Reece dated 14 April 1948 and Reece letter to E.A. Graham dated 24 April 1948 in Folder 3, BCR Papers, Box 3.

[41] Newspaper Article dated April 1948 in Scrapbook 32, BCR Papers, Box 42; "Reece Lets Friends in South Back Him," *New York Times*, 19 March 1948, p. 46.

[42] Transcript of the 1948 Republican National Committee in Folder 14, BCR Papers, Box 14.

[43] *The Republican News* dated June 1948 in Scrapbook 7, BCR Papers, Box 28.

[44] Reece letter to E.F. Spring dated November 1947 in Folder 12, BCR Papers, Box 8.

[45] Newspaper Article dated 28 January 1948 in Scrapbook 27, BCR Papers, Box 39; "Reece May Make Run in Senate Primary," *New York Times*, 1 July 1948, p. 13; Newspaper Article dated 2 July 1948 in Scrapbook 33, BCR Papers, Box 43.

[46] Campaign tract titled the "Story of Carroll Reece" dated 1948 in Folder 5, BCR Papers, Box 13.

[47] Charles L. Fontenay, *Estes Kefauver: A Biography* (Knoxville: The University of Tennessee Press, 1980), Chapters 3-7.

[48] Fontenay, *Estes Kefauver*, p. 130-152; Newspaper Article in Scrapbook 33, BCR Papers, Box 43; Newspaper Article in Scrapbook 39, BCR Papers, Box 47.

[49] Reece Speech dated 1948 BCR Papers, Box 22:5; Reece Speech dated 2 November 1948 BCR Papers, Box 22:6.

[50] Newspaper Articles in Scrapbook 35, BCR Papers, Box 44; "Reece is Egg Target at Tennessee Rally," *New York Times*, 8 September 1948, p. 22.

[51] Newspaper Articles in Scrapbook 34, BCR Papers, Box 43.

[52] Newspaper Articles in Scrapbook 34, BCR Papers, Box 43; Newspaper Articles in Scrapbook 35, BCR Papers, Box 44; Reece Speeches dated 2 November 1948, 10 September 1948, and 22 September 1948 in BCR Papers, Box 22:6.

[53] Newspaper Articles in Scrapbook 34, BCR Papers, Box 43; "Brownell Urges Reece for Senate," *New York Times,* 25 October 1948, p. 15.

[54] Newspaper Article in Scrapbook 34, BCR Papers, Box 43; Newspaper Articles in Scrapbook 35, BCR Papers, Box 44; Newspaper Article in Scrapbook 40, BCR Papers, Box 47.

[55] Newspaper Article in Scrapbook 34, BCR Papers, Box 43; Newspaper Articles in Scrapbook 35, BCR Papers, Box 44.

[56] Kefauver telegram to Reece dated 3 November 1948 in Folder 15, BCR Papers, Box 2.

Chapter 6

[1] Newspaper Articles in Scrapbook 39, BCR Papers, Box 47; W.H. Lawrence, "GOP Foes of Scott Try to Join Forces," *New York Times*, 25 January 1949, p. 1; Taft letter to Rentfro B. Creager dated 5 January 1949 in Charles Wunderlin, *The Papers of Robert A. Taft, Vol. 4, 1949-1953* (Kent: The Kent State University Press, 2006): 6-7.

[2] "Reece and Spangler Join Attack," *New York Times*, 25 January 1949, p. 7; W.H. Lawrence, "Scott Keeps Post as GOP Chairman by 4-Vote Margin," *New York Times*, 28 January 1949, pg. 1.

[3] Newspaper Articles in Scrapbook 42, BCR Papers, Box 48.

[4] Newspaper Articles in Scrapbook 42, BCR Papers, Box 48.

[5] Newspaper Articles in Scrapbook 42, BCR Papers, Box 48; "Reece Purchases Paper," *New York Times*, 22 February 1950, p. 20. Reece sold the newspapers to General Newspapers, Inc. in April 1951 for an undisclosed amount in order to devote more time to his official duties and the "emergency confronting our country." Newspaper Article dated 2 April 1951 in Scrapbook 44, BCR Papers, Box 49.

[6] Newspaper Articles in Scrapbook 42, BCR Papers, Box 48; Newspaper Article dated 11 February 1947 in Scrapbook 21, BCR Papers, Box 36.

[7] "Reece Enters Race for Congress Seat," *New York Times*, 21 May 1950, p. 45; Reece speech dated 20 May 1950 in BCR Papers, Box 22:5; Article in *Knoxville Journal* dated 21 May 1950 in Scrapbook 42, BCR Papers, Box 48.

[8] Newspaper Articles in Scrapbook 42, BCR Papers, Box 48; Clayton Knowles, "G.O.P. in the South Defended by Taft," *New York Times*, 30 May 1950, p. 21; Robert Taft letter to Reece dated 2 June 1950 in Scrapbook 43, BCR Papers, Box 49.

[9] Reece speeches dated 8 July 1950, 20 July 1950, and 27 July 1950 in BCR Papers, Box 22:5; Newspaper Articles in Scrapbook 42, BCR Papers, Box 48; James A. Huston, *Outposts and Allies: U.S. Army Logistics in the Cold War, 1945-1953* (Cranbury: Associated University Presses, 1988), 226-228.

[10] Reece speech dated 27 July 1950 in BCR Papers, Box 22:5.

[11] Newspaper Article dated 25 June 1950 in Scrapbook 42, BCR Papers, Box 48; Newspaper Articles in Scrapbook 42, BCR Papers, Box 48.

[12] Newspaper Article in Scrapbook 44, BCR Papers, Box 49; "Browning Leading in Tennessee Vote," *New York Times*, 4 August 1950, p. 36; Newspaper Articles in Scrapbook 34, BCR Papers, Box 43.

[13] Representative Frank Fellows letter to Reece dated 25 September 1950 in Scrapbook 38, BCR Papers, Box 46; Newspaper Articles in Scrapbook 34, BCR Papers, Box 43.

[14] Newspaper Articles in Scrapbook 44, BCR Papers, Box 49; John N. Popham, "G.O.P. Forces Split in Tennessee Race," *New York Times*, 5 November 1950, p. 74.

[15] Newspaper Articles in Scrapbook 44, BCR Papers, Box 49; Newspaper Article in Scrapbook 34, BCR Papers, Box 43; John N. Popham, "G.O.P. Forces Split in Tennessee Race," *New York Times*, 5 November 1950, p. 74.

[16] *Congressional Elections, 1946-1996* (Washington: Congressional Quarterly, Inc.): 7.

[17] Michael J. Ybarra, *Washington Gone Crazy: Senator Pat McCarran and the Great American Communist Hunt* (Hanover: Steerforth Press, 2004), 485-489, 506, 537-539, 547, 569-571; Powers, *Not Without Honor*, 236.

[18] Newspaper Article in Scrapbook 43, BCR Papers, Box 49; Newspaper Articles in Scrapbook 45, BCR Papers, Box 49; "House Foreign Aid Debate," *The Congressional Digest* (30 November 1951): 286.

[19] Newspaper Articles in Scrapbooks 44 and 45 in BCR Papers, Box 49.

[20] Newspaper Article in Scrapbook 38, BCR Papers, Box 46; Newspaper Article in Scrapbook 46, BCR Papers, Box 50.

[21] Patterson, *Mr. Republican*, 511-530; Newspaper Articles in Scrapbook 45, BCR Papers, Box 49; Newspaper Articles in Scrapbook 44, BCR Papers, Box 49; Robert B. Dishman, "How It All Began: The Eisenhower Pre-Convention Campaign in New Hampshire, 1952," *The New England Quarterly* 26 (March 1953), p. 5.

[22] Newspaper Articles in Scrapbook 45, BCR Papers, Box 49; Newspaper Article in *Knoxville News Sentinel* dated 11 October 1951 in Scrapbook 23, BCR Papers, Box 37; "G.O.P. in South Solid for Taft, Says Reece," *New York Times*, 17

December 1951, p. 41; Reece letter to Professor Kenneth Colegrove dated 1 July 1958 in BCR Papers, Box 16:20.

[23] Newspaper Articles in Scrapbook 45, BCR Papers, Box 49; Newspaper Articles in Scrapbook 23, BCR Papers, Box 37; Reece Speech "Republic of the United States" dated 2 February 1952 in BCR Papers, Box 23:9.

[24] Newspaper Article in Scrapbook 45, BCR Papers, Box 4; Reece speech "Nation's Defense" given 19 June 1952 in BCR Papers, Box 23:3; Reece Speech "Eisenhower's Hand in Our Air Power Reduction" dated 19 June 1952 in BCR Papers, Box 22:17; Newspaper Article in Scrapbook 23, BCR Papers, Box 37.

[25] Newspaper Article in Scrapbook 47, BCR Papers, Box 50; Booklet published by the Taft Committee, "The True Facts of the Texas Republican Convention" in BCR Papers, Box 23:24; Newspaper Article in Scrapbook 45, BCR Papers, Box 49; Reece letter to Professor Kenneth Colegrove dated 1 July 1958 in BCR Papers, Box 16:20.

[26] Reece letters to Fred W. McWane dated 14 December 1951, 1 March 1952, 17 April 1952, and 21 May 1952; Fred W. McWane letter to Reece dated 5 March 1952; and *Human Events*, Frank C. Hanighen, ed. dated 11 June 1952 all in Box 11, Papers of Frederick William McWane, Special Collections Library, University of Virginia, Charlottesville, Virginia.

[27] "Taft Campaigners: Ingalls, Hamilton, Reece and Coleman, Old Masters—Newcomer Wedemeyer," *U.S. News & World Report* 13 June 1952, 42. 44; Newspaper Article in Scrapbook 43, BCR Papers, Box 49.

[28] Vincent P. DeSantis, "The Presidential Election of 1952," *The Review of Politics* 15 (April 1953), p. 131-132; Robert B. Dishman, "How It All Began: The Eisenhower Pre-Convention Campaign in New Hampshire, 1952," *The New England Quarterly* 26 (March 1953), p.13-14, 22.

[29] Newspaper Article in Scrapbook 34, BCR Papers, Box 43; Taft letters to Reece dated 18 July 1952 and 14 August 1952 in BCR Papers, Box 11:4; Reece letter to Professor Kenneth Colegrove dated 1 July 1958 in BCR Papers, Box 16:20. Taft's memo was not discovered until 1959, and a copy of it is in the Reece Papers. Newspaper Article dated 24 November 1959 in Scrapbook 57, BCR Papers, Box 55.

[30] Newspaper Article dated 5 November 1952 in Scrapbook 34, BCR Papers, Box 43; Newspaper Article in Scrapbook 47, BCR Papers, Box 50; Invitation to 1953 Presidential Inauguration and Nixon letter to Reece dated 28 February 1953 in Scrapbook 49, BCR Papers, Box 51; *Congressional Elections, 1946-1996* (Washington: Congressional Quarterly, Inc.): 9.

[31] Vincent P. DeSantis, "Eisenhower Revisionism," *The Review of Politics* 38 (April 1976), p.190-191, 195; Chester J. Pach, Jr. and Elmo Richardson, *The Presidency of Dwight D. Eisenhower* (Lawrence: University Press of Kansas, 1991), xi-xiii, 23, 31-32, 45-47, 124-126, 237-239.

[32] Newspaper Article in Scrapbook 43, BCR Papers, Box 49; "Political Eclipse Faces Taft Aides," *New York Times*, 12 July 1952, p. 6.

Chapter 7

[1] Reece memo to Rene Wormser dated 29 June 1955 in BCR Papers, Box 19:1.

[2] "Cox Heads Tax Exemption Study," *New York Times*, 1 May 1952, p. 41; "Investigation Set on Tax-Free Funds," *New York Times*, 16 November 1952, p. 75; "Reece Assails Acheson," *New York Times*, 4 October 1952, p. 2.

[3] "Investigation Set on Tax-Free Funds," *New York Times*, 16 November 1952, p. 75; "Questionnaire submitted by the Select Committee of the House of Representatives of the Congress of the United States," in BCR Papers, Box 16:13; "Stenographic Transcript of Hearings: Special Committee to Investigate Tax Exempt Foundations (House Resolution 217), House of Representatives" (Hereafter "Transcript of Hearings"), Volume 1, May 10, 1954, p. 32-77 in BCR Papers, Box 20:5; Final Report of the Select Committee to Investigate Foundations and Other Organizations dated 1 January 1953 in Container 150, Folder 11, J. Robert Oppenheimer Papers, Manuscript Division, Library of Congress, Washington, D.C.

[4] "Questionnaire submitted by the Select Committee of the House of Representatives of the Congress of the United States," in BCR Papers, Box 16:13.

[5] Dwight MacDonald, *The Ford Foundation: The Men and the Millions* (New York: Reynal & Company, 1956): 28-9.

[6] George B. de Huszar, "Subversive and Un-American Propaganda Activities of Foundations," pp. 7-9, in BCR Archives, Box 18:5; Printed Final Report of the Select Committee to Investigate Foundations and Other Organizations for the House, 82nd Congress, 2nd Session, BCR Papers, Box 19:9; Final Report of the Select Committee to Investigate Foundations and Other Organizations dated 1 January 1953 in Container 150, Folder 11, J. Robert Oppenheimer Papers, Manuscript Division, Library of Congress, Washington, D.C.

[7] Newspaper Article in Scrapbook 23, BCR Papers, Box 37; Taft letter to Reece dated 14 August 1952 in BCR Papers, Box 11:4; Reece letter to Fred W. McWane dated 1 August 1952 in Box 11, Papers of Frederick William McWane, Special Collections Library, University of Virginia, Charlottesville, Virginia.

[8] Excerpt from the Congressional Record of the House dated 23 April 1953 in Container 150, Folder 11, J. Robert Oppenheimer Papers, Manuscript Division, Library of Congress, Washington, D.C.

[9] Memorandum to Board of Trustees of The Twentieth Century Fund dated 8 May 1953 in Container 150, Folder 11, J. Robert Oppenheimer Papers, Manuscript Division, Library of Congress, Washington, D.C.; Helen Hill Miller, "Investigating the Foundations," *The Reporter* 9 (24 November, 1953), 38; Aaron Sargent letter to Reece dated 21 June 1953 in BCR papers, Box 18:4; Macdonald, *The Ford Foundation*, 29.

[10] "Speech of Carroll Reece, Republican, of Tennessee, In Connection with the Introduction Today of a Resolution to Appoint a Special Committee to Investigate Tax-Exempt Foundations and Other Comparable Organizations," undated, in BCR Papers, Box 15:8.

[11] Reece letter to George B. de Huszar dated 2 July 1953 in BCR Papers, Box 15:8; Letters between Reece and Edward A. Keller, dated April – June 1953 in BCR Papers, Box 15:8.

[12] Helen Hill Miller, "Investigating the Foundations," *The Reporter* 9 (24 November, 1953), 38; Newspaper Article in Scrapbook 34, BCR Papers, Box 43; Dwight Macdonald, *The Ford Foundation: The Men and the Millions.* (New York: Reynal & Company, 1956), 31; Frank K. Kelly, *Court of Reason: Robert Hutchins and the Fund for the Republic* (New York: The Free Press, 1981), 25.

[13] House Congressional Record of 27 July 1953 in Container 150, Folder 11, J. Robert Oppenheimer Papers, Manuscript Division, Library of Congress, Washington, D.C.

[14] House Congressional Record of 27 July 1953 in Container 150, Folder 11, J. Robert Oppenheimer Papers, Manuscript Division, Library of Congress, Washington, D.C.; *American Foundations News Service,* Volume III, No. 7 dated 11 August 1953 in Container 150, Folder 11, J. Robert Oppenheimer Papers, Manuscript Division, Library of Congress, Washington, D.C.

[15] "Request to the Ford Foundation" dated April 1951 in Southern Regional Council Papers, Series I, Reel 12:432; David Freeman letter to Marion A. Wright dated 26 September 1955 in Southern Regional Council Papers, Series I, Reel 11:369.

[16] Leslie W. Dunbar, "The Southern Regional Council," *Annals of the American Academy of Political and Social Science,* 357 (January 1965), p. 109-110; Manning J. Dauer, "Recent Southern Political Thought," *The Journal of Politics* 10 (May 1948), p. 340-1; Rene A. Wormser, *Foundations: Their Power and Influence* (New York: The Devin-Adair Company, 1958), p. 276; Robert J. Norrell, "Triangles of Change: The Southern Regional Council in the Civil Rights Movement," unpublished paper, used with permission of the author.

[17] House Resolution 217, 83rd Congress, 1st Session, undated in BCR Papers, Box 15:8; Helen Hill Miller, "Investigating the Foundations," *The Reporter* 9 (24 November, 1953), 40.

[18] "The Man Who Talks Back," *The New Republic* 130 (28 June 1954): 12-13; Frank K. Kelly, *Court of Reason: Robert Hutchins and the Fund for the Republic* (New York: The Free Press, 1981): 49. By 1976 Hays had secured the position of chairman of the House Administration Committee, which controlled members' allowances for office and travel expenses. He had become one of the most powerful leaders in the House. Later that year, he faced accusations of misappropriating funds to pay the salary of a woman he formerly dated. Hays denied the allegations, but the public, fresh from the Watergate Scandal, could not be convinced of his innocence. He resigned three months later. Warren Weaver, Jr. "But He Also Knows How to Say 'Yes' to Win Support," *New York Times* 22 February 1976, p. E4; "Text of Hays's Statement to the House," *New York Times* 26 May 1976, p. 16; James Reston, "Reform by Scandal," *New York Times*, 4 June 1976, p. 19; "Farewell to Hays," *New York Times,* 5 September 1976, p. 114.

[19] Helen Hill Miller, "Investigating the Foundations," *The Reporter* 9 (24 November, 1953), 37; Newspaper Article in Scrapbook 48, BCR Papers, Box 51;

Thomas C. Reeves, *Freedom and the Foundation: The Fund for the Republic in the Era of McCarthyism* (New York: Alfred A. Knopf, 1969), 309; Kelly, *Court of Reason*, 25-6.

[20] "Propose New Probe of Foundations," *The Christian Century* 70 (12 August 1953), 908; "The Un-Tory Activities Probe," *The New Republic* 129 (10 August 1953): 3; Newspaper Article in Scrapbook 34, BCR Papers, Box 43.

[21] Memo to Board of Trustees of The Twentieth Century Fund dated 10 September 1953 in Container 150, Folder 11, J. Robert Oppenheimer Papers, Manuscript Division, Library of Congress, Washington, D.C.; Reece letter to Aaron Sargent dated 30 July 1953 in BCR Papers, Box 18:1; Rene Wormser letter to Reece dated 27 April 1953 in BCR Papers, Box 19:1; Rene A. Wormser, *Foundations: Their Power and Influence* (New York: The Devin-Adair Company, 1958): vi, 347.

[22] Murrey Marder, "Staff Selection Stirs Clash Between Foundation Probers," *The Washington Post,* 17 October 1953 and Copy of Statement issued by Congressman Carroll Reece dated 16 October 1953 in Container 150, Folder 11, J. Robert Oppenheimer Papers, Manuscript Division, Library of Congress, Washington, D.C.

[23] Release from the Special Committee to Investigate Tax-Exempt Foundations dated 13 November 1953 in Container 150, Folder 11, J. Robert Oppenheimer Papers, Manuscript Division, Library of Congress, Washington, D.C.; Various letters to Reece Committee dated 1953 and 1954 on the Kinsey Report in BCR Papers, Box 18:1; Articles on Kinsey Study in BCR Papers, Box 18:8; Norman Dodd letter to American Statistical Association dated 12 February 1954 in BCR Papers, Box 18:7; "Those Other Hearings," *The Reporter* 10 (8 June 1954), 3; Reece letter to Rene Wormser dated 10 December 1953 in BCR Papers, Box 20:3.

[24] Ellen Schrecker, *Many Are the Crimes: McCarthyism in America,* (Boston: Little, Brown and Company, 1998), 408-410; C.P. Trussell, "House Votes to Renew Private Funds Inquiry," *New York Times*, 28 July 1953, p. 1; "President Opens Files of Tax-Exempt Groups," *New York Times*, 13 February 1954, p. 6; "Propose New Probe of Foundations," *The Christian Century* 70 (12 August 1953): 908.

[25] Macdonald, *The Ford Foundation,* 70; Reeves, *Freedom and the Foundation,* 56; Kelly, *Court of Reason*, 20, 28-9.

[26] Thomas C. Reeves, *Freedom and the Foundation: The Fund for the Republic in the Era of McCarthyism* (New York: Alfred A. Knopf, 1969), 9, 17; Kelly, *Court of Reason*, 14.

[27] Kelly, *Court of Reason*, 4, 21, 28-9; Reeves, *Freedom and the Foundation,* 11.

[28] Waldemar A. Nielson, *The Big Foundations* (New York: Columbia University Press, 1972), 123-4; Reece letter to Joseph N. Pew dated 3 April 1958 in BCR Archives, Box 19:2; Reece letter to Richard Rimanoczy dated 18 November 1955 in BCR Archives, Box 17:20.

[29] Newspaper Articles in Scrapbook 47, BCR Papers, Box 50; Article in *The Washington Post* dated 3 August 1953 in Scrapbook 47, BCR Papers, Box 50; "They Work Together," *The New Republic* 130 (24 May 1954): 4-5.

[30] David H. Price, *Threatening Anthropology: McCarthyism and the FBI's Surveillance of Activist Anthropologists* (Durham: Duke University Press, 2004),

Chapter 2; Ellen Schrecker, *No Ivory Tower: McCarthyism and the Universities* (New York: Oxford University Press, 1986), 11, 96, 190-218, 282, 340.
[31] Kelley, *Court of Reason*, 53.
[32] Reeves, *Freedom and the Foundation,* 25, 63-65; Thomas C. Reeves, *The Life and Times of Joe McCarthy: A Biography* (New York: Stein and Day, 1982), 423.
[33] David M. Oshinksy, *A Conspiracy So Immense: The World of Joe McCarthy* (New York: The Free Press, 1983), 134; Haynes Johnson, *The Age of Anxiety: McCarthyism to Terrorism* (Orlando: Harcourt, Inc., 2005), 253-281; John N. Thomas, *The Institute of Pacific Relations: Asian Scholars and American Politics* (Seattle: University of Washington Press, 1974), 68-73; Reeves, *The Life and Times of Joe McCarthy*, 423, 488-490; Waldemar A. Nielsen, *The Big Foundations* (New York: Columbia University Press, 1972), 82.
[34] Oshinsky, *A Conspiracy So Immense*, 417.

Chapter 8

[1] "A Report from Norman Dodd, Director of Research, covering his direction of the staff of The Special Committee of The House of Representatives to Investigate Tax-Exempt Foundations" in Container 150, Folder 11, J. Robert Oppenheimer Papers, Manuscript Division, Library of Congress, Washington, D.C.
[2] "Transcript of Hearings," Volume 1, May 10, 1954, p. 37-42, in BCR Papers, Box 20:5; "Transcript of Hearings," Volume 2, May 11, 1954, p. 56-115, 155-6, in BCR Papers, Box 20:6; C.P. Trussell, "Tax-Free Foundations Held Threat to Education in U.S.," *New York Times*, 12 May 1954, p. 1,23.
[3] "Transcript of Hearings," Volume 3, May 18, 1954, pp. 211-217, 219-223, in BCR Papers, Box 20:7; C.P. Trussell, "New House Study on Funds Opened," *New York Times*, 11 May 1954, p. 15; C.P. Trussell, "Tax-Free Foundations Held Threat to Education in U.S.," *New York Times*, 12 May 1954, p. 1; Newspaper Article in Scrapbook 50, BCR Papers, Box 52.
[4] Newspaper Article in *Washington Post* dated 10 May 1954 in Scrapbook 48, BCR Papers, Box 51; "The Reece Investigation," *New York Herald Tribune* dated 15 May 1954 and "Foundation Inquiry No. 2," *New York Times* dated 13 May 1954 in Container 150, Folder 11, J. Robert Oppenheimer Papers, Manuscript Division, Library of Congress, Washington, D.C.
[5] "Transcript of Hearings," Volume 4, May 19, 1954, p. 354, in BCR Papers, Box 20:8; Newspaper Article in Scrapbook 48, BCR Papers, Box 51; C.P. Trussell, "Power of Grants Scored in Inquiry," *New York Times*, 20 May 1954, p. 26; "Transcript of Hearings," Volume 5, May 20, 1954, p. 440, in BCR Papers, Box 20:9; Wormser, *Foundations,* 86-7.
[6] "Transcript of Hearings," Volume 6, May 24, 1954, pp. 476-480, 501, 502-504, in BCR Papers, Box 20:10; Wormser, 143, 160, 358.
[7] "Transcript of Hearings," Volume 6, May 24, 1954, pp. 509-520, in BCR Papers, Box 20:10; C.P. Trussell, "Two Democrats Bolt Foundation Inquiry," *New York Times*, 25 May 1954, p. 1.
[8] "Random Notes From Washington: Capital Runs High Inquiry Fever," *New York Times*, 31 May 1954, p. 6; "Transcript of Hearings," Volume 7, May 25, 1954, pp.

599-607, in BCR Papers, Box 20:11; C.P. Trussell, "Democrats Back at Funds Inquiry," *New York Times*, 26 May 1954, p. 21; Pamphlet "Exhibit A (Attached to Resolution Before the Special Committee of the House of Representatives to Investigate Tax Exempt Foundations," dated 25 May 1954, in BCR Papers, Box 17:10; *American Forum of the Air: Should Foundations Remain Tax-Exempt?*, prod. by Theodore Granik, 29 min., NBC Television Network, 1954, videocassette..

[9] "Transcript of Hearings," Volume 8, May 27, 1954, pp. 806-807, in BCR Papers, Box 21:1; C.P. Trussell, "Democrats Back at Funds Inquiry," *New York Times*, 26 May 1954, p. 21; Newspaper Article in Scrapbook 48, BCR Papers, Box 51.

[10] C.P. Trussell, "Tax-Free Funds Backed at Inquiry," *New York Times*, 3 June 1954, p. 21;"Transcript of Hearings," Volume 11, June 4, 1954, pp. 1154, in BCR Papers, Box 21:3; "Transcript of Hearings," Volume 12, June 8, 1954, pp. 1232-1233, in BCR Papers, Box 21:4.

[11] "Transcript of Hearings," Volume 10, June 3, 1954, pp. 1011, in BCR Papers, Box 21:2; "Aid to Socialists by Funds Charged," *New York Times*, 4 June 1954, p. 18; "Transcript of Hearings," Volume 13, June 9, 1954, in BCR Papers, Box 21:5; "Inquiry Aide Calls Writings 'Red,' Then Learns they are by 2 Popes," *New York Times*, 10 June 1954, p. 1; T.M. McNiece letter to Reece dated 14 June 1954 in BCR Papers, Box 2:15.

[12] "Transcript of Hearings," Volume 13, June 9, 1954, in BCR Papers, Box 21:5; "Inquiry Aide Calls Writings 'Red,' Then Learns they are by 2 Popes," *New York Times*, 10 June 1954, p. 1; "C.P. Trussell, "Defense of Funds Begun by Witness," *New York Times*, 17 June 1954, p. 19.

[13] C.P. Trussell, "Tax-Free Funds Backed at Inquiry," *New York Times*, 3 June 1954, p. 21; "A.D.A. Scores Reece's Inquiry," *New York Times*, 13 June 1954, p. 59; "Cool Off Voted on Foundations," *New York Times*, 18 June 1954, p. 23;

[14] "Investigating the Foundations," *Business Week,* 19 June 1954, 180; "The Man Who Talks Back," *The New Republic* 130 (28 June 1954): 12-13.

[15] Newspaper Article in *Washington Post* dated 3 June 1954 in Scrapbook 48, BCR Papers, Box 51; ""Inquiry on Grants Closes Hearings," *New York Times*, 3 July 1954, p. 1.

[16] "Inquiry on Grants Closes Hearings," *New York Times,* 3 July 1954, p. 1; Russell Porter, "Carnegie Foundation Assails Congress Inquiry on Grants," *New York Times*, 12 July 1954, p. 1.

[17] Reece letter to R.A. Wormser dated 19 June 1954 in BCR Papers, Box 22:27.

[18] Transcript of "American Forum of the Air," dated 3 August 1954 in Scrapbook 48, BCR Papers, Box 51; *American Forum of the Ai: Should Foundations Remain Tax-Exempt?*, prod. by Theodore Granik, 29 min., NBC Television Network, 1954, videocassette.

[19] Transcript of "American Forum of the Air," dated 3 August 1954 in Scrapbook 48, BCR Papers, Box 51; *American Forum of the Ai: Should Foundations Remain Tax-Exempt?*, prod. by Theodore Granik, 29 min., NBC Television Network, 1954, videocassette.

[20] Copy of Reece Remarks, "Point of Personal Privilege," undated in BCR Papers, Box 17:17.

[21] "'Tax Dodging' Laid to Smaller Funds," *New York Times*, 9 August 1954, p. 1; "Press Criticized on Funds Inquiry," *New York Times*, 24 August 1954, p. 21; Newspaper Article in Scrapbook 23, BCR Papers, Box 37; "Another Stupid Inquiry," *New York Times*, 5 July 1954, p. 10.

[22] "Foundation Head Defends 5 Studies," *New York Times*, 12 July 1954, p. 7; C.P. Trussell, "Carnegie Protest Jolts house Unit," *New York Times*, 13 July 1954, p. 25; "House Unit Held Unfair to Funds," *New York Times*, 16 July 1954, p. 7; Russell Porter, "Fund Head Makes Slander Charge," *New York Times*, 21 July 1954, p. 30.; John Chabot Smith, *Alger Hiss: The True Story* (New York: Holt, Rinehart, and Winston, 1976), 140-142, 232-234, 385; Powers, *Not Without Honor*, 223-225.

[23] Luther A Huston, "Ford Fund Scores Inquiry Charges," *New York Times*, 25 July 1954, p. 1; Dean Rusk telegram to Reece dated 2 July 1954 and Reece telegram to Dean Rusk dated 3 July 1954 in BCR Papers, Box 21:11; "Foundation Gives Details on Grants," *New York Times*, 5 August 1954, p. 15; "Rockefeller Fund Answers Charges," *New York Times*, 5 August 1954, p. 1.

[24] John J. McCloy letter to Reece dated 12 July 1954, Reece letter to McCloy dated 15 July 1954, McCloy letter to Reece dated 29 July 1954 in BCR Papers, Box 17:14.

[25] Reece letter to George B. de Huszar dated 3 July 1954 in BCR Papers, Box 17:9; J.K. Javits letter to Leo E. Allen, Chairman of the Rules Committee, dated 24 July 1954, Reece letter to Javits dated 26 July 1954, Javits letter to Reece dated 29 July 1954, and Javits letter to Allen dated 16 August 1954 in BCR Papers, Box 21:11.

[26] C.P. Trussell, "New House Study of Education Set," *New York Times*, 18 July 1954, p. 41; C.P. Trussell, "Inquiries Facing Test at the Polls," *New York Times*, 20 September 1954, p. 15;

[27] Newspaper Article in *Knoxville News Sentinel* dated 14 February 1954 in Scrapbook 23, BCR Papers, Box 37; Newspaper Article in Scrapbook 47, BCR Papers, Box 50; Newspaper Articles in Scrapbook 51, BCR Papers, Box 52.

[28] Reece interview, undated, in BCR Papers, Box 23:8; Newspaper Articles in Scrapbook 51, BCR Papers, Box 52.

[29] Reece radio address dated 4 August 1954 in BCR Papers, Box 22:5; Reece letter to Arthur Conrad of The Heritage Foundation dated 11 October 1954 in BCR Papers, Box 16:8; Newspaper Articles and Dwight Eisenhower telegram to Reece dated 31 October 1954 in Scrapbook 51, BCR Papers, Box 52;

[30] Robert Griffith, *The Politics of Fear: Joseph R. McCarthy and the Senate*, (Lexington: The University of Kentucky Press, 1970), 315-317; Reeves, *The Life and Times of Joe McCarthy*, 654; C.P. Trussell, "Socialist Trend Laid to Big Funds," *New York Times*, 30 November 1954, p. 24.

[31] "Tax-Free Foundations: A New Controversy," *U.S. News & World Report*, 31 December 1954, 84, 90; Rene Wormser letter to Reece dated 10 December 1954 and Reece letter to Angier Goodwin dated 23 December 1954 in BCR Papers, Box 19:8.

[32] "Tax-Free Foundations: A New Controversy," *U.S. News & World Report*, 31 December 1954, 84-89.

[33] "Tax-Free Foundations: A New Controversy," *U.S. News & World Report*, 31 December 1954, 90-92.

[34] "Tax-Free Foundations: A New Controversy," *U.S. News & World Report*, 31 December 1954, 93-96.

[35] "Tax-Free Foundations: A New Controversy," *U.S. News & World Report*, 31 December 1954, 95-102.

[36] "Tax-Free Foundations: A New Controversy," *U.S. News & World Report*, 31 December 1954, 102-103.

[37] Charles Grutzner, "Foundations Call Charges Untrue," *New York Times*, 20 December 1954, p. 1.

[38] "Reece Committee Report," *New York Times*, 21 December 1954, p. 26; Newspaper Article dated 23 December 1954 in Scrapbook 48, BCR Papers, Box 51.

[39] "Thought Control," *Time,* 3 January 1955, 15-16; Paul Blanshard, "Malice in Blunderland, Report on the Foundations," *The Nation* 180 (15 January 1955): 51-52; Bernard DeVoto, "Guilt by Distinction," *Harper's Magazine,* April 1955, 15-19.

[40] Carroll Reece, "Investigating Foundations," *New York Times*, 1 January 1955, p. 12; "Reece Hits Critics of Study on Funds," *New York Times*, 22 January 1955, p. 4.

[41] Wayne L. Hays, "Hearings on Foundations," *New York Times*, 12 February 1955, p. 14; "Reece letter to Editor of *New York Times* dated 29 February 1955, *New York Times* letter to Reece dated 22 February 1955, and Wormser letter to Reece dated 14 February 1955 in BCR Papers, Box 21:8.

[42] Reece letter to Norman Dodd dated 5 January 1955 in BCR Papers, Box 15:10; Reece Speech, "Remarks Before the National Press Club Luncheon" dated 23 February 1955 in BCR Papers, Box 23:1; Reece letter to Sister Margaret Patricia McCarran dated 22 July 1955 in BCR Papers, Box 17:2.

[43] Reece Speech "Commonwealth Club of California" dated 11 March 1955 in BCR Papers, Box 22:9; Reece Speech, "Remarks Before the National Press Club Luncheon" dated 23 February 1955 in BCR Papers, Box 23:1; Reece letter to Arthur Conrad dated 24 July 1954 in BCR Papers, Box 16:8.

Chapter 9

[1] Letters to and from Reece in BCR Papers, Box 16:7, Box 16:18, and Box 20:1; Reece letter to Fred Drexel dated 16 April 1956 in BCR Papers, Box 17:5; Copy of letter from Dean Rusk to general R.E. Wood dated 5 May 1955 in BCR Papers, Box 16:15.

[2] Newspaper Article dated 14 December 1955 in Scrapbook 53, BCR Papers, Box 53; Reece letter to Carey McWilliams of *The Nation* dated 8 February 1956 in BCR Papers, Box 15:10; George Mitchell letter to Marion Wright dated 27 December 1955 in Southern Regional Council Papers, Series I, Reel 24:483.

[3] "Hutchins Decries Reece Fund Study," *New York Times*, 27 January 1955, p. 12; Thomas C. Reeves, *Foundations under Fire* (Ithaca: Cornell University Press, 1970), 117, 112; Reeves, *Freedom and the Foundation*, p. 103-104; Kelly, *Court of Reason*, 48; "Remarks of Robert M. Hutchins, President of the Fund for the Republic, before the National Press Club, Washington, D.C., 26 January 1955" in Container 150, Folder 11, J. Robert Oppenheimer Papers, Manuscript Division, Library of Congress, Washington, D.C.

[4] C.M. Bertollette Letter to Reece dated 5 June 1955 and Reece letter to Bertollette dated 15 June 1955 in BCR Papers, Box 16:19; "Remarks of Carroll Reece of Tennessee in the House of Representatives, The Ford Fund for the Republic, Dr. Robert Maynard Hutchins," undated, in BCR Papers, Box 16:6; Reece Speeches "The Ford Fund for the Republic" dated 21 July 1955 and "Ford Foundation Fund for the Republic," undated in BCR Papers, Box 22:22 and 22:23; "Ford Fund Accused of Aid to Leftists," *New York Times*, 22 July 1955, p. 13; "Reece, In Reply to Dr. Hutchins, Says Foundations Aid Socialism," *New York Times*, 24 February 1955, p. 12.

[5] Letters from Dana Coggins of the Harvard Law School Form to Reece dated 17 October 1955 and 11 January 1956 and Letters form Reece to Coggins dated 28 November 1955 and 17 January 1956 in BCR Papers, Box 10:4.

[6] Correspondence between Reece and Robert Hutchins dated March 1956 and correspondence between Richard Rimanoczy and Reece dated March 1956 in BCR Papers, Box 15:10.

[7] "Foundation Asks Fund-Report Law," *New York Times*, 30 September 1955, p. 17; Jay Walz, "Legion Head Proposes Boycott of Fund for Republic Projects," *New York Times*, 12 September 1955, p. 1; Robert E. Bedingfield, "Ford Fund Faces Cash Indigestion," *New York Times*, 13 November 1955, p. F1; Russell Porter, "Foundation Gains Since 1944 Noted," *New York Times*, 26 January 1956, p. 21.

[8] Transcript of "Listen to Washington" broadcast dated 28 March 1955 in BCR Papers, Box 21:12; Congressional Record, 84th Congress, 1st Session, undated, in BCR Papers, Box 22:24; Reece Speech "Socialism by Way of Tax-exempt Foundations," dated 6 April 1956 in BCR Papers, Box 23:18.

[9] Transcript of "Listen to Washington" broadcast dated 28 March 1955 in BCR Papers, Box 21:12; Letters from Dr. Karl E. Ettinger to Reece dated 10 February 1955 and 9 May 1955 in BCR Papers, Box 17:9; Rene Wormser letter to Reece dated 24 May 1955, 26 October 1955, 27 February 1956, 8 March 1956, and 17 May 1956 in BCR Papers Box 19:1.

[10] Reece and Wormser correspondence dated 1957-1958, Reece letter to Devin A. Garrity dated 20 May 1958 in BCR Papers, Box 19:2.

[11] Rene A. Wormser, *Foundations: Their Power and Influence* (New York: The Devin-Adair Company, 1958), 82, 139, 200, 218, 234, 239, 253.

[12] Wormser letter to Reece dated 6 March 1959 and Reece letter to Wormser dated 17 March 1959 in BCR Papers, Box 15:1; Reece Speech "American Crisis in Education," undated in BCR Papers, Box 22:1.

[13] Correspondence between Kenneth Colegrove and Reece dated 1955-1958 and Congressional Record Appendix dated 29 July 1955 in BCR Papers, Box 16:20; Reece letter to Arthur Conrad dated 6 June 1956 in BCR Papers, Box 19:7; Congressional Record with Reece's insertion of Speech "Address of Rev. Edward A. Keller, C.S.C.," dated 27 February 1951 in BCR Papers, Box 22:30.

[14] Reece Speech "American Crisis in Education," undated in BCR Papers, Box 22:1; "Are Today's Public Schools Failing to Serve the Best Interests of the Nation?" *The Congressional Digest* 37 (August 1958): 204-210; Newspaper articles dated 12 December 1957 and January 1958 in Scrapbook 55, BCR Papers, Box 54.

[15] Reeves, *Foundations Under Fire*, 17-18; Macdonald, *The Ford Foundation*, 34.

[16] Waldemar A. Nielsen, "How Solid Are the Foundations?" *New York Times*, 21 October 1962, p. 243.

[17] Will Lissner, "Patman Inquiry on Funds Assailed," *New York Times*, 22 December 1968, p. 28; "Witness Walks Out at Patman Inquiry," *New York Times*, 14 November 1967, p. 34; Eileen Shanahan, "Foundations Face Sweeping Inquiry by a House Panel," *New York Times*, 17 February 1969, p. 1; Reeves, *Foundations Under Fire*, 19-25.

Chapter 10

[1] "Reece in Taft Memorial Post," *New York Times*, 8 August 1954 (p. 36); "Memorials to Taft," *New York Times*, 9 September 1954, p. 33.

[2] "A Taft Carillon at Capitol Urged," *New York Times*, 9 January 1955, p. 71; Reece Speech "Remarks to the National Press Club Luncheon," dated 23 February 1955 in BCR Papers, Box 23:1; John F. Kennedy, *Profiles in Courage* (New York: Harper Perennial, 1956, 1964), 221-235.

[3] Reece letter to Sterling Morton dated 14 April 1958 in BCR Papers, Box 19:2; Allen Drury, "President Dedicated Memorial to Taft; Hoover in Tribute," *New York Times*, 15 April 1959, p. 1; Reece Speech "Robert A. Taft Remarks" dated 14 April 1959 in BCR Papers, Scrapbook 23:21; Newspaper Articles dated 21 April 1959 in Scrapbook 52, BCR Papers, Box 53.

[4] Newspaper Article dated 3 November 1955 in Scrapbook 53, BCR Papers, Box 53; Congressional Record, 77th Congress, 1st Session dated 13 March 1941 in BCR Papers, Box 22:29; Notes, Confederate Bond Sheet, and Newspaper Articles in BCR Papers, Box 2:11; Reece Speech "Andrew Johnson: Man of Indomitable Courage and Incorruptible Integrity," undated, in BCR Papers, Box 22:29; Newspaper Articles in Scrapbook 55, BCR Papers, Box 54.

[5] Newspaper Article in Scrapbook 23, BCR Papers, Box 37; B. Carroll Reece, *The Courageous Commoner: A Biography of Andrew Johnson* (Charleston: Education Foundation, Inc.), 1962.

[6] Newspaper Articles in Scrapbook 23, BCR Papers, Box 37; Newspaper Articles in Scrapbook 53, BCR Papers, Box 53.

[7] Newspaper Articles in Scrapbook 23, BCR Papers, Box 37; Newspaper Articles in Scrapbook 53, BCR Papers, Box 53; Newspaper Articles in Scrapbook 55, BCR Papers, Box 54.

[8] Newspaper Articles in Scrapbook 23, BCR Papers, Box 37; William S. White, "Unity of Democrats Points to a Victory in Tennessee," *New York Times*, 10 October 1956, p. 1.

[9] Newspaper Article in Scrapbook 54, BCR Papers, Box 53; Newspaper Article dated 17 April 1958 in Scrapbook 55, BCR Papers, Box 54; Newspaper Articles in Scrapbook 23, BCR Papers, Box 37; Campaign advertisement in *Knoxville Journal*, 7 August 1958, p. 13.

[10] Cole C. Kingseed, *Eisenhower and the Suez Crisis of* 1956 (Baton Rouge: Louisiana State University Press, 1956), 81-101, 134-141; Newspaper Articles dated 15-23 July 1958 in Scrapbook 56, BCR Papers, Box 54; "Reece Wins Smashing Victory," *Knoxville Journal*, 8 August 958, p. 1.

[11] Newspaper Articles in Scrapbook 56, BCR Papers, Box 54; Newspaper Article in Scrapbook 52, BCR Papers, Box 53.

[12] Newspaper Articles in Scrapbook 56, BCR Papers, Box 54.

[13] Reece speech "Communists behind Attacks on Nixon," dated 22 May 1958 in BCR Papers, Box 22:10; Reece speech "Cuban Crisis," undated in BCR Papers, Box 22:12; Reece Speech "United Nations," undated in BCR Papers, Box 23:26

[14] Letter to Reece from Chairman of the Board of *The American Mercury* dated 27 February 1956 in BCR Papers, Box 15:11; B. Carroll Reece, "Your Private War on Communism," *American Mercury* 88 (March 1959): 65-69.

[15] Reece speech "Responsibilities of Freedom" dated 31 May 1959 in BCR Papers, Box 23:11.

[16] Newspaper Article dated January 1958 in Scrapbook 55, BCR Papers, Box 54; Newspaper Article dated February 1960 in Scrapbook 57, BCR Papers, Box 54.

[17] Newspaper Article in Scrapbook 57 dated 25 May 1960 in Scrapbook 57, BCR Papers, Box 54; Tom Wickers, "House Unit Backs 975-Million Bill on Aid to Schools," *New York Times*, 20 May 1960, p. 1; Newspaper Article dated 23 June 1960 in Scrapbook 58, BCR Papers, Box 55; "Tom Wicker, "School Kill Blocked in House; Committee Vote Stuns Backers," *New York Times*, 23 June 1960, p. 1.

[18] Reece letter to John J. McCloy dated 2 August 1956 in BCR Papers, Box 17:14; Reece letter to Rene Wormser dated 22 May 1957 in BCR Papers, Box 19:1; Eric Pace, "Prince Louis Ferdinand, 86, Grandson of Kaiser, Is Dead," *New York Times*, 27 September 1994, p. B14; B. Carroll Reece, *Peace Through Law: A Basis for an East-West Settlement in Europe* (New Canaan: Long House, 1965); Jedrzej Giertych, *Poland and Germany: A Reply to Congressman B. Carroll Reece* (London: Jedrzej Giertych, 1958).

[19] Newspaper Articles in Scrapbook 60, BCR Papers, Box 56;

[20] Newspaper Article dated 25 May 1960 in Scrapbook 5, BCR Papers, Box 54; Newspaper Article dated 7 June 1960 in Scrapbook 58, BCR Papers, Box 55; Newspaper Article in Scrapbook 43, BCR Papers, Box 49; Newspaper Article in Scrapbook 57, BCR Papers, Box 54.

[21] Newspaper Article dated 25 May 1960 in Scrapbook 57, BCR Papers, Box 54; Newspaper Article dated 7 September 1960 in Scrapbook 58, BCR Papers, Box 55; Newspaper Article dated 18 July 1960 in Scrapbook 48, BCR Papers, Box 55.

[22] Reece speech at Salt Lake City, dated 27 January 1960 in BCR Papers, Box 23:15; Newspaper Articles in Scrapbook 58, BCR Papers, Box 55; Newspaper Articles in Scrapbook 57, BCR Papers, Box 54.

[23] Newspaper Articles and Kefauver telegram to Reece dated 18 January 1961 in Scrapbook 57, BCR Papers, Box 54; Newspaper Article in Scrapbook 62, BCR Papers, Box 57.

[24] Newspaper Article in Scrapbook 62, BCR Papers, Box 57; Newspaper Articles in Scrapbook 61, BCR Papers, Box 56.

[25] Newspaper Articles in Scrapbook 60, BCR Papers, Box 56; Newspaper Articles in Scrapbook 61, BCR Papers, Box 56; Newspaper Articles in Scrapbook 62, BCR Papers, Box 57; Clipping from Senate and House Congressional Records dated 20 March 1961 in the Estes Kefauver Collection, Series X, The University of Tennessee Special Collections Library, Knoxville, Tennessee; Newspaper Articles in Scrapbook 61, BCR Papers, Box 56.

[26] Newspaper Articles in Scrapbook 59, BCR Papers, Box 55; Form letter from James Quillen to "Colleague" dated 16 August 1963, Letter from Clarence Brown to Robert Taft, Jr. dated 17 October 1963, Letter from Thomas E. Coleman to Robert Taft, Jr. dated 21 October 1963, Letter from W. Harnischfeger to Robert Taft, Jr. dated 21 October 1963, and Letter from Robert Taft, Jr. To Louise Reece dated 7 November 1963 in Container 7, Folder 6, Robert Taft, Jr. Papers, Manuscript Division, Library of Congress, Washington, D.C.

[27] Newspaper Articles in Scrapbook 61, BCR Papers, Box 56; Newspaper Articles in Scrapbook 63, BCR Papers, Box 57; Newspaper Articles in Scrapbook 59, BCR Papers, Box 55.

INDEX